THE HISTORY OF THE CHURCH
IN FRANCE

THE HISTORY
OF THE
CHURCH IN FRANCE
A.D. 950–1000

*Being a Study in Mediaeval
Christianity*

BY
DOUGLAS W. LOWIS, D.D.

*THESIS APPROVED FOR THE DEGREE OF
DOCTOR OF DIVINITY IN THE UNIVERSITY
OF LONDON*

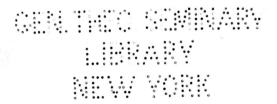

LONDON
THE EPWORTH PRESS
J. ALFRED SHARP

*Publication aided by a grant from
the Publication Fund of the
University of London*

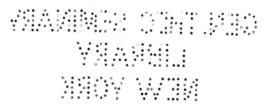
First Edition 1926

———

*Made and Printed in Great Britain by
The Camelot Press Limited,
London and Southampton*

TO MY WIFE

WITHOUT WHOSE CONSTANT SYMPATHY
AND ACTIVE CO-OPERATION THIS BOOK
COULD NEVER HAVE BEEN WRITTEN

PREFACE

In presenting this treatise to the public I am very conscious of its limitations, but trust that it may prove to be a contribution to the knowledge of one of the most obscure periods of Church history.

I formed an early interest in the events connected with the passing of the Carolingian dynasty of kings in France, and this interest was strengthened during the war, when I realized that these events were associated with an early stage in the Franco-German quarrel concerning Alsace-Lorraine. From these beginnings I advanced to the study of the Church in France as illustrating Mediaeval Christianity in an obscure epoch.

My thesis is that the Mediaeval Church, with all its faults, represented the best life of the world, and that it did preserve civilization from total collapse. I write from the standpoint of a convinced believer in the Protestant Reformation, but I suggest that Protestants of to-day can learn something from the Mediaeval Church.

I wish to express my gratitude to Professor Bett of Handsworth for reading through the MSS. and for valuable comments and criticisms ; and also to the Rev. Arthur Rudman, my colleague in the Headingley Circuit, and my brother, Mr. O. R. Lowis, LL.B., for reading the MSS. in part, and for suggestions offered. I wish to place on record my indebtedness to Dr. Williams's Library, from whose valuable collections of mediaeval literature in Migne, Pertz, &c., I have derived great help. Among many who have encouraged me in these labours, I must place the one to whom this book is dedicated, my mother, and my father who, though he has passed to Higher Service, is an inspiration and honoured memory to his children.

This treatise was prepared in the busy life of the circuits, whilst I was stationed at Hartley Wintney in the Sandhurst

7

Circuit, and at Kirkstall in the Leeds Headingley Circuit, and published whilst stationed at Leeds, Beeston Hill. I have received great kindness in these circuits, as in all the circuits in which I have travelled, and I trust that absolution will be granted if in any respect these studies have encroached upon the duties of preacher or pastor.

D. W. L.

BEESTON HILL, LEEDS.

CONTENTS

INTRODUCTION

THE France of A.D. 950 was a kingdom ruled by the last descendants of the Emperor Charlemagne, known as the Carolingian dynasty. Gaul, originally a purely Celtic confederacy, had been thoroughly Latinized by the Roman conquerors, and had become Latin in language, customs, law, and religion. The Franks, who broke in the Roman frontier, and finally settled in the country, giving their name to it, were a confederacy of German tribes. Under Clovis they established a powerful and personal monarchy, dispossessing Visigoths and Burgundians who had preceded them. The country was divided into a number of 'Pagi' under Counts. The baptism of Clovis, and his respect for the Roman Church and civilization, produced a dual system. Roman law was allowed to exist alongside Frankish custom, and the local bishop was regarded as the representative of the Romans, who lived mostly in the towns, whilst the Franks contented themselves with the rural areas.

The decline in physique and morale of the successors of Clovis, known as the Merovingian Kings, gave influence to the Mayors of the Palace, who, from being household officials, rose to the height of power. The office was vested in certain families springing from the more easterly portions of the country.

Finally Pepin le Bref displaced the last Merovingian, and his son Charlemagne ruled an immense empire, covering half the Continent of Europe, till his death in 814. His son Louis shared his empire among his sons, and at last, after fratricidal conflict, the treaty of Verdun divided Western Europe into three main divisions. Charles ruled in the western portion over an area roughly corresponding with modern France; Louis ruled in the east over what later came to be known as Germany; whilst Lothaire took Italy and a strip of country comprising Belgium, Lorraine, and Provence. The brothers continued to quarrel furiously, and on the death of Lothaire's son, the Kings of France and Germany, as we may now call them, divided this middle territory between them.

The French language made its appearance in the wording of an oath which Charles took at Strassburg in 840. It was a mixture of Celtic, Latin, and German, in which the Latin predominated. The successors of Charles the Bald had to meet the invasions of the Northmen, who harried the coast, swept up the rivers, and devastated the country generally. In order to bring peace to the country, Charles the Simple surrendered a portion of the country, known later as Normandy, to Rollo, one of these pirate chiefs. He was an ancestor of William the Conqueror. In these times the Feudal System made great headway at the expense of the King's authority.

The son of this Charles was Louis IV, whose reign from A.D. 936–54 was one prolonged struggle against strong barons, frequently helped by the Northmen of Rouen. He was once a prisoner at Rouen, but, by courage and perseverance, and with help from Otho I of Germany, prevailed over his foes, and handed his kingdom over to his son Lothaire in A.D. 954. This now brings us to the period under review, which will be considered in the following chapters.

I

FRANCE OF THE TENTH CENTURY

To understand France in 950 we must note the feudal estates and study the boundaries of the kingdom. Now, France was not in the tenth century the France we find in the atlas of to-day. In some points the boundaries extended farther, at others they were considerably reduced.

The whole district east of the Rhone consisted of the independent kingdom of the Arelate. This kingdom was constituted by the union of two small kingdoms, Provence and Burgundy, which originally formed part of the dominions of Emperor Lothaire I. The kingdom of Provence was founded in 879 by Count Boso of Vienne, husband of Lothaire's grand-daughter Hermengarde, and was united, on the death of his son, Louis the Blind, with the kingdom of Upper Burgundy, which had been founded by a Count Rudolf at the end of the ninth century. This kingdom included such towns as Geneva, Lausanne, and Besançon. The first King of the united kingdom was Count Rudolf's grandson, Rudolf, and the latter was succeeded by his son Conrad in 937. Conrad married Matilda, sister of Lothaire of France, and reigned till 993. He was ever a close friend of the Carolings. This kingdom retained its separate existence till 1032, when Rudolf III died without an heir, and surrendered his kingdom to the Emperor Conrad of Germany. There was some dispute between the kingdoms of Burgundy and France concerning the possession of Vienne and Lyons, which, however, were finally apportioned to Conrad as the dowry of his wife Matilda. This large kingdom thus stretched from Basle to Arles, and embraced the valleys of the Rhone and Doubs, including Savoy, and much of modern Switzerland.

Then we have the duchy of Lorraine, originally Lotharingia (Lothaire's kingdom), consisting of the districts east of the Meuse, including Verdun, Toul, Nancy, Brussels, &c. On the death of Lothaire II, by the treaty of Mersen, 870, renewed later at Kiersy, 877, this kingdom was divided between France and Germany. Charles the Bald secured the western portions, Toul, Verdun, and Cambrai. After the death of Charles the Fat, Lorraine fell into the hands of Arnulf of Germany, who formed it into a separate kingdom for his son Zwentibold. Once more, under Charles the Simple, it became French, only to be reconquered for Germany by Henry I, who made it a duchy, with Gilbert as duke. In 944 Conrad the Red, son-in-law of Otho, became duke; but, proving disloyal, was succeeded by Bruno, brother of the Emperor and Archbishop of Cologne, who at a later stage divided the duchy into two parts, the southern portion of which he gave to Frederick, Count of Bar. Louis IV's son Charles received in 976 the duchy of Lower Lorraine as a fief of the Empire, which after his death and the death of his son Otho passed to the family of Godfrey, Count of Verdun. It is thus to be noted that at the end of the tenth century Lorraine, both Upper and Lower, formed part of the German Empire, in spite of the efforts of French kings to secure it. Various counts appeared in the history of Lorraine, and the impression made is that Lorraine was unusually cursed by a large number of semi-independent lords like Isaac of Cambrai, Godfrey of Verdun, Reginald of Roucy and Hainault, &c., who caused the duke great anxiety by their feuds. The frontier towns of the French kingdom were Chaumont, St. Dizier, Vong, and Hirson, whilst Cambrai, Mezières, and Mouzon lay well within the German frontier. At Cambrai the frontier passed north-east, following the Escaut to the sea. Thus the frontiers of the kingdom lay for the most part well to the west of the Meuse.

But if France in 950 did not include Lorraine and Provence, it stretched beyond modern boundaries in two instances. The county of Barcelona, or the Spanish march, included the land north of the Ebro, and the march of Flanders included the land between the Escaut and the North Sea, with the towns of Tournai, Ghent, Bruges, and Courtrai.

For the rest, the kingdom of France consisted of a large number of great feudatories, which in their turn contained a much larger number of smaller counties. In theory the King's authority extended over the whole area from the Escaut to the Ebro, from the Rhone and Meuse to the Atlantic, and he had a nominal claim upon the homage of all the barons, great and small, with rights on investiture and confirmation. The King's name appeared on the coins and the year of his reign on the charters, but in reality his direct sovereignty was confined to the cities of Laon, Compiègne, and Rheims, and certain estates in the ecclesiastical provinces of Bourges, Rheims, Tours, Sens, and Lyons, which were in part under his influence by reason of certain ecclesiastical appointments which he controlled. He had to make good these nominal claims, however, by ceaseless fighting and much use of statecraft.

The Duchy of Normandy corresponded with the ecclesiastical province of Rouen, and consisted of the land north of the River Epte. The duke was practically independent in this region, and Rollo and his successors knew how to hold in check the smaller barons, and kept tight hold of all Church patronage.

Brittany also lay outside the actual jurisdiction of the French king, and under their Celtic chiefs the tribesmen resisted the claims of the Duke of Normandy and the King of France, and the ecclesiastical pretensions of the Archbishop of Tours. Certain counts fought their way to the title of duke, but the story of Brittany is one of constant feudal friction. There were few signs of civilized life. The Celtic population, however, maintained a separate national existence to a much later period.

The marquisate of Flanders included, not only Western Belgium and towns like Bruges and Ypres and Ghent, but also Douai, Arras, and Lille. The first Count Baldwin was husband of Charles the Bald's daughter, Judith, and was originally a Carolingian official who received territories because of successful defence against the Normans, and the county became hereditary in his family, with the Counts of Boulogne and St. Pol as vassals. Count Arnulf, who figures largely in the reign of Louis IV and Lothaire, was his descendant, and a number of Baldwins held the marquisate for many years in succession.

To the south of Flanders lay the county of Vermandois, which also touched the royal domain on the north. The Herberts, who ruled here, were thorns in the side of the Carolings, and the menace was increased when Troyes was added to Vermandois, but on the death of Herbert II the area was divided between his sons. Albert took Vermandois and

married one of Lothaire's sisters.   Robert took Meaux and
Troyes, and, on his death, was succeeded by his brother
Herbert.   The marriage of his sister to Count Theobald of
Blois, Chartres, and Tours, led eventually to the formation
of a very powerful domain of Blois and Champagne, which
caused much trouble to the Capetians in the persons of Eudes I
and Eudes II.   Eudes I shared the dowry with his cousin
Herbert III, and they were very active in the closing scenes
of the Caroling dynasty.   A glance at the map will show how
dangerous was this union of Chartres, Blois, Troyes, and
Meaux, allied as these counties were with Vermandois, for
the royal domain was almost completely surrounded by this
powerful alliance.

The Duchy of France is, however, the most powerful of these
large feudatories.   There has been some controversy about the
meaning of this term, but the contemporary writers like Richer
refer to the Franks, Burgundians, and Aquitanians as if they
formed together the kingdom of France, so that probably the
Duke of France had the same kind of vague suzerainty over
the counts and barons north of the Loire that the Duke of
Aquitaine had in the south, and the Duke of Burgundy in the
east.   Whether this be so or not—and Professor Lot believes
that the title ' Duke of France ' applied wherever the title
' King of France ' applied, and that the Duke was a kind of
viceroy—the original duchy carved out by Robert the Strong
certainly consisted of land between the Loire and the Seine,
and included the counties of Paris and Orleans, with suzerainty
over Anjou, Blois, and Tours.   The first ruler of this illustrious
house was Robert, a Carolingian official of Saxon origin,
who received his lands from Charles the Bald on condition
of defending them from the Northmen.   His sons were Eudes
(888–98) and Robert (923), who both reigned as kings, rivals
of Charles the Simple; and his grandson was Hugh the Great.
Flodoard (in his note for 924) tells us that Hugh possessed
land between the Seine and the Loire.   Rudolf (923–36), his
brother-in-law, gave him Maine, farther west, in 944 ; Louis IV
recognized him as Duke of France (Fl. 943).   Later he was
invested with Burgundy by Louis IV and Aquitaine by Lothaire
(Fl. 954), but he certainly never made good his claim to
Aquitaine, and Blois, Chartres, and Anjou soon gained practical
independence ; but the Norman dukes did homage to Hugh,

and his power was further increased by the possession of certain great abbeys of which he became lay abbot, such as St. Martin of Tours and St. Germain and St. Denis, and certain other abbeys like St. Riquier and Corbie which he controlled. The title ' Duke of the Franks ' may easily have facilitated the ultimate accession of this family to the throne of France.

The County of Anjou, originally part of the inheritance of the Roberts, eventually became a powerful and hereditary county. The first hereditary count was a brave soldier of humble origin. Among his descendants were Fulk the Good, a deeply religious man and a great lover of St. Martin of Tours, who died in 960 ; and Geoffrey Grisonelle, who still recognized the Duke of France as his lord, but nevertheless was consistently faithful to the Caroling Kings, supporting them in their Norman and German wars. Fulk the Black, 987–1040, was in constant conflict with Eudes of Champagne and the Counts of Brittany. A descendant of his was Henry II of England.

The Duchy of Burgundy, as distinct from the kingdom, had been formed as a separate march for Richard the Justiciar in 877. The duchy lay between the Loire and the Rhone, and included counties like Autun, Dijon, Avallon, Langres, Mâcon, Auxerre, Nevers, and Troyes, and great monasteries like Cluny and Vezelay. Richard's son Rudolf became king after the deposition of Charles the Simple, and his brother Hugh the Black maintained his position as duke, though challenged by the Duke of France, and was succeeded in 952 by his brother-in-law Gilbert, Count of Avallon, Autun, and Chalons. It was the marriage of Gilbert's daughter Luidgarde and Otho son of the Duke of France that brought the duchy at last into the hands of Hugh's family, though the power of the Duke of Burgundy was always limited by the practical independence of numerous counts.

South of the Loire there had been a great undefined area called Aquitaine, which claimed to be a duchy. This area had developed differently from the lands of the north. A separate kingdom had been formed here by the Visigoths, and Charlemagne bestowed it upon his son. The title of duke was disputed by many counts. At one time it was held by the Counts of Auvergne. Then Raymond of Toulouse, who died in 950, appears to have been confirmed in possession of the title by Louis IV, and, after his death, William, son of Ebles, Count of

B

Poitiers, appears to have received investiture. Hugh the
Great sought to use his influence with Lothaire to secure the
duchy, but he failed to dislodge William, who later became
reconciled to the king, and handed on the duchy to a long line
of dukes all called William, till at last the heiress Eleanor
brought it to Henry II of England as a dowry. Meanwhile,
when Aquitaine became attached to Poitiers, its area became
more narrowly defined, though it still included Limousin,
Perigord, Auvergne, Angoulême, Saintonge, Poitou. The
various counts and viscounts were very powerful, and the
Duke's authority even in this restricted portion was sometimes
very limited.

Farther to the east there was the powerful county of Toulouse
under counts generally called Raymond, the first hereditary
count of which, Raymond I, died 864. We have seen that one
Raymond actually held the title of Duke of Aquitaine in 940 ;
and when the Duchy of Aquitaine became attached to Poitiers,
Toulouse drew away Givaudan, Velay, Albi, and Quercy into
a quite separate and powerful county, which later became the
centre of a rich and luxurious civilization of art, poetry, music,
and free thought. Life was altogether gayer than in the more
rugged north. Roman influences prevailed over Teutonic, and
the towns in many cases preserved their old Roman institutions,
and became wealthy by Mediterranean trade. The Romance
dialect, the *langue d'oc*, as distinct from *langue d'oeil*, spoken
to the north of a line drawn from Bordeaux to Lyons, was
spoken in its purest form, and eventually gave its name to the
country. Though nominally part of the kingdom of France—
and the counts appear to have recognized the Caroling and
Capetian kings, dating their charters by the year of the king's
reign—Langue d'oc formed in reality a separate country,
differing in language, manners, and institutions. A member
of the same family, named Raymond, ruled over the county
of Rouerque, to which was attached at this stage the Marquisate
of Gothia, which had been formerly united to Auvergne. A
whole host of viscounts, e.g. Narbonne, Nimes, &c. contested
the authority of the Count.

South of the Garonne there remained the Duchy of Gascony,
founded about 870. The rulers, frequently called Sancho, are
little known, and the history is very obscure. A William
Sancho ruled in the time of Hugh Capet, and had relations with

Abbo of Fleury, but life was proverbially wild in those districts. In 1062 Gascony became part of the Duchy of Aquitaine. The capital of the duchy was Bordeaux, which was originally a city of Aquitaine. It has been suggested by Lot that Gascony had been conquered by the Franks fighting from Bordeaux as the basis of operations, and that the conquered territory had drawn Bordeaux into its orbit. The Basques formed a portion of the population, and Gascony had relations with Spain. The authority of the Kings of France was very slight, and Gascony lived its own life very much to itself ; and here, as elsewhere, the Duke had to make what headway he could against numerous warlike barons.

Beyond the Pyrenees lay the March of Spain, and here the Counts of Barcelona, also called Marquises of Spain, menaced by Saracens, preserved intimate relations with the Kings of France. The first hereditary Count, Wilfred le Velu, was a Carolingian official, and at the end of the tenth century Count Borell was prominent. The march extended to the Ebro and included Rousillon, to the north of the Pyrenees, and numerous counties to the south.

Thus France in the tenth century was a highly feudalized society. A short account of the origin and growth of the feudal system should now be given.

The two great statutes which marked the progress of feudalism were the *Edict of Mersen*, 847, which allowed every man to choose his own lord, and the *Edict of Kiersy*, 877, by which hereditary succession in fiefs and royal offices was permitted. These edicts simply confirmed a situation arising from the breakdown of the centralized system of Charlemagne. The private and personal character of Teutonic law, together with the preference of the invaders for rural life, tended towards feudalism. Certain suggestions of feudalism can be found in the character of early Gallo-Roman country estates, and there is a sense in which feudalism might be termed a partial return to the tribalism which preceded Roman domination, with the chieftain's place emphasized at the expense of the tribesmen's rights.

It is, however, not necessary to examine carefully such historic origins, because feudalism, as history knows it, was the result of the breakdown of centralized government, the discrediting of public law, the invasion of barbarians, and the general insecurity which followed.

In spite of efforts of such men as Clovis and Charlemagne to rebuild the Roman state, Charles the Bald, for the sake of some temporary advantage, such as the securing of the Imperial Crown at Rome or the acquiring of portions of Lorraine, and for the sake of countering the rebellion of some powerful count, surrendered one royal right after another to his afore-time officials, who thus became semi-independent lords instead of royal functionaries. The counts and viscounts, who had held office as officials of the King, in these days of insecurity, with the central power divided and weakened by internal strife or invasion, asserted themselves in their counties, and, by a convenient and inevitable confusion between their official and personal positions, carved out for themselves private domains which they ruled no longer by royal appointment, but by the strength of their own right arm. The Count accepted the homage of the free men of his county and conferred land on others, land which in theory he only held in the name of the King as a royal official. The dues and returns which he once rendered to the King's treasury he now retained for himself, whilst he administered justice in his own name, at his own courts, and called up his armed men to fight for himself rather than for the King. When these powers were increased by the granting of the hereditary title, the official had indeed become a feudatory, and the local courts and levies had usurped the place once occupied by royal justice and royal troops.

The King, therefore, had weakened his position: (1) By alienating land in the form of benefices. (2) By surrendering regalian rights to his officials. (3) By recognizing the hereditary rights of these officials.

But this is not the whole story. We must not suppose that France had thus become a number of well-organized counties at peace within their borders, even if at war with other counties. The disintegration extended much further. There were viscounts who resisted the authority of the count ; there were powerful rural magnates and barons living in strong castles, who refused allegiance both to the count and viscount ; and the story of France is the story of division and sub-division, from the king downwards through marquis, duke, count, viscount, and baron, till we reach the lowest level of the feudal nobility in direct contact with the peasantry. The free-man who once owned his land had wellnigh disappeared, and each man was the vassal of the man above him and lord of the man below him.

We can easily see now what had happened. The invasions of Normans and Hungarians, and the proved inability of the king, or even the count, to protect the people, had created for them a terrible problem. The free-man was at the mercy of every robber or corrupt official, and he could secure neither justice nor protection from the king. Ideas of private law and personal loyalty were prominent in the mind of the age. As the power of the State was weakened, a free-man was compelled to place himself under the protection of a more powerful neighbour, and so he did homage and became a vassal, and as the ' man ' of the other accepted investiture of his land. The allodial land became a fief, and the once free landowner the vassal of another. The lord of the castle, on the other hand, promised personal help and protection on condition of military service being rendered and the payment of certain dues. The vassal therefore received protection from armed foes, the lord enjoyed power and prestige and a claim on the armed service of the other.

Originally, then, feudalism meant the personal relationship of the vassal to the lord, but it became inevitably connected with a system of land tenure by an economic necessity. Life had become increasingly rural. Insecurity, war, and bad government had reduced the trade of the country and therefore the value of town life. The possession of land became an absolute necessity in such a rural society. The vassal needed land in order to live, the bigger landowner had lands to bestow which he could not cultivate himself. Hence vassalage became also associated with the fief or benefice. Industry became domestic, and was largely confined to the private domain, whilst the villa became more important than the city. Thus an ascending scale of relations, all private and personal, the link being the oath of fealty, and the promise of protection, and the giving and receiving of land, at last bound the humblest chevalier to the lord in one vast system of vassalage and feudal tenure.

Society came to be one vast pyramid, at the apex of which was the king, and at the base of which were thousands of barons, and, lying between these, layer upon layer of feudal ranks. The pledge of allegiance and the promise of protection, implying in theory a pledge of mutual loyalty, alone prevented anarchy. A rough code of honour developed among the feudal nobility. A religious sanction came to be associated with the investiture of the young knight, and vows of purity and loyalty were taken after the lonely vigil in the church. Again, there can be no doubt that feudalism provided a local defence in those wild days, and therefore some measure of security for the people. In some cases a real loyalty would unite the village to the castle ; personal relationships also existed, and in a personal relationship the human element counts for something. Man dealt with man, not with machines and companies, and some real family life became possible when the lord was forced to spend so much time in his castle with his own people. When the roads were so difficult to travel upon, and life so insecure in the forests and marshes and even the open ways of the country, men were tempted to stay at home with their families. Then, instead of huge factories and a complicated industrialism, there were village industries, for the domain would be largely self-supporting. There would be village artisans, the workers on the land, and those spinning and weaving in the home.

We think of the rural life of the village, the woods, the fields, the lanes, and the vineyards, and the imagination is presented with a picture of beauty and peace ; but the real life was not so picturesque. Let us not forget that beneath the lowest layer of the feudal pyramid there lay masses of crushed, degraded peasantry at the mercy of the feudal lord. It is difficult to realize the life of this underworld, for contemporary writers are more concerned with the doings of kings and lords, but occasional glimpses reveal a background of woe.

We read of 'servi,' 'coloniae,' and 'franci' (Actes de Loth. x.). The lowest stratum of all consisted of serfs, a population of immense misery, deprived of civil and political rights, bound to the soil, at the mercy of the lord, who could do what he liked with his own. We read in charters of serfs (Actes de Loth. xii., xiv.), male and female, who pass over with the estate, classified with the animals, meadows, forests, watercourses, &c., as so much wealth belonging to the estate. Serfdom was hereditary. The serf could not marry outside the domains, could not leave property to any but direct heirs.

There were different degrees of serfdom, and in some cases the 'formarriage' and the 'mainmorte' restrictions were qualified. The serf in the field would have more personal liberty than the domestic serf, and, indeed, the tendency to regard the serf as belonging to the land prevented the arbitrary sale of his person, as in the earlier days of Roman slavery and in the later days of American slavery, and gave him fixity of tenure and the possibility of a home life. He was the property of his master as part of the estate. He had no protection at law against his master's cruelty. His one friend was the Church. He had no civil rights, but he was liable to criminal prosecution, and this meant his responsible personality was at any rate recognized.

A stage above the serfs we find the 'coloniae,' as they were called. Now life was very immobile in those days of the self-contained domain, but not entirely so. There were, for instance, pilgrims moving from shrine to shrine, there were students passing from school to school, and there were still merchants in the land.

There were vast areas of waste and forest land, and into these areas certain peasants frequently wandered, who cut down the forests, and made for themselves patches of cultivated land. Many of the barons, occupying areas depopulated by war, pestilence, and famine, welcomed such mobile labour and gave it generous terms. Thus, many of these 'coloniae' secured a living by clearing forest land or cultivating the waste places for the local barons, securing thereby certain rights and privileges bordering on freedom, for which they rendered services or paid dues. These new clearings in time developed into new villages and towns.

One stage higher we find the free peasantry. They were nominally their own masters and had legal rights, but their freedom was more nominal than real. They had to pay rent for the soil, and, in addition, immense dues, or returns on produce. Further, they had to give actual time to the service of the lord in the form of corvée, and there were limitations on free buying and selling. It seems possible, then, that the actual difference between the condition of the serf and the free peasantry was not great. Bishop Asceline in his *Carmen* (Migne 141) makes no distinction between them, grouping all workers under the name of serfs, whose duty it is to furnish for all 'gold, nourishment, and clothing.' He says, 'They possess nothing which hard work does not buy,' and further adds, ' Who will be able to count the pains, the fatigues, which the poor serfs have to bear ? Alas, there is no limit to the tears and groans of these unfortunate people.' And this is the testimony of a proud aristocratic bishop, who thinks the threefold order of society, those who pray, those who fight, and those who work, natural and satisfactory. Abbo, Abbot of Fleury, also distinguishes between the fighters, by which he means the nobility, and the workers, by which he means serfs and free-men grouped together, whilst in many Diplomata we read of two classes, ' ingenui ' and ' servi.'

It is certain that Asceline did not exaggerate. Apart from exploitation by cruel barons, the peasantry bore the brunt of all the evils of the time. Rudolf Glaber (Migne 142) and Aimon (Miracles of Benedict, Migne 139) in their writings give lurid details of tragedy and pain. We read of sweeping pestilences, of terrible famines, and the horrors of war ; and the people, unprotected by the stout walls of castle or town, are always the first to suffer. Richer (iii. 74, iv. 37), for example, tells us how Otho burned and depopulated the country through which he passed on his way to Paris, and how Hugh Capet, in his wars with Charles of Lorraine, ravaged the land round Laon, Rheims, and Soissons with such ferocity that he did not ' leave a hut inhabited by the old man childish with age.' Such burning and slaughter meant appalling suffering, and must have had a direct connexion with those famines and plagues which swept the country, making possible the cannibalism which R. Glaber describes in such terrible detail. This burning of crops and vineyards seems to have been the usual method of waging war, and war was the chronic condition of feudalism.

Aimon (Migne 139) shows us how the people suffered also by floods and storms. He tells us of a sudden rise of the Loire, which involved in its sudden ruin labourers, those journeying on horseback, sheep, cattle, horses, fathers, mothers, sons ; and the same writer gives us numerous instances of the violence of the local barons, leading to pillage, cattle-lifting, and murder. There are robberies by the wayside, fierce barons preside at rough tribunals, men are hanged and blinded on little evidence, and exploited by the feudal nobility. They become victims of pestilence, war, and famine, and the lot of the peasantry is pitiful enough. We are not surprised to read of a great revolt of the Norman peasantry, who claimed representative government and the right to the fruits of their own labour, and the possession of land, which revolt, however, was ruthlessly crushed (William of Jumièges, Migne 149).

We have now to consider one aspect of society which was in principle non-feudal, and which was ultimately to undermine feudalism. Society was largely rural, but the cities and towns still existed, though reduced in population and influence. The ancient Roman cities had suffered enormously by the general insecurity and decline of trade. Yet they did not disappear. The bishop continued to dwell there, as also did the count, and this meant numerous officials such as lawyers, tax-collectors, soldiers, policemen. Here also were to be found schools, connected with episcopal churches, with their teachers and students. Such a gathering of people, not directly engaged on land or in trade, would inevitably mean that an artisan and merchant class would be formed to meet their wants. Thus Richer (iii. 8) shows us a wall-repairing scheme in operation at Mons, with labourers carrying cement and stone. There were also workers in wood (R. iii. 103, iv. 18), stone, and iron required for military purposes. These cities also proved to be the most convenient centres for what trade had survived the break-down of Roman society. We read of a fair at Chalons (Fl. 963), also one at St. Philibert de Tournus (Dip. x.), and we read of the suburb of merchants attached to Verdun, connected with the city by bridges across the Meuse (R. iii. 103). Trading towns grew up alongside the bishop's city, and at a later stage formed themselves into guilds and corporations, and some of these guilds may go back to Roman times. The chandlers of Étampes, the bakers of Pontoise, tanners of Senlis, the tavern-keepers of Orleans, and the shoemakers and butchers of Paris, were really corporations of merchants or artisans. The respective positions of Paris and Orleans on the Seine and the Loire gave these cities special commercial advantages, and both were royal cities and the sees of bishops. Rouen was also famous for its sailors, and enjoyed trade with Britain. Many cities like Laon and Lyons also owed their importance to their being on great trade routes, and these cities developed into those half-feudal entities called ' communes.' Some towns grew up

round great monastic foundations like St. Denis or St. Riquier
or St. Philibert de Tournus—for the presence of a monastery
possessing relics would not only attract the trader, but the
sick person, the pilgrim, the devotee. We also learn that the
fruitful soil and healthy climate of Centule had much to do
with the choice of that site for the monastic settlement of
St. Riquier (Chr. i. 5).

These towns, possessing wealth and the advantages of
corporate life, were able to obtain charters which confirmed the
economic or even political privileges they had secured. It is
doubtful whether these ancient cities retained any of their
original republican form, for the ruling authority was either
the bishop or the count or the monastery. Sometimes the bishop
was also the count, as in Langrès, Laon, Le Puy. At the same
time the citizens were not without power, and often
asserted themselves against the bishop, count, and even the
king.

The citizens of Rheims and Laon are often mentioned. We
find citizens gathering for church festivals, such as the translation of relics, or the consecration of a church, and evidently
they had some share in the election of bishops. Thus Hugh
Capet (R. iv. 26) addressed the citizens of Rheims concerning
the election of Archbishop Arnulf, whilst the people of Sens
were able to make known to Lothaire their desire for the
election of Anastasius. The citizens of Laon resisted their
bishop on an economic question (R. iv. 15). The citizens of
Cambrai openly revolted against their bishop appointed from
Germany, and the inhabitants of St. Denis attacked the bishops
gathered in council in the town. We know little of the life
they lived, and know not by what means the mass of citizens
could make their presence and influence felt ; but it is clear
that they had interests of their own which they could assert,
and they were feeling their way after economic and ultimately
political freedom, though for a time they had to contend against
the feudal lord who wished to exploit them.

It was a long struggle, but in the markets and fairs and
guilds the towns preserved a certain non-feudal character.
Their trade and their corporate life gave them advantages
not enjoyed by their brethren of the country-side. They
were necessary for the impoverished baronage, and behind their
walls could maintain some standard even of luxury, whilst

they could make full use of woods, pastures, and vineyards lying close to the walled city. Thus we read of a citizen of Chartres who possessed pigs in a wood close by, and also of horses which were brought out of Laon (R. ii. 89) and watered in the country near by. There were the wheat-fields and vine-yards round the city, which satisfied the city's wants. It is certain that the various charters confirming the liberties of these towns date from the twelfth century, but they only confirm an existing state of things, and refer to ' ancient rights,' and these liberties must have been steadily developing during the unrecorded history of the tenth century. There may have been commercial as well as ecclesiastical links between Roman Gaul and Feudal France.

The urban element was but the exception which proved that feudalism was the rule ; and, when all has been said that can be said in its favour, feudalism stood for (1) *A vast system of class and caste distinctions* based on landed possessions and noble blood. Birth and lands counted for more than education or character. Such an aristocracy, contradicting the Christian ideal of brotherhood, could not but produce tyranny and oppression. (2) *The arbitrary authority of the baron's will.* There was no state strong enough to coerce him. His authority was only limited by expediency, otherwise there was no right beyond his might. He owned the land, and therefore the people who lived on it. (3) *The supremacy of force.* As Asceline and Abbo remind us, the duty of the noble was to fight, and culture and labour were outside his province. ' Ours to fight, theirs to toil for us,' was their motto. They lived on the earnings of the labour of the so-called inferior man, and despised the man by whose labour they lived. They fought because they loved fighting, but fighting for fighting's sake meant a vast callousness to human pain, and life was very hard. (4) *Incompetency.* There was no clearly marked purpose, no science of government. War has never helped learning, for science and trade are the expression of the productive, con-structive genius ; war is the destructive tendency gone mad. Just because feudalism was ignorant, unsocial, it had within itself the certainty of perishing. So feudalism fought itself out on battlefield or in sordid intrigue. Mutual jealousies played into the hands of shrewd kings who did appreciate character, culture, labour ; and a centralized monarchy rose on the ruins of a broken feudalism, finding its principal support in the Church and the trading classes.

The reigns of Louis IV and Lothaire show us how the anarchical tendencies of feudalism were kept in check by a hero king dependent on the Empire and the Church, both institutions anti-feudal and Roman in theory. We must notice another tendency in feudalism which counteracted the infinite sub-divisions, for big fiefs gradually appeared. The strong overcame the weak. Some of the estates like Flanders, Normandy, France, were large original endowments arising out of military necessity. Sometimes one family married into another, thus uniting counties. The wealth of these dukes, and their vast landed estates, gave them a special pull in dealing with the nobles in their territory. Thus by force of arms, by skill in diplomacy, by chance of successful warfare, by intermarriage, by the possession of wealth, by the encouragement and protection of non-feudal elements, and by securing the support of the Church, the strong mastered the weak, till, in the course of time, power at last returned to the King.

The influence of feudalism on the change of dynasty is apparent. The Capetians did not take the crown because they presented a national policy against foreign influence, for we shall find that the Capetians at the moment were more pro-German than the Carolings, and national feeling scarcely existed. To say this is not to deny that a dynasty arising out of the central portions of France had better promises to offer the future than a dynasty with an Imperial tradition behind it ; but one must emphatically deny that Hugh Capet came to the throne because he was a Frenchman and Lothaire a German. Moreover, the Caroling dynasty did not pass because their kings were weak, for they were men of energy and courage with few exceptions. But one reason for the change can be found in the fact that, through the surrender of regalian rights, the Carolings had become a family without land in a society where landed possessions gave power. Yet, though the Carolings passed, the kingship survived, partly because the feudal pyramid required an apex, a supreme lord, in fact one who could grant investiture and receive the homage of all his vassals. The Capetians were helped to the throne by their vast landed estates, but we shall see that the change of dynasty owed more to the Church than to feudalism, and there is reason to believe that the feudal aspects of the change of dynasty have been exaggerated. The Capetian kings are not conscious of any prerogative which the Caroling kings did not enjoy, and they speak of themselves in the charters in the same language which the Carolings had used before them. Their accession meant the union of Capetian and Caroling estates, but we find that the Capetians had also to struggle against disintegrating movements, and it is doubtful whether they enjoyed increased authority over their vassals. Apart from other considerations, the Capetian would have hardly resisted the pressure of aggressive Feudalism, but the Capetians were supported by powerful Church interests both episcopal and monastic.

II

THE REIGN OF LOTHAIRE, 954 TO 987

Note
R.   = Richer.
Fl.   = Flodoard.
G.P.C.= Gesta Pontificum Camaracensium.
Th.   = Thietmar.
G.   = Gerbert's Letters.
Dip.   = Diplomata of Lothaire, Louis V.

WE need to take a short survey of the reign of Lothaire and his son Louis, which covers the greater part of the fifty years under review, for throughout this period the relations between Church and State are very close, and indeed so mingled that the bishop continually enters into the political life of the State, whilst the king's activities affect the Church. The untimely death of Louis IV left an anxious situation for the Carolings. Two sons survived, Lothaire, aged thirteen, Charles aged three, and it appeared likely that Duke Hugh of France would now claim the throne for himself and his family, but there were facts which promised well for the Carolings. Queen Gerberge lived, and, possessing the qualities so marked in the great Saxon family from which she sprang—energy, courage, and wisdom—was prepared to defend her son's claim as she had defended her husband's. She was on good terms with her brothers, the Emperor Otho I and Bruno, Archbishop of Cologne and Viceroy of Lorraine, who, though for the moment preoccupied with internal revolt and Eastern wars, was nevertheless prepared to help her and her son.

What was more important for the moment was the decision of Hugh the Great to support Lothaire. The reasons for this step are a little obscure, and there is no need to suppose that he was animated by any pity for the young King. He was a shrewd man, who loved the reality of power better than the mere name, and he probably realized that the Feudatories might resent his accession, as being one of themselves. Then he would have to allow for the opposition of the Saxon house and the respect for the Caroling blood, whilst the experience of his own relatives, Eudes and Rudolf, in precarious sovereignty, had not been very encouraging, and undoubtedly there was much power to be exercised behind the scenes, especially if he could secure fresh territory from the king as a condition of support. So when Gerberge appealed for his help he promptly responded with a promise of loyalty on conditions.

A great meeting was held at St. Rémy of Rheims, consisting of nobles and bishops from Burgundy, Aquitaine, and France, and Lothaire was elected and then crowned and consecrated by Archbishop Artold of Rheims November 12, 954. In this election we see three principles applied :

1. The hereditary right of the son to succeed the father.
2. The rights of the nobles to elect their king.
3. The claim of the Church to declare the divine right of kings.

These principles were mutually contradictory, yet little outward conflict appears, and the king continued to reign by hereditary right, election of the princes and right divine.

As for the conditions, Lothaire bestowed upon Hugh Aquitaine and Burgundy, and the Duke at once took steps to secure possession. He was quite prepared to negotiate with Gilbert of Burgundy by arranging a marriage between his son Otho and the heiress of Gilbert, Luidgarde, thus ensuring the succession for his family. But Aquitaine could only be secured by war. It was at the time ruled by William, Count of Poitiers, who had been confirmed in possession by Louis IV in 951, and was determined to defend his claims by arms. Hugh took the young king and Gerberge to Paris for Easter celebrations, and then together they visited Orleans, Chartres, and Blois (R. iii. 3) that the Duke might demonstrate his own influence with royalty to his own people.

The king and duke then invaded Aquitaine and attacked Poitiers. Count Reginald of Roucy burned the camp of St. Radegond by a sudden onset, but the attack on the city failed, and after two months the siege was raised. Duke William gathered troops in Auvergne and attacked the retreating invaders, but was heavily repulsed. Negotiations took the place of hostilities, and, hostages being given, Aquitaine, with Poitiers, remained in the hands of William. The king and the duke returned to Laon (R. iii. 4, Fl. 955).

Meanwhile, in spite of this repulse, the power of Hugh was very great. He had married Hadwig, sister of Otho and Gerberge, and his daughter Beatrice had married in 954 Frederick, Count of Bar, who became later Duke of Upper Lorraine. Gilbert of Burgundy had recognized him as Duke of Burgundy, and he had ensured possession for his family by his son's marriage, and his daughter Emma was betrothed to the Duke of Normandy. Gilbert died in 956, and Hugh succeeded without difficulty or challenge. He was preparing for a renewed attack upon Poitiers, but death came to him at the height of his power at Dourdain on June 17, 956 (R. iii. 5, Fl. 956). His sons were too young to inherit full sovereignty, and Bruno, who was both their uncle and uncle of the king, administered the whole county on behalf of his nephews. Hugh's sons were not immediately confirmed in their nominal inheritance of the duchies of France and Burgundy respectively, which shows that the hereditary right of the feudatories was still checked by the need of a fresh royal investiture, which in this case was delayed. A terrible plague, from which probably Duke Hugh died, also removed the Archbishop of Trèves and possibly the Bishops of Noyon and Cambrai, who passed away about the same time. Hadulf, a cleric of Laon, was elected bishop of Noyon in 955, whilst Berengarius succeeded at Cambrai.

Numerous diplomas were granted by Lothaire during these years at the request of his mother and various dukes and bishops and abbots. Thus he confirmed the restoration of St. Bavon of Ghent (Dip. i., ii.) conceding free election to the monks, confirmed the restitution of Corbery to St. Rémy of Rheims (Dip. iv.) and the immunities to that church granted by his father, and renewed the diploma of King Rudolf granting to Notre Dame of Le Puy (Dip. v.) immunity and full property of the bourg attached to the church. These immunities were granted at Laon in the early part of 955. At Compiègne (May 21) he confirmed the reforms and gifts of Archbishop Artold to St. Basil (Dip. vi.) ; whilst in October (Dip. vii.) he confirmed to Aimard possessions and privileges of Cluny, and to the same monastery, in November, the gift of Notre

Dame of Huillaux (Dip. viii.) in Auvergne, made originally
by one Stephen and his wife. About this period he also
renewed a diploma of his father confirming reforms at the
Abbey of Homblières, and in November 956 he confirmed
possession of privileges of St. Philibert of Tournus accorded by
his predecessors (Dip. ix., x.). In 958, at his mother's request,
he conceded to Abbot Pons the monastery of St. Michel of
Cuxa, confirming the possessions, and, whilst at Dijon, to
Cluny the deserted monastery of St. Amand in Provence
(Dip. xi.).

Meanwhile the Emperor was quite willing to befriend the
young king, provided that his rights to Lorraine were
respected. Apart from natural family feeling, his own troubles
with powerful barons made him realize the danger of
encouraging disloyalty abroad. Two great assemblies were
held in 956 at Ingleheim and Cologne respectively, and hostages
were given by the towns of Lorraine. Bruno's task was to
rule effectively his own duchy, where there was a large number
of turbulent counts who threatened his authority, and at the
same time to preserve peace between his nephews, Lothaire and
the sons of Hugh the Great. On the whole he succeeded in his
difficult task. Renier, Count of Hainault, took away Chiers
from a Chevalier of the Church of Rheims named Ersmar, and
sought to dispossess Gerberge of some domains she possessed
in right of her first husband. Lothaire captured Chiers, and
Rudolf, father of the historian, Richer, by a stratagem took
Mons, capturing the wife and children of Renier (R. iii. 8).
Bruno intervened, and brought about an agreement whereby
Renier recovered his wife and family on condition that he
restored the possessions of Gerberge. A further revolt in 957
led to strong action on the part of Bruno. Lothaire was at the
time in Burgundy, but he advanced to the help of his uncle at
Cambrai. Renier surrendered to Bruno, and, when he refused
to give hostages for future conduct, Bruno delivered him to the
Emperor, and he died an exile in Bohemia. His sons Renier
and Lambert were taken to the Court of Lothaire and brought
up there.

In the same year there was trouble between Arnulf of
Flanders and Roger, Count of Ponthieu, about Amiens. Some
of the bishops of whom we read in these days were men of war.
A certain castle of Roucy belonging to Artold, Archbishop of

C

Rheims, was seized by Theobald, Count of Chartres and Blois. The Archbishop retook the town, but Harduin, a certain baron, held the castle for Theobald until Lothaire and Artold, with bishops and nobles, compelled him, after two weeks' siege, to purchase liberty by delivering his nephews as hostages. Theobald, too late to save the town, ravaged the Soissons district and took La Fère by treachery. Rorico, Bishop of Laon, arrived on the scene with soldiers of the Church of Rheims, and besieged La Fère till Lothaire arrived, when, the Counts of Troyes and Meaux mediating, Theobald surrendered the place.

On the death of Hugh the Great, it was understood that Otho, his second son, betrothed to Luidgarde, would succeed, but Lothaire hesitated formally to invest him, possibly hoping to secure possession for himself. He visited Burgundy in 957 and again in 958, taking possession of certain towns like Dijon. This created trouble between Lothaire and his cousins. Bruno had to call them together at Compiègne, where the dispute was settled by the mutual interchange of hostages. Lothaire and his mother celebrated Easter 959 at Cologne, where the King gave the Emperor assurances concerning Lorraine.

Difficulties arose in Lorraine. Bruno had taken strong action against the many baronial castles. He ordered several of these to be destroyed, and called upon the lords to pay heavy taxes to the Treasury, with the result that one Immon headed a revolt. Bruno ensured for himself powerful support by granting Upper Lorraine to Frederick, Count of Bar and Metz and husband of Hugh's daughter Beatrice. A great revolt against the King's authority followed. Robert of Troyes had married a daughter of Duke Gilbert, but had no part of the inheritance. He now captured Dijon by treachery, expelling the King's men. Ansigisus, Bishop of Troyes, also quarrelled with Robert and fled to Bruno, who had arrived in the district with troops from Lorraine. Bruno besieged Troyes, whilst Lothaire besieged Dijon, but the appearance of another fighting prelate complicated matters.

Lothaire had nominated Archembald, son of Count Robert, to the see of Sens, 958. He was a great soldier, but an utterly unworthy bishop, and evidently his appointment was due to a feudal interest. The Chronicles of Sens strongly condemned his destruction of the monastery and his worldly life. Now, with the Count of Sens and his father, he attacked Helpon, Bruno's General, and completely defeated him. Both sieges were raised for the time, but were resumed next year. Robert consented to treat for peace and surrendered hostages, one of whom, Odelric, the traitor of Dijon, was hung by royal orders. Bishop Ansigisus then recovered his bishopric and Lothaire once more held Dijon.

Bruno paid another visit to Burgundy and brought about a reconciliation between his nephews. Hugh and Otho did homage to Lothaire, who formally invested the former with his father's lands, to which he added Poitou, and the latter with the Duchy of Burgundy. Lothaire had been able to vindicate his right of investiture, but apparently had to surrender any hope of personally ruling the duchy. The solemn investiture of Otho followed at Easter 961 in the presence of French and Burgundian nobles. It is doubtful whether Hugh sought once more to take possession of Poitiers, but, if he tried, he completely failed, and the Counts of Poitiers successfully vindicated their claims to Aquitaine. Meanwhile Bruno had further trouble with Immon, Count of Cambrai, and Artold had to contend with brigands in his diocese, a certain number of whom were seized by his nephew Manasses and hung.

In the same year in which Otho received the Duchy of Burgundy, the old Norman trouble broke out. It began with a dispute between Duke Richard, who had now married Emma, sister of Hugh Capet, and Theobald, who had married Richard's stepmother, and was in revolt against Hugh Capet, who was his suzerain. Theobald drew towards Lothaire. A conference was summoned at Soissons to deal with the case. There is some difficulty in interpreting motives in this Norman war, because we have conflicting accounts of the same event. Dudo (Migne 141) the Norman chronicler, writes in a florid rhetorical vein, greatly biassed in favour of Duke Richard, who is to him the ideal king of knightly propensities. Flodoard gives the French view in the studied moderation of the annalist, and he was of course contemporary with the events described. Dudo says Richard was drawn to Soissons by the treachery of his enemies. Flodoard says he drew near to break up the conference. Whoever was the real aggressor, it is certain that a battle was fought at Soissons in which the Normans were defeated, and that Lothaire, with Geoffrey of Anjou and

Baldwin of Flanders, now ruling in place of his father, Arnulf the Old, pursued them beyond the Eaulne.

Lothaire was then called away to Burgundy, where he met certain Aquitaine princes at Conde, and possibly reconciled himself with them. In 961 Guy, Bishop of Auxerre, died and was succeeded by Richard on the nomination of Lothaire, and in the same year Archbishop Artold of Rheims died on September 30. Meanwhile Lothaire, at his mother's request, made a gift of Conde to St. Rémy of Rheims, and also confirmed donations to St. Martin of Savigny made by a woman, Emmena, December 10, 960 (Dip. xiii.), showing, therefore, that he had some influence in the Lyons district. During this journey he permitted his sister Matilda to marry Conrad, the King of Burgundy, and abandoned his rights over Vienne and Lyons as her dowry (Hugh of Flavigny, Migne 154).

The following year Lothaire was in friendly contact with Duke William of Aquitaine, and, meeting him at Vitry, October 14, 963 (Dip. xx.), granted confirmation of the cession of Curtis Furga, near Poitiers, made by a certain Robert to Duchess Adela, mother of the duke, who had died thirty years before. The death of Duke William III the following year seemed to cause some interruption of relations between Laon and Poitiers, though there is every reason to believe that Lothaire was recognized by Duke William IV. However, in 970 Hugh Capet married Adelaide, sister of the new Duke, and thus the two rival houses became at last reconciled. It is possible that the young Count Raymond II of Rouerque and Gothia, who succeeded his father that year, was among the Aquitaine princes who visited Lothaire in Burgundy.

The Norman war continued. Theobald, with royal troops, captured Evreux ; Richard replied by devastating Chartres and Dunois, and he utterly defeated Theobald at Hermentruville by a surprise attack. The defeated Count fled to Evreux, whilst his troubles were increased by the death of his son and by the destruction of Chartres by fire on August 5, 962. Theobald in distress sought help from Lothaire, which he obtained. Harduin, Bishop of Chartres, had lately died, and Lothaire gave the see to the learned and gifted Wulfald, Abbot of his own royal abbey of Fleury, in whose reign the church and city were rebuilt magnificently. Richard

succeeded as Abbot of Fleury. Richard of Normandy, heavily
pressed by Theobald and his royal troops, called in the Danes,
and for years these pirates of the sea laid waste the country
bordering on Normandy with pitiless cruelty, sparing neither
sacred nor secular buildings.

Meanwhile the King had succeeded in increasing his influence
in Flanders, where the Count, the enemy of the Normans, was
always friendly. Lothaire had at an early stage confirmed the
restoration of the monastery of St. Bavon, and Arnulf had
generously endowed St. Rémy of Rheims. The old Count
resigned the government to his son Baldwin, but on the
latter's death in 961 he resumed it. Lothaire had to mediate
in a quarrel between him and his ' nepos ' Arnulf, whom he
accused of having murdered his brother. The ' nepos ' may
refer either to a nephew, Arnulf of Boulogne, or, more likely
still, the old Count's grandson, also called Arnulf. The older
Arnulf now resigned all into the hands of Lothaire on condition
that he was allowed the enjoyment of it for his life. Lothaire's
close relations with the old Count are reflected in the diplomas
given. In 962 Lothaire renewed the immunities of St. Bertin
of Ghent (Dip. xv.), and accorded immunity to St. Peter of
Ghent, which he extended in 963 and renewed in 964 (Dip. xvi.,
xxi., xxii.). He also confirmed the old Count's gift of Kiersy
to Homblières (xviii). Other royal diplomas confirmed gifts
of Villa Mazella to St. Thierry of Rheims (xvii.), and subscribed a chart by which Count Herbert, Abbot of St. Medard
of Soissons, authorized the Abbot of Homblières to buy at
Rumigny an estate dependent on St. Medard (xix.).

The death of Archbishop Artold had provoked a disturbance
which lasted through 962. A strenuous effort was made by
the Vermandois Princes to secure the election of their brother
Hugh, and they were supported by Hugh Capet. This Hugh
had been a nominee of these princes before the election of
Artold of Rheims. He had already held the see as a child,
but had been rejected by Rudolf and Louis IV and the Pope
as unworthy of the position. A synod of thirteen bishops of
the provinces of Sens and Rheims met under the presidency
of Archbishop Archembald of Sens, at a place unknown near
the Marne. The Bishops of Orleans, Senlis, and Paris, who
were nominees of Hugh Capet, supported the claims of Hugh ;
but Rorico of Laon and Gibuin of Châlons vehemently opposed

on the ground that Hugh, having been excommunicated by such a Council as that of Ingleheim in 948, could not be absolved by a smaller body. The matter was referred to Pope John, who decided against the Vermandois party at a synod held in Rome. Hugh died soon afterwards at Meaux, a town belonging to his brother Robert.

Odelric, called by Flodoard an illustrious cleric, and described by Richer (R. iii. 18) as a Canon of Metz and memorable for his knowledge of letters, was elected by the clergy of Rheims, with the favour of Lothaire and Bruno. Odelric was ordained by the Bishops of Soissons, Laon, Châlons, Noyon, and Verdun. This prolonged effort to introduce Hugh to Rheims was a political move throughout. No question of spiritual fitness could apply, but it was an effort to advance the Vermandois family at the expense of royalty, the landed possessions of Rheims and its political influence being the prize at stake. The recognition of the appellate jurisdiction of the Papacy has a special interest. The Vermandois Princes did not easily forgive Odelric, and the latter had to defend his rights by force of arms. Heribert of Troyes seized Épernay, whilst Theobald laid hands on Coucy. Heribert and Robert of Troyes also attacked Châlons in the absence of the bishop, and burnt it at the time of the Fair (Fl. 963). The defenders were, however, able to retire to the Tower. Odelric threatened excommunication, and his threat was so far successful that Heribert surrendered what he had taken, and Theobald gave up Coucy, which, however, was granted as a fief to his son.

Arnulf the Old died in 965. Lothaire claimed the heritage, but Flanders opposed his claims in the interests of the grandson Arnulf the Second, and eventually Lothaire granted him possession on condition of retaining for himself what he had occupied—Arras, Douai, and St. Amandus. Rorico of Laon seems to have acted as mediator. Dudo's statement, that Richard of Normandy intervened, and forced Lothaire to give up these conquests, is not borne out by other evidence, for in 966 Lothaire received Arnulf at Arras, and on May 5 (Dip. xxv., xxvi.) at St. Waast of Arras, he accorded diplomas for the monasteries of St. Bavon and St. Peter the Great, and in 968 granted or sold the Abbey of St. Amandus to Rathier of Verona.

Lothaire had been accompanied by his mother and his

brother Charles, and it has been thought that there was some plan for endowing the landless Charles with the additional territory ; but in May 965, Lothaire, with both mother and brother, Archbishop Odelric and Hadwig, mother of Hugh Capet, visited Cologne, when there was held a great family gathering. The Emperor Otho presided, accompanied by his wife Adelaide, his mother Matilda, and Archbishop Bruno. Emma, daughter of Adelaide by her first husband, Lothaire of Italy, was also present, and it is likely that a marriage with Lothaire was discussed. The Life of Empress Matilda (Migne 135) tells us that a suggested marriage of Emma with Henry of Bavaria had been vetoed by the aged Empress herself. Emma was eighteen, Lothaire twenty-five. Both were of royal blood, and such a marriage might strengthen the tie between Germany and France. Lothaire had apparently two sons already by a Lorraine lady of title ; but this irregular union, or morganatic marriage, was not allowed to stand in the way, and Lothaire and Emma were duly married in 966. At Cologne, Otho was at the height of his power, and Lothaire signed an Imperial diploma, as a vassal king might do, in 965 (xxiii.), granting to Bishop Heraclius of Liège certain privileges.

On his return to Laon, Lothaire speedily quarrelled with his cousins. Otho of Burgundy had died during the year, and the lords of the duchy had chosen his brother Henry without even consulting the King. This ignoring of his feudal rights roused the King. Bruno arrived on the scene, and, for the last time, by a supreme effort established peace. He was, however, taken ill at Compiègne, and died at Rheims on October 10, whilst his body was taken by Bishops Thierry of Metz and Wilfred of Verdun to its last resting-place in Cologne. His death was a great loss to the Carolings, and proved a turning-point in the reign of Lothaire. Bruno had proved himself a great statesman, animated by the purest motives.

The Norman wars continued. The ravages of the heathen Danes extended even to Brittany. Norman chronicles describe the ruin as so great that not even a dog was left to bark (William of Jumièges, Migne 149). Highways disappeared, and there was no ploughing. Starvation and pestilence followed ; castles and villas were burnt. Normandy escaped the ravages, but the adjoining territories must have suffered terribly. The King, whose territory lay some distance away, did not take the matter too seriously, and as we have seen, found time to deal with questions affecting Flanders and Burgundy. The bishops, however, gathered at Laon, and decided to send Bishop Wulfald of Chartres to interview Duke Richard. The Duke stated his wrongs, but nevertheless expressed himself willing to meet the Bishop at Jeufosse, and to do his best to relieve the land of the invaders. Theobald, hearing that peace was in the air, justified once more his name of Trickster, secretly approached Richard, gave back Evreux, and, unknown to the King, reconciled himself to the Duke. Some indignation at the King's apparent indifference may have had something to do with this change of front, but he undoubtedly felt that his own interests might be sacrificed now that peace had become urgent and was being pressed for by the bishops of the land. The fact that the bishops took the initiative from Laon may suggest that they were acting in conjunction with the King.

The meeting was held at Jeufosse in due course. According to Dudo the princes and bishops laid the blame for the whole trouble upon Theobald, and pleaded with the Duke to deliver the land from the pagans, promising that the rights of the duchy would henceforth be respected. The Duke had great difficulty in prevailing upon the Danes to withdraw, and, according to Dudo, he sought to impress upon them the truths of Christianity. Some yielded to his arguments and stayed, but the others were at last bribed by money, and the promise of guides for the way to pass over into Spain. The Duke was probably glad to be relieved of them, but there is some inconsistency in the ducal character as depicted by the admiring biographer. This most highly Christian Prince, according to Dudo, was relying on pagans whose delight was the burning of churches and the robbery of people. Dudo extols him for his encouragement of monastic reform, and yet the Duke, who was said to deplore the depravity of the monks and canons, and who compelled them to serve God strictly, had nevertheless two sons by a concubine during the life of his duchess. Later on he married his concubine and had a large family. It is said he rebuilt churches burnt by the Danes, and gave his wife's dowry for the support of churches in the Duchy of France.

The case of Duke Richard is only one illustration of the breach between religion and morality in mediaeval life. Another Assembly followed at the River Epts, near Gisors. Lothaire, Richard, Theobald, Hugh Capet, and Gozlin, the Abbot of St. Denis, were all present, and swore eternal friendship. Lothaire, as a sign of peace, confirmed reforms at St. Michael's Mount (Dip. xxiv.), and at the same Assembly Abbot Gozlin reclaimed Berneval, which the Duke restored. The pact was well maintained, and no further quarrel is recorded between the King and the Duke. Lothaire confirmed the reforms undertaken by Geoffrey of Anjou at St. Aubins (Dip. liv.), and the latter made peace with the Duke of France, who is described as his 'lord' in the charter.

Now we lose the invaluable guidance of Flodoard. In the last entry, 966, he mentions the marriage of Lothaire, and then proceeds to state that Archbishop Odelric excommunicated Count Reginald of Roucy, because the latter had retained certain towns belonging to the Church of Rheims. Richer, after a brief statement about the succession of Adalberon to Rheims, confines his attention to matters purely ecclesiastical, such as the doings of Adalberon in his diocese and the work of Gerbert.

In 968 Lothaire sustained serious loss. His mother, Gerberge, left the Court after his marriage, and, accompanied by her son Charles, aged fifteen, retired to the estates of her first husband in Lorraine. This retirement may have been due to the wise appreciation of the new situation by Gerberge, or it may have been caused by the growing influence of Queen Emma. Gerberge, on her arrival in Lorraine, in the presence of Bishop Gerard of Toul, the Emperor Otho, and many counts, made a solemn gift of all her Lorraine possessions to the Church of St. Rémy on condition that the monks prayed for her soul and the soul of her first husband. Her landless son Charles was strangely neglected in her will, and this may have embittered the spirit of the young man. Gerberge did not long survive. She died on May 5, 968, and was buried at St. Rémy. Her mother, the aged Empress Matilda, had only preceded her by two months. Gerberge was a worthy sister of the great Otho. She had twice saved the Caroling dynasty. The best tribute that can be made to her is to say that she was a loyal wife and mother and retained the affectionate loyalty of husband and son.   Her will shows us that she was deeply religious, and her name often appears in religious donations.   Her tact, judgement, and wisdom had been a tower of strength, and were much missed in the immediate future.

The same year, Odelric, another stalwart friend of the Caroling dynasty, passed away.   As a Canon of Metz and nominee of Bruno, he had been a link with the Empire, and united courage and loyalty with culture.   The choice of a successor proved unfortunate to the King.   He found purity of life but not loyalty in his nominee, Adalberon, brother of Count Godfrey of Hainault.   The new Archbishop's connexion with the nobility of Lorraine and his Imperial sympathies involved him in political difficulties, and eventually in something like actual treason.   Lothaire made a gift of the forest of Wasda in Waas to Thierry (Dip. xxxii.), Count of Holland, which shows a northerly extension of his authority.   Sonier (Dip. xxxi.), Bishop of Elne, son of the Count of Rousillon in the Pyrenees, came to Lothaire at Laon and obtained permission to rule during his life two Benedictine monasteries, St. Paul at Maritime and St. Felix at Jescal.   Sunifred, Count of Barcelona, had constructed a monastery, St. Michael at Cuxa, in 953, and had given numerous domains to the Abbey of Ripole.   His successor, Count Borell, also visited Laon and recognized Lothaire.   We find Lothaire moving about the kingdom with his Queen, and her name appears frequently in diplomas.   We note her presence in 967 in both Flanders and Burgundy.   Lothaire conceded the city of Langres to the Church, granting to Bishop Achard the authority of Count, with political and economic control (Dip. xxix.), and, at the request of the citizens of Sens, he nominated Anastasius to succeed Archembald, an appointment which was in every way satisfactory, as Anastasius was a good pastor.   He also granted two immunities to Fleury (Dip. xxvii. and xxviii.) and renewed them again in 974, with promise of free election of Abbot (xxxiv.) at the request of Abbot Richard.   We gather from these diplomas that the King had an influence upon the religious life of the country, and that he was seconded by his wife, who enjoyed her husband's confidence and was greatly interested in Church affairs.

In 972 the celebrated Gerbert arrived from Italy and became

scholasticus at Rheims. The relations between Lothaire and his cousins remained friendly for the time. In 970 Hugh Capet married Adelaide, sister of the Duke of Aquitaine, and this ended the long feud between the two houses, whilst his half-brother Herbert became Bishop of Auxerre. This prelate spent his time in building castles, in hunting, and wasting the possessions of the Church. In fact Duke Henry of Burgundy was more religious than his brother. In 974 Lothaire gave the Duke the renewal of privileges for St. Columba of Sens (Dip. xxxv.) and the Duke brought St. Germain of Auxerre under Cluny influence.

The Emperor Otho I died in 973, and from this date can be easily traced the weakening of the friendship between the Courts of Laon and Aachen. The new Emperor, Otho II, was a cousin of the King and half-brother of the Queen, but this double relationship was not sufficient to preserve cordiality. Otho II was eighteen. He was married to Theophania, a Greek Princess, and, whilst influenced by Byzantine ideas of power, lacked the real greatness of his father. Students of the Great War will be interested to learn that during the next twenty years there were two invasions of Germany to the Rhine, an invasion of France to the suburbs of Paris, two sieges of Verdun and one battle of the Aisne, and the quarrel was then about the possession of the Lorraine and Alsace portions of the old Emperor Lothaire's central kingdom.

No sooner was the strong hand of Otho I removed than the two exiled sons of Renier left Lothaire's Court and defeated at Peronne the counts who had been placed by the Emperor over their father's original inheritance of Hainault. They took the castle of Boussoit and pillaged the surrounding country. Otho II, advancing to the relief of his counts, drove Renier and Lambert back into French territory and then gave Hainault to Godfrey of Verdun and to Arnulf, the son of Isaac, Count of Valencienne and Cambrai. Lothaire was still friendly with the Capetians, for in 974 he accorded to Hugh Capet a diploma for the monks of St. Riquier (Dip. xxxvi.).

All through this period Lothaire was on excellent terms with Geoffrey of Anjou, and in 975 he bestowed the bishopric of Le Puy on Guy, Abbot of Cormerie, brother of Geoffrey. Meanwhile events tended towards a break with the Emperor.

Lothaire received the sons of Renier on French territory, thereby justifying suspicion that he was accessory to their attack on Peronne. They commenced to conspire, and in 976 they had formed a confederacy consisting of Charles, the King's brother, and Eudes of Vermandois, the King's nephew. Counts Arnulf and Godfrey were shut up in Mons. A battle followed, in which Godfrey was seriously wounded, from which wound he never quite recovered, whilst Arnulf fled hurriedly to his own county. The authorities favourable to the Emperor claim a victory for Godfrey, but the *Additions of Flodoard* show that the victory was to the other side. Eudes took possession of Le Gouy, which had belonged to Arnulf, whilst Lothaire advanced with an army to Douai, where he lingered to restore to the monastery of Marchienne the village of Haine, at the request of the Queen (Dip. xxxix.). Here he threatened the weak Bishop Theudo of Cambrai, who, panic-stricken, sought the help of the neighbouring lords, but they only took advantage of his weakness to rob his church (G.P.C. i. 99).

Lothaire returned to Laon, and at his wife's request restored the monastery of St. Amandus (Dip. xli.) of Marolle near Arras, which had been destroyed by Bishop Theudo of Cambrai, and also confirmed the immunity of St. Quentin (xlii.) at the request of Arnulf, the young Count of Flanders, and this was followed by the solemn translation of the bones of St. Thierry at Rheims.

In December 976 Lothaire lost another good friend, the faithful Rorico of Laon. He was a prelate, sympathetic with reform movements, a Caroling by birth, a soldier and a statesman, and his position in the royal town had been a source of strength to the King, who had recently confirmed the possessions of St. Vincent at his request (Dip. xxxvii. and xxxviii.).

In choosing a successor, Lothaire made a tremendous blunder in nominating Adalberon, better known as Asceline, who was raised quickly from the sub-diaconate to episcopal dignity. Apparently he was of noble birth, perhaps brother to Counts Bardo and Gozilo of Lorraine. He had been secretary to Lothaire for three years and enjoyed the monarch's confidence, but he was utterly false, and proved to be an evil genius to the Caroling dynasty. Had the Queen any voice in this election ? Asceline, as secretary to the King, must have been a frequent visitor at the palace, where he enjoyed the friendship of the Queen as well as of the King. He had not been long appointed before sordid rumours connected his name with the Queen. A synod was called to consider the Bishop's case, and once more Richer (iii. 66) comes to our help after a long silence. His reference to the synod is cut short in the middle of a sentence, and certain dots show that something has been left out of set purpose : ' Considentesque et quaeque utilia pertractantes prius quam metropolitanus.' . . . We know not what the metropolitan said. Was Richer hiding evidence proving the guilt of the Bishop ? This is not likely to be the case ; and though later events would lead us to expect almost anything of Asceline, there is much to suggest that the Bishop was innocent of the charge preferred.

1. He and Emma continued to enjoy the King's confidence. She continued to accompany the King in his journeys and to assist him in his correspondence, whilst Asceline continued to hold the bishopric under the eyes of the King. Indeed, Asceline and Emma are associated in a diploma issued at Laon 980 (xxix.).

2. Richer uses one significant phrase, ' Nullius manifesto intentionis teste,' which implies that no proof was forthcoming at the synod.

3. Emma strongly pleaded her innocence in a letter to her mother (G. 97), whilst Asceline equally repelled the charge (G. 98).

4. Thierry of Metz (G. 31, 32) roundly accused Charles, the King's brother, of libelling the Queen: ' Dum turpia in Remensium archepiscopum turpiora in reginam ementiendo serpentino sibilo effudisti.' Charles in his reply does not repel this charge. Richer tells us that Charles felt that Emma had driven him from his brother's Court (R. iv. 18), and this may have been the motive for issuing a libel. In view of these facts we must say that at any rate the charge is not proven, and we may further suggest that Lothaire's complete confidence in her is her best plea. Nevertheless the brilliant, unscrupulous young Bishop, with his insinuating ways, had by some indiscretion, if not actual crime, given ground for such rumours. The silence of Richer shows that the evidence was not altogether creditable to the parties concerned. Emma impresses

us in the various diplomas as a woman interested in church life, and her prayer-book was in existence until quite recently in Rheims. She made her second son a canon. Did Asceline therefore presume upon the religious feelings of the Queen, who turned to him as Bishop of the city for advice ?

Certain matters of ecclesiastical importance must be mentioned. Theobald, Bishop of Amiens, had been condemned at Rome by Benedict VII. He refused to appear before a provincial council in July 977, and was therefore excommunicated and deposed by Adalberon in conjunction with Stephen, the Papal Legate. In the same year the good Bishop Anastasius of Sens passed away and was succeeded by Seguin, whose entrance into the see was opposed by his maternal uncle, and Seguin threw an interdict over the country from October 977 to February 17, 978. The death of Bishop Hadulf of Noyon removed another friend of the Carolings. Lothaire nominated his own nephew, Liudolf, son of Albert of Vermandois. This appointment incidentally added to the power of the Vermandois House, whose possessions could be found in Noyon, Soissons, Tournai, Beauvais, Laon, and Meaux. About this time Walter became Bishop of Autun and Guy of Soissons.

The relations between Lothaire and Otho became more and more strained. Lothaire had his eye on Lorraine. Why should not Lothaire possess ' Lothaire's kingdom ' ? Was it not part of the Caroling inheritance ? It is to be remarked that at this time Lorraine and Alsace formed part of the German Empire. It is a problem of the middle kingdom created by the Treaty of Verdun and accentuated by the death of the Emperor Lothaire's sons without male issue. Lorraine had, however, been faithful to Charles the Simple, and Lothaire, for dynastic rather than national reasons, could not resist the temptation to seize Lorraine from the Saxons. Otho suspected the designs of Lothaire, and, by a master-stroke of diplomacy, brought a hostile confederacy to his side. He restored to Renier and Lambert their paternal inheritance, and secured their support. Godfrey kept Mons, Bouillon, and the County of Verdun. His boldest stroke was the winning over to his side of Charles, Lothaire's brother. He must have known of the domestic troubles at Laon, and, hearing that Charles had been expelled from the kingdom

because of his libels on the honour of the Queen, he offered
to him the Duchy of Lower Lorraine, provided that he did
homage for it and used his position to thwart his brother's
design. Charles, angry and landless, readily consented. By
thus supporting Charles, Otho had taken part in a family
quarrel, and Queen Emma's natural German sympathies
would be quite overshadowed by the strength of her indignation
against Otho, the supporter of her slanderer.

Lothaire was in Burgundy in the spring of 978 with Bishop
Seguin of Sens and Gibuin of Châlons, when he suddenly
called a secret council of the lords, including Duke Hugh, and
proposed an attack on Lorraine. Lothaire's army advanced
rapidly by the left bank of the Sambre and divided into companies of a hundred strong, when they had crossed the Meuse.
There seems to have been considerable attention to military
formation, but the army was too big and progress too slow
to prevent information going before. Otho and his wife were
keeping the feast of St. John at Aachen. At first he refused
to credit the news, but finally left the city by one gate as
Lothaire and his army entered the other. The Emperor,
with his pregnant wife, hurriedly fled, abandoning the royal
insignia, but he escaped, and to that extent Lothaire's plan
had miscarried. Lothaire had staked everything on the
surprise and was not prepared for a further pursuit, so after
plundering the palace and turning the eagle on the roof of the
palace so that it faced west, he hurriedly retreated after only
three days in Aachen. It had been a sensational advance and
a blow at the Imperial prestige, but otherwise a Pyrrhic victory.

Otho had escaped, and determined on revenge. He began
by issuing a protest against the attack, called his nobles
together and threw himself on their loyalty. Alpert of Metz
(Migne 140) shows us that opinion was not unanimous for
reprisals, but Otho soon found himself at the head of a sub-
stantial army. Lothaire on his return made an unsuccessful
attack on Metz, with the result that Bishop Thierry entered
the contest and brought Charles of Lorraine into the
struggle against his brother (G. 32). Otho invaded
Lothaire's territory, burning and laying waste the districts
through which he passed. Attigny was burnt, and Compiègne,
and at Laon Charles was proclaimed King (G. 31). The piety
of the Emperor spared the churches, and when the monastery

of Chelles was burnt, unknown to him, he indemnified the monks. Lothaire withdrew to Étampes to gather fresh troops. Otho advanced to the suburbs of Paris, but could not cross the Seine. Winter was approaching, Paris was well defended by Hugh Capet, and Lothaire was advancing with an army. Otho decided to retreat, but, according to one authority (G.P.C. i. 97), he caused the ears of the defenders to tingle by chanting an Alleluia on the heights of Montmartre—strange mixture of piety and cruelty, sincerity and empty bombast.

The retreat was rapid, but disaster came upon them on the banks of the Aisne. Apparently the river was flooded by heavy rain, and Otho, accepting the advice of Count Godfrey and Bishop Wulfgang, crossed with the greater part of the army, leaving the rearguard to follow in the morning with the baggage. Lothaire, pursuing hotly, arrived on the scene and destroyed the rearguard, the swollen river making it impossible for help to be sent across from the other side. The story is told that Otho challenged Lothaire to a duel, and there is a reported dialogue between Geoffrey of Anjou and Godfrey of Verdun in which the latter refused to allow the Emperor to risk his life, but these may be later embellishments. It is said that Geoffrey of Anjou was a prominent supporter of Lothaire and held some high office in the royal ranks. His greatness can be seen through the midst of much legend in the Chronicles of Anjou. We gather that Lothaire had also the support of the Dukes of France and Burgundy, and thus may suppose that the King, in face of an actual danger, had exercised his feudal rights by summoning the great feudatories. Otho continued his retreat, and Charles of Lorraine joined him in his flight. Theudo of Cambrai, who had fled to Cologne on the advance of Lothaire, died there, and the see remained vacant for some time, as Otho II was called away to the east.

Meanwhile Lothaire took steps to associate his eldest son Louis in the kingdom. The boy could not have been more than thirteen, but the proclamation of Charles as King at Laon had evidently frightened Lothaire. Moreover he knew the reverence felt for the crowned head, and, anxious to secure the position of his dynasty, he obtained the assent of the princes, and Louis was crowned by Adalberon, Archbishop of Rheims, June 979 (R. iii. 91).

At this time the relations between Lothaire and Hugh were

friendly, as can be seen by a glance at the diplomas. Louis V on the day of his coronation granted an immunity to Arnulf of Orleans, and also the renewal of one to the Abbey of Fleury (Dip.). Then Adalberon of Rheims, Hugh, and Queen Emma joined together in securing from Lothaire and Louis a confirmation of donations made to Notre Dame by Bishop Elisiard of Paris (Dip. lvi.).

Lothaire now threatened the vacant see of Cambrai, and laid hands upon the see of Arras, which at that time was united to Cambrai, claiming Regalian rights. Counts Godfrey and Arnulf, knowing that Otho was far away, turned to Duke Charles of Lorraine, and asked him to occupy the town of Cambrai. Charles agreed, but according to the Cambrai Chronicles (G.P.C. 100) his conduct in the city was disgraceful. He and his wife occupied the Bishop's bed, the church was pillaged, its possessions alienated, prebends were sold, and there was a general trade in ecclesiastical offices. Only the return of Otho from the east brought the scandal to an end. In estimating the accuracy of this statement, it must be remembered that it comes from an enemy source, and that other writings describe Charles as a glorious duke who sought to improve the condition of the Lorraine churches.

On the advice of Bishop Notker of Liège, the Emperor nominated Rothad to the vacant see. The new bishop was a former student of Gorz and a friend of Adalberon of Rheims. He came of noble family and bore a high character. He had difficulties to face, but when Eudes of Vermandois endeavoured to weaken his power by constructing a castle at Vinchy, Counts Godfrey and Arnulf intervened and destroyed the castle. Lothaire confirmed the reforms of Bishop Liudolph at Noyon (Dip. lv.) and confirmed, at the request of the Queen and Asceline and Gibuin, a donation made by Count Herbert to the monastery of Deventer (Dip. xliv.). Guery, Bishop of Langres, died in 980, and Lothaire nominated his nephew Bruno, son of Richard of Roucy, to the vacant see. He was only twenty-four, but proved to be one of the best of reforming prelates. It was in the same year that Hugh Capet secured the relics of St. Valerie and St. Riquier from Count Arnulf as the price of peace.

The good relations between Lothaire and Hugh Capet, which had lasted some time, were suddenly disturbed. The

D

King feared the growing power of the Duke and his influence with the Church and people. Perhaps he perceived that the Duke might make a separate peace with the Emperor, and that, by alienating the German Emperor, he had placed himself in the power of his feudatories. Perhaps he also realized that, by quarrelling with Otho, he was risking trouble with the Church. If he had meditated breaking with Otho, he should never have placed Adalberon, an Imperialist by birth and sympathy, in the important church of Rheims. It was freely rumoured that Adalberon had provided guides for Otho on his homeward way from Paris. A war between Lothaire and the Empire could not but lead to complications. Emma, for example, was a daughter of the Empress Adelaide, and therefore half-sister of Otho, and it is quite probable that by now she wished for peace between her husband and her brother. Perhaps Adelaide, who always professed her special love for her son-in-law, worked for peace. It is certain that Lothaire proposed secretly terms of peace, and, as a basis for general reconciliation, surrendered his claims to Lorraine. The treaty was signed at Margot on the Chiers, July 980.

Otho and Lothaire never met again, for Otho was soon called away to Italy, where, in conflict with the Greeks and Saracens, he met his death, defeated and broken, before he had reached thirty. Lothaire returned to Laon to hear the first muttering of indignation from the followers of Hugh Capet. Hugh himself was greatly vexed, and, calling his sympathizers together, denounced what he regarded as the King's perfidy. The barons were annoyed because they had not been consulted in the treaty. They feared the increased power that the King might secure by renewed alliance with the Empire, but we may possibly find in this resentment some trace of a national spirit, as distinct from a merely dynastic or feudal ambition, slowly emerging. Hugh was urged to meet Otho in Italy, which he did in company with Arnulf of Orleans and Count Burchard. There is a significant break in Richer's sentence (R. iii. 84), and it is possible that Adalberon of Rheims and Gerbert, who were in Italy in 980, were members of the party. Hugh was also Otho's relative, and had greater material resources even than the King. Otho himself could not forget the unprovoked attack of Lothaire, and he knew the power of Hugh, so an alliance was definitely formed. After visiting

Rome and receiving Papal confirmation of his work at St. Riquier, Hugh was conducted to the foot of the Alps.

News of this secret agreement reached Lothaire, who realized that he had been tricked in his turn. Efforts made by Lothaire and his wife to entrap Hugh in the Alps, referred to by Richer (iii. 86, 87), failed, though Hugh narrowly escaped capture on one occasion. He was travelling in disguise in a peasant's garments, but he happened to stay one night at a hospice, and the innkeeper, looking through a chink of the door, observed the attention paid to him by his servants. Fortunately for Hugh, the innkeeper was observed, and, having been seized, was threatened with death if he gave the alarm. Hugh and his friends, escaping in the night, took the innkeeper with them till they reached the place where he could be safely left. So Hugh arrived safely home. Lothaire's letter to Conrad of Burgundy refers to his discovery of the secret enmity of Hugh ; and the letter of Emma to her mother, which shows her place in the confidence of the King and her active co-operation with him in the administration of affairs, and which makes it difficult to believe the sordid rumours which were afloat, describes the figure and dress of Hugh in great detail. Lothaire's position was not an enviable one, though two diplomas for Duke Guifred of Roussillon in 981 (Dip. xlv., xlvi.) show his influence in the south, for he had quarrelled with Hugh without securing the friendship of the Emperor, and he had seriously endangered his friendship with the most powerful ecclesiastic of the kingdom, the Archbishop of Rheims. Nevertheless, the nobles grew weary of the subtle warfare of intrigue and plot and counter-plot. So the wise men on both sides assembled and sought to reconcile the King and the Duke ; and though there was too much suspicion for cordiality on both sides, an agreement was patched up between the parties ; and thus in 982 Lothaire confirmed Duchess Adelaide's gift of a church to the monastery of the Holy Trinity, Poitiers (Dip. xlviii.).

Geoffrey of Anjou and his brother, Bishop Guy of Le Puy, both favourably disposed towards the Carolings, had a sister Adelaide, the widow of Count Stephen of Gevaudan, a powerful Aquitaine heiress who, with her sons, Pons and Bertrand, had great influence in that area. Now if Louis, the King's son, could be married to this heiress, the King's power

would be strong in the south ; and, by securing such a point
of vantage, he would be in a position to threaten the Duke of
France from the south. A marriage proposal was therefore
made to Lothaire through Emma, and negotiations were
carried to a successful conclusion unknown to Hugh. The two
kings and Emma proceeded with an army to Brioude, where
the marriage was solemnized and Adelaide crowned. A few
diplomas date from this time, for Lothaire, at the wish of
Ildesond (Dip. l.), Bishop of Elne and Abbot of St. Peter of
Roses, confirmed to him the possessions of that monastery, and,
at Parontignac (Dip. xlix.) in Auvergne, he also confirmed the
possession of the monastery of Ripoli to Abbot Seniofred.

The marriage scheme may have been a master-stroke of
political strategy, but it broke down on the passions of human
nature. The bride was much older than the bridegroom, and
the disparity of years rendered mutual affection impossible.
Their habits differed and they never shared the same house,
and always conversed in the open air. Louis was only twenty,
and the unequal marriage and the separation from the wiser
counsels of his father completely spoilt the young prince. As
he grew in wild extravagance, his resources were so reduced
that he came to poverty. Open quarrels broke out between
the ill-assorted pair, until Adelaide, after two years of shameful
quarrelling, separated from her young husband (R. iii. 92, 93).
Lothaire came with an army to Brioude and took his son back
to Laon. He stopped at Limoges on the way, and ordered Abbot
Guigue of St. Martial to surround the abbey with ramparts
(Adhemar, Ch. of St. M.). Adelaide married William, Count of
Arles, and became mother of Constance, wife of Robert II.
A brilliant scheme had thus miscarried, and one last opportunity of building up a strong Caroling appanage in the south
had failed. The strategy of the scheme may have been sound,
but it did not sufficiently allow for the wayward influences
of a young man's emotional nature.

The Emperor Otho II met his death in 983. He had
sustained a severe defeat at the hands of the Greeks, and
narrowly escaped death on the field. He escaped only to die
a year later, baffled, heart-broken, leaving behind him a child
of three to inherit the crown. The Empress Theophania had
openly shown her sympathies with the Greeks. She had
Byzantine ideas of royalty, and was greatly disliked by the

proud baronage of Germany, who claimed that she was more Greek than German. Otho III was crowned at Aachen by Archbishop John of Ravenna and Archbishop Willegesus of Mayence ; but as Theophania was still in Italy, Henry of Bavaria, cousin of Otho II, secured the person of the new King and claimed the right to rule in his name. Opposition to the Empress grew in volume. Egbert, Archbishop of Trèves, rejected her as a Greek, and was supported by Ware, Archbishop of Cologne, Gisilo of Magdeburg, and Thierry of Metz, all of whom rallied to Duke Henry.

Henry of Bavaria was no mean opponent. He possessed gifts of body and mind, but he was ambitious and covetous of power. He met his supporters at Magdeburg, and was saluted as King at Quidlinburg (Easter Sunday, 984). The followers of the young King met at Asselburg, and it would seem that Lothaire put himself forward as guardian of the child King.

For the events that follow Gerbert is our guide. His correspondence is not clearly dated, and there is some uncertainty as to the order of events, but Havet and Lot have worked out a reasonable scheme which can be followed. Gerbert was the power behind all these secret negotiations. He had been made Abbot of Bobbio in 983 by the Emperor Otho II, but, being fiercely opposed by a former abbot, who resisted his efforts at reform, Gerbert returned to Rheims. He resumed his work as *scholasticus* at the episcopal school, but he never forgot that he had taken an oath of allegiance to the Saxon Emperor, by which oath he felt committed. He therefore joined heartily with Archbishop Adalberon and other bishops and barons in the furtherance of Lothaire's advocacy of the young King Otho III. Hostages, including Adalberon, son of Count Godfrey and nephew of the Archbishop, were given as security for Lorraine.

Writing to the Lady Imiga, Gerbert says (22), ' Go, tell Theophania that the Kings of the Franks favour her son, and that their only end is to destroy the tyranny of Henry.' Again, writing to Gerard of Aurillac, he refers to the son of the Empress ' under the tutelage of the Kings of the Franks.' Correspondence between Thierry of Metz and Charles of Lorraine (G. 32) shows that Lothaire and his brother were at that time on the side of Otho III, whilst Adalberon in his defence

against a charge of treason (G. 57) refers to the time when
Lothaire claimed to be Otho's guardian.

Henry, losing ground, consented to meet his opponents at
Rava, June, A.D. 984, and there delivered up Otho III to his
mother. A peace was signed at Worms October, A.D. 984.
Then there followed a change of policy. Henry began to
negotiate with Lothaire, offered him Lorraine as the price of
his support, and arranged to meet him on the Rhine at Brisach,
February, A.D. 985.

Gerbert is well informed about the plan, and writes : ' We
know the dark designs of Henry, and the fierce attacks of the
Franks. We are not ignorant of their intentions, for the
Kings of the Franks approach secretly the Rhine at Brisach,
and Henry meets the enemies of the State ' (G. 92). Henry
failed to keep the appointment, for he found that such active
support of Lothaire would weaken his position in Germany,
and he returned to the policy of negotiating with the party
of the Empress till at last, by the Treaty of Frankfort, Bavaria
was once more restored to him (Th. iv. 6).

Meanwhile Lothaire, deserted by Henry, found himself in a
critical position, with the Vosges and a hostile people between
him and his country. Nevertheless, by the use of light infantry
he cleared the heights, removed obstacles that had been thrown
in his path, and brought his troops safely across the passes.
Having failed to secure Lorraine by agreement with Henry,
or in the disguise of guardian of Otho III, Lothaire determined
to pursue his own course. As Richer (R. iii. 99) puts it :
' Having obtained opportunity, Lothaire meditated another
invasion of Lorraine in order that he might bring it back to
his own rule, as Otho had no power and the barons were
divided.' He secured the services of the Count Eudes of
Chartres and Herbert of Vermandois. He captured Verdun
in an eight-day siege, and, leaving Emma in charge, returned
to Laon. A successful revolt of the lords of Lorraine, in
collusion with the Empress, followed. Emma and the French
garrison were driven out of Verdun, and the city was prepared
for further siege by the requisitioning of the wealth of the
merchants and the services of the peasantry, whilst a great
amount of timber was brought from the Argonne (R. iii. 103).
Among the Lorraine lords were Thierry of Upper Lorraine,
Godfrey of Verdun, Sigebert of Luxemburg, and two barons,

Bardo and Gozilo, brothers, possibly, of Asceline, Bishop of Laon.

Meanwhile certain changes in the bishops of Verdun should be noted here. Wigfrid, a friend of Bruno, had died in 983 (August 31). Adalberon, son of the Duchess Beatrice of Lorraine, had succeeded to the bishopric, but, on the death of Thierry of Metz, September 7, 984, he was transferred to that see. Adalberon, son of Godfrey, and nephew of the Archbishop Adalberon, a cleric of Rheims, and, incidentally, a hostage of Lorraine's good faith, was sent off to Worms and received the appointment of bishop of the city from the Empress in the name of her son. His uncle released him from service at Rheims, and, as he was only a sub-deacon, rapidly passed him through the various grades of the ministry, and sought consecration for him from the Archbishop Egbert of Trèves, the metropolitan. Lothaire was incensed. As the nominal advocate of the Emperor, he claimed to be consulted in these matters. Moreover, this action revealed to him the real sympathies of the Archbishop and his party, and their real disloyalty to him. Lothaire never forgave the Archbishop, and his influence with Egbert secured at any rate the postponement of the consecration.

Lothaire renewed his attack on Verdun in the early months of 985, with 10,000 men. Richer (iii. 105) describes the great machines used by the opposing forces. The attack was fierce and sudden, but it apparently failed, and operations developed into a regular siege. Lothaire was wounded in the upper lip as he approached too near the wall. Verdun, with the exception of the merchants' quarter, which was connected by a bridge with the rest of the city, lay within the territory enclosed by the windings of the river, and was a strong position ; but Lothaire succeeded in capturing the city, along with the lords of Lorraine. Adalberon, the new bishop, and his brother escaped to Germany. The prisoners were committed to the care of Eudes and Herbert, but no other vengeance was taken on the city. No lives were forfeited, and unusual leniency seemed to have characterized the policy of Lothaire throughout this campaign. There was a strong party favourable to him in the city, and opposed to the new bishop, and the friendship of that party he obviously intended to maintain, so that he could reign by general consent. After this success the King

pursued his campaign in the north, and threatened Cambrai.
Bishop Rothad, humbly approaching, secured as a favour an
arrangement by which he was only to surrender Cambrai in
the event of Liège being captured (G.P.C. i. 105). Richer
(iii. 107) informs us that Lothaire was engaged in schemes for
enlarging his borders at the time of his death, and the campaign
against Cambrai and Liège was evidently part of a general
scheme of conquest whereby he hoped to bring all Lorraine,
Upper and Lower, including Belgium, under his sway.

Now this attack on Germany for the sake of the Middle
Kingdom was open to grave criticism. It certainly provoked
the opposition of Archbishop Adalberon and Gerbert, who
were both heavily committed to Otho III, and probably
encountered the opposition of the Queen. Lothaire would have
been well advised to refuse the tempting bait, and to have
retained the friendship of the Empire, and, what was more
important still, the friendship of Adalberon. This new war,
successful in a military sense, was a tremendous blow at the
dynasty. Adalberon might give lip service and send his troops
to the siege, but his heart was elsewhere. A great secret
movement against Lothaire was engineered by Gerbert.
Treason deep and desperate is seen in every page of Gerbert's
letters. He finds out what is happening, and hastens to give
information to the enemies of his sovereign. He brings Hugh
Capet into the conspiracy, and states that Hugh, not Lothaire,
is the real king (see Letters 47–52).

After the capture of Verdun the conspiracy strengthened.
Gerbert is in constant correspondence with the Empress
Theophania and the relatives of the captured counts, and
is always protesting his loyalty to Otho III. He secures
access to the prisoners by the connivance of the jailers, and
acts as a medium between them and their friends in Germany.
He urges these friends, in impassioned letters, to be careful
not to sacrifice the Imperial interest in order to liberate the
captives. The treason of Adalberon was proved. He was
metropolitan and chancellor of the kingdom of Lothaire, and
he ought to have resigned these posts or remained loyal to
his oaths. He did neither, and as Lothaire's chancellor he
corresponded with Lothaire's enemies. Even at Verdun
his loyalty was not beyond suspicion, for he refused to pull
down the Monastery of St. Paul at the King's request, on the

plea that it was of no advantage to the enemy, and that, even
if it were, he would not as Archbishop do such a thing, and,
whilst protesting his loyalty, complained that his soldiers
were suffering from undue exposure in a long campaign (G. 53).
Adalberon publicly wrote letters at the command of Lothaire
and disavowed them by secret letters. Thus (G. 49) 'In
these letters he did not write what he wished, but simply
what the tyrant commanded,' says Gerbert. 'I do not wish
to conceal the fact that I sent the former letters to your
Paternity (Egbert of Trèves) only by order of my
King' (54). Another letter contains the sentence, 'The
silence of your friend Adalberon indicates his own condition and at the same time the condition of the Church,
the Lords, and the Palace of the Franks,' and, in the letter to
Theophania, Gerbert speaks of Adalberon as 'faithful to
you' (59).

Lothaire gravely suspected the prelate. Gerbert and the
Archbishop knew their King's attitude when Gerbert wrote to
the Empress (52), 'Also you know that the Kings of the Franks
do not regard me with a favourable eye, on account of our
loyalty to you and because we do not feel as they do, and
because we enjoy so much familiarity with the Archbishop
of Rheims, whom they blame for similar reasons and think
disloyal to themselves.' In another letter, Adalberon himself
asserts, 'I am charged with the crime of perfidy (57) and
infidelity to the King's Majesty.' Proof was not at once
available, and Lothaire bided his time. The King's position
in such treason-laden atmosphere was serious enough. Hugh
Capet was being drawn into the conspiracy.

'If you will seek out his friendship and unite the son of
Caesar to his son, you will not have, for long, hostile Kings of
the Franks' (48), writes Gerbert, and again to the son of Count
Sigebert : 'When you have united yourself to Hugh in friendship, you will be strong enough to resist the attacks of the
Franks' (51) ; again, 'You must not delay in seeking the
friendship of Hugh' (60). Thus the greatest churchman,
the greatest scholar, the ablest feudal lord, were arrayed
secretly against the King.

Lothaire was watchful, prepared if necessary to strike, a
rather noble kingly figure. At last he revived the question
of the licence given to Adalberon of Verdun, and

denounced the Archbishop, in an assembly at Compiègne, as traitor in May 985. Gerbert (58) gives information about this citation. There were present Duke Charles, Renier of Hainault, Herbert of Troyes, Gibuin, Bishop of Châlons, and Asceline of Laon, when suddenly Hugh Capet descended with six hundred men and dispersed the assembly. Adalberon had a plausible defence, and Lothaire did not proceed further, but came to an agreement with Hugh (59), which, however, did not prevent the latter from continuing his correspondence with the Empress (G. 60, 61). Lothaire also consented to release his prisoners on conditions—Godfrey alone refusing liberty, at the price of relinquishing Mons and Hainault to Renier, and of depriving his son of the see of Verdun.

Lothaire was pressing his campaign in the north, and Gerbert writes mysteriously of perils and invasions (G. 59). Egbert of Trèves was acting with Lothaire (62), who also received ambassadors from beyond the Pyrenees (70). The Saracens had burnt Barcelona, and Count Borell asked help of the King, a tribute to his reputation in the south. The King may have at this time confirmed to Eudes, Abbot of St. Cucufat (Dip. li.), gifts made to that monastery by Charlemagne and Louis I. Lothaire was fighting successfully in the north, and making his name to be respected in the south, but the end was near. He was seized with violent colic, took to his bed in Laon, and there he died. Louis was present to hear his father's dying behests, in which he was warned against Adalberon and advised to seek help from Hugh, a council of despair to a young man in the midst of foes.

Louis V had been crowned at Compiègne, and there was no opposition. Queen Emma now made her appearance. She was last seen at Verdun. She would probably be at her husband's side. The story that she poisoned her husband must be rejected. It appears for the first time in Adhemar's writings, and Richer and Gerbert know nothing of such a story. Gerbert's letters include one written in the Queen's name expressive of great sorrow at her husband's death. ' O bitter day, which snatched my husband from my side and precipitated me into such miseries ' (G. 74). ' Whilst he flourished, I flourished, &c.' It is clear from this letter that Emma is with her son as guide and confidante, for she says that the barons have taken the oath to her and her son.

She, however, deprived of her husband's advice in perilous days, seeks peace with the Empire by appealing to her mother, the Empress Adelaide, and asks for an interview with her uncle, King Conrad. The Queen had probably been adverse to the continuance of the war which embroiled her with her mother, but there is no evidence that she had ever been disloyal to her husband's policy during his lifetime ; but the removal of his strong hand made restoration of peace essential, and there is little doubt that her policy was really the wise one. The approach to the Empire meant reconciliation with Adalberon and Gerbert, and thus we are not surprised that the latter is acting as her secretary and the former is rejoicing in a new-found favour (G. 73). All of the Lorraine lords except Godfrey were now released.

Louis lacked his father's character. He had energy, but the wild spirit he had shown in Aquitaine revealed itself in a series of rash, ill-judged activities which only increased the number of his enemies. Lothaire had trusted his wife and banished Charles, his brother, for libel. Louis seems to have believed all these rumours concerning his mother's infidelities, which were probably revived by the death of Lothaire. Emma was living at Laon, the episcopal see of Asceline. She may have turned to him as spiritual adviser in her sorrow, but sordid rumour was soon afloat. Louis broke with his mother, and banished Asceline, who took refuge with Hugh Capet at Dourden. Moreover, remembering his father's behests, he broke furiously with Adalberon, charged him with treason, and besieged him at Rheims. The Archbishop only escaped by offering hostages and agreeing to appear at a council summoned for March 27, to answer the charges, which, as before, related to the election of his nephew to Verdun. Louis then returned to Senlis, and Adalberon took refuge in the German parts of his diocese. Meanwhile Asceline issued a letter of passionate defence, and, refusing to resign, pleaded his innocence and pronounced curses on any one who would undertake his duties (G. 98). ' As the charges are false there is no cause for remorse,' he says. Emma, now entirely out of favour, though at liberty in Laon, wrote her mother another passionate letter (G. 97). Her son has now become her enemy. ' They charge the Bishop of Laon with disgraceful crimes to my shame. They persecute him and try to deprive him of all

honour, so that endless shame may rest upon me.' She asked
for the intervention of her mother, in order that Theophania
and Otho III may become favourable to her, and refers
to the loyalty of Eudes and Herbert in the emergency. ' My
enemies boast that I have neither brother, neighbour, nor
friend to help me.' She is a pathetic figure deserted by her
son, persecuted by her brother-in-law, and in her despair
throws herself on the counsels of her mother and seeks help
from the country's foes. Louis had received so far the outward support of Duke Hugh, but the young King soon learnt
how precarious that support was. He began to realize that
his mother's policy of peace was not so foolish, and possibly
he also came to see that he had too readily believed the stories
told against her. At any rate, he began to retrace his steps,
and sought to be reconciled with the Empire. The Duchess
Beatrice seems to have acted as mediator, and there is a letter
which mentions a conference to be held on May 25, 987, at
Montfauçon, on the Meuse. The Empress Adelaide, Emma,
Hugh, Conrad of Alsace, and Louis were to be present.
The plan failed because, for some reason or other, the Empress
Theophania had not been consulted, but it is clear that
Louis, reconciled with his mother, was seeking peace.

The council at which Adalberon was to plead was postponed
from March to May through the influence of Duke Hugh, and
Richer indicates that the conference was fixed for the very day
on which Louis died. The young King, impetuous as ever,
fell from his horse whilst hunting, and died soon afterwards.
He was the last of the Caroling kings and had only reigned
fourteen months. Whether he could have made headway
against the treachery and intrigue around him it is impossible
to say. He was only twenty at his death. Certainly he did
not lack vigour and courage, and there might have come with
years of experience that tact, discernment, and restraint
which were so sorely needed in those days. The conference
met, heard Archbishop Adalberon, and acquitted him. He in
his turn declared his loyalty to Hugh, and suggested a council
for the election of a new king, hinting that Hugh should be
elected. The record suggests a pre-arranged scheme. Hugh
would secure the acquittal of Adalberon, and he would support
the Duke's claim to the throne.

The council was summoned to meet at Senlis. The only

legitimate heir, Charles, at once addressed himself to Adalberon. He pleaded for his rights, his fitness by birth and character, and pathetically recounted his wrongs and his exile. He recalled that no share of his father's kingdom had fallen to him, and yet he had been loyal to his brother. 'Whither can I go? To whom shall I appeal beside you? Have compassion on me, wearied by so many injuries.' It was in vain Adalberon threw the responsibility for election upon the princes, roundly accused Charles of keeping disreputable company, and at the great council opposed his election on grounds that (1) character, not blood relationship, constituted fitness, (2) Charles possessed neither character nor energy, (3) he had received a duchy from a foreign monarch, (4) he had married a wife of inferior status, so that he would be unable to sustain the royal dignity before the princes. The speech was effective, and Hugh was elected.

We cannot suppress sympathy with Charles, driven from his brother's Court, landless and friendless, though we can recognize the wisdom which sought to preserve the unity of the Caroling heritage under one head, and can well believe that Charles's treatment of his sister-in-law had hardened Lothaire's attitude. The objections raised by the Archbishop have a certain interest. (1) His criticism of the hereditary principle on imperialistic and ecclesiastical grounds certainly did not coincide with the general ideas of that feudal world, but apparently corresponded with the genuine convictions of Adalberon's mind and the theory of the Church. (2) Charles certainly possessed energy, and his character was probably no worse than that of the dark, unscrupulous man who supported him. (3) The reference to the German intimacy came with ill grace from the man who was in close relation with the Court of Aachen. (4) The Duke's marriage, whilst subject to severe criticism from the proud aristocracy of Church and State, which gave so much attention to purity of blood, &c., would doubtless commend him to a more democratic age. However, it seems obvious that these objections only veiled the actual situation. Adalberon and Gerbert were committed to Hugh, and were determined to remove the Carolings from power. The Church had thrown over the dynasty, and it was doomed.

Just a word is needed in regard to the character of Lothaire, whose long reign covered so large a portion of this period. He was only forty-four at his death. There was a magnificent funeral, and many expressions of a people's grief. ' The whole house resounded with lamentations.' Princes carried the pall, and bishops and clerics carried their insignia of office. There was a crown flashing with jewels. The soldiers followed, weeping, for he had been a warrior king, and so he was buried in the Monastery of St. Rémy at Rheims by the side of his father and mother. It was a day of crisis fateful for the dynasty. ' O bitter day, which has robbed me of my husband,' sobs his widow. It was the day on which the most ' brilliant star ' was taken from the world, according to the testimony of an enemy (G. 73). History judges that with him there passed the glory of the Caroling Dynasty.

It is not easy to estimate in full measure the character of Lothaire, but unquestionably he was one of the greatest of his line. R. Glaber, writing in the eleventh century, says he was ' agile in body, and in mind sound and vigorous ' (i. 3). In the book of discovery of Judocus, written also in the time of King Robert, we are told that he was by no means inferior to his ancestors, and that he was ' strong in nobility and uprightness of character, eager for glory, sagacious in industry, a man who governed happily for many years.' These opinions are borne out by a study of the life of Lothaire. He displayed considerable ability as a soldier and general. His military qualities were displayed in the attack on Aachen, which only just missed being a brilliant achievement. The retreat from Brisach and the sieges of Verdun, and his military formations, showed knowledge of military science. He shared the hardship of the campaign, whilst his personal bravery is vouched for by the wound he received at Verdun. His statesmanship has been criticized, especially in regard to his attack on the Empire and the break with the Church which followed. In regard to the attacks on Lorraine, he may have found it necessary to find employment for the fighting elements within his kingdom, and certainly the lure of Lorraine to a Lothaire, a Caroling, was natural enough, whilst his expedition to Aquitaine was a quite reasonable endeavour on the part of the King to strengthen the position in the south. His hesitation in re-granting Burgundy to the Capetian princes, his unwillingness to divide the royal patrimony with his brother, show that he was fully alive to the real weakness of the Carolings. His crowning of his son Louis was in the interests of his dynasty and secured a peaceful succession. Whatever mistakes he made, Lothaire was certainly working consistently for the Caroling interest. He would stoop to intrigue and secret diplomacy, but he was surrounded by treachery, and there was no prince, either ecclesiastical or secular, whom he could fully trust. It is true he countered plot with plot, but he maintained the royal supremacy, and advanced the reputation of his dynasty, caused fear in the Palace at Aachen, and received recognition both in Lorraine and beyond the Pyrenees. Adalberon of Rheims dared not openly break with him. Hugh found neutrality a safer policy than an open breach. A union of activity and restraint alone could have secured such results. Lothaire's diplomas prove that he believed in the Divine Right of Kings, and, though he was prepared to consult the clergy and nobles, he claimed to reign by the grace of God. In his attitude to the Church, he showed himself favourable to attempted reformation in the manners of clergy and a believer in the mediaeval type of Christian piety, revealed in a veneration for relics. He used his royal power to select certain bishops from his own friends, but of these, Bruno of Langres and Liudolph of Noyon were reformers. His choice of Adalberon for Rheims, Asceline for Laon, show that his discernment was often faulty, and both appointments were thoroughly disastrous. Nevertheless, these appointments were not without reason. The reputation of the Lorraine clergy stood very high, and both these men were Lorraine clerics and men of ability and knowledge. Had Lothaire been able to keep peace with his German cousins, the appointment of Adalberon, the greatest churchman of the day, would have been in every way satisfactory and creditable. Lothaire's trust in Asceline is difficult to understand, for he ought to have estimated his character, as he had been secretary to the King for some time before his appointment to the see. A singular, subtle charm must have pervaded Asceline's personality, otherwise his immunity from penalty in spite of oft-repeated treason would remain a mystery indeed.

In his private life, Lothaire had been a devoted son to Gerberge, and he seems to have been an equally devoted husband. Both Gerberge and Emma figure largely in the correspondence of the reign, and evidently took a large share of the administration. In spite of sordid rumour, he trusted

his wife absolutely, and her influence on him was strong. She
accompanied him in his royal journeys and shared his State
secrets.   He writes of her in official documents as ' sweetest,'
' most-loved wife.'   These expressions may have more than
a formal meaning.   He seems to have been devotedly attached
to her, and her grief at his passing was very great.   His two
sons, Arnulf and Richard, by the Lorraine lady, were probably
born before his marriage with Emma.   Hugh Flavigny states
definitely that Arnulf was born first.   He had two sons by
Emma—Louis, who succeeded him, and Otho, who was a
canon at Rheims and died young.   The fact that two of his
sons were clerics may indicate a strong Church interest in
Lothaire's life.   In estimating his character, we must also
recollect Emma's statement that he was on most affectionate
terms with his mother-in-law, the Empress Adelaide, who
greatly loved him (G. 87).

Another personal trait is his humanity.   No act of cruelty
is charged to his account, and his generosity to the Verdun
captives is particularly noticed by Richer.   He obviously
retained the confidence of his son, the love of his nephew
Bruno, and the respect of even his enemies.   As to his personal
appearance, the book of hours of Emma, which was destroyed
in 1774, contained a miniature representing the King with
his wife and sons, but this book fortunately had been copied
by Mabillon before its destruction, and we see a rather imposing
bearded figure representing the King.   We cannot be certain
that this is a correct copy, neither can we be sure that the
prayer-book miniature would be a really true portrait of the
King.   We may safely conclude that Lothaire's break with
the Church was not on moral or religious grounds, but rather
on political grounds, and was due to the important political
influence of the Church in those days.   This break with the
Church was an important cause of the fall of his dynasty.
This was due to no new principle of government, but a
temporary alliance between leading churchmen, the Empire,
and the Capetian House secured the throne for the Capetians.

III

THE CHURCH IN THE TIME OF HUGH CAPET AND CHARLES OF LORRAINE, 987 TO 990

Note
R. = Richer's History.
G. = Gerbert's Letters.

HUGH CAPET had now been called to the kingdom, but his elevation to the throne was to bring him no ease, and the difficulties were immense. The Duke was elected by the consent of all sections of feudal France. Richer (R. iv. 12) describes him as a King of Gauls, Bretons, Danes, Aquitainians, Goths, Spaniards, Gascons, and this list comprises the whole area of the kingdom. It is, however, not necessary to say that in some of these districts his authority, like the authority of Lothaire, was little more than nominal, even though, surrounded by these various princes, he did issue decrees in which he also promised to preserve the rights of the Church and grant justice to the people.

Adalberon had rejected the hereditary principle, and had thus paved the way for the election of Hugh, but Hugh himself had already acknowledged the hereditary principle when he had agreed openly to the crowning of Louis V in his father's lifetime (R. iv. 8) and allowed him quietly to succeed. Indeed, he declared at a later period that if Louis had had issue he would have regarded such issue as heirs to the crown. He was thus acting consistently with this profession when he determined to provide himself with a crowned heir by inducing the Archbishop to crown his son Robert (R. iv. 12). Adalberon's advocacy of free election at any rate emphasized the Church's part in the choice of the sovereign, but the Archbishop soon perceived the significance of Hugh's desires. It meant that he was prepared to throw down the ladder by which he had ascended and commit himself to the hereditary principle.

Adalberon at first refused consent, but Hugh out-manœuvred him. A call for help which came from Borell, Count of Barcelona, who was pressed by the Saracens, proved opportune. Hugh declared that it was necessary that there should be two kings, in case one were drawn away into foreign wars. Adalberon reluctantly yielded, and Robert was duly crowned, and thus the hereditary right was reasserted and the right of free election quickly shelved. Robert was crowned at the Church of the Holy Cross in Orleans. Hugh, having secured his ends, never found it convenient to engage in this campaign on behalf of Borell. He wrote him a letter (G. 112) asking for a repetition of an oath of allegiance when the armies should meet in Aquitaine, but the armies never met, for other events intervened, and Borell had to fall back on his own resources.

About this time a marriage alliance with the Eastern Empire was in the mind of the Kings, and there is a letter (G. 112) bearing on the question ; but nothing came of the suggestion, and Robert was married to Susannah, widow of Arnulf of Flanders, early in 988.

Hugh's first steps had been in the direction of friendship with the Empire, perhaps in the fulfilment of secret obligations. He delivered up Verdun (G. 100), made peace with Germany, and secured the release of Count Godfrey. Apparently Eudes and his jailer only released him on conditions, for his son Adalberon was held as hostage, and Godfrey had agreed to give up some villas pertaining to the Empire. Thus the Archbishop wrote to the Empress Theophania expressing his hope that she would not ratify the agreement, and in another letter warned her against the conspiracies of Eudes and Herbert (G. 100), who were seeking to secure her person by guile. The details of these negotiations are not known, though we have a letter from Adalberon to his brother inviting him to an interview at Bouillon (G. 129).

These letters show us the intrigue of the two Counts, and the extraordinary knowledge of their schemes which, nevertheless, the Archbishop possessed through an efficient spy service. In spite of this peace with Germany, secured through the surrender of Lorraine and Verdun, Hugh had enemies. Albert of Vermandois revolted, and was only reconciled through the intervention of Richard of Normandy (Dudo). The Archbishop of Sens was slow to recognize the change of dynasty, and apparently his city remained a centre of opposition to the Capetians. The sympathy shown by the Chronicles of Sens with Charles and Arnulf is most striking, and Hugh is termed usurper and rebel against the rightful King Charles. The reference to trouble with Aquitaine can be treated with reserve. Adhemar's story may represent a confusion with events of 955, and the charters of that period seem to recognize without hesitation the sovereignty of Hugh. But there was more serious trouble at hand.

Charles of Lorraine was not idle (R. iv. 14). He returned to his duchy and gathered his friends together, stated his wrongs, and asked for support. Steps were taken for the purpose of conquering the kingdom unjustly snatched from him. His tears and pleadings won their sympathy and support. He determined to test the feeling of the citizens of Laon. Spies were sent, and it was soon discovered that Asceline, the Bishop, was not popular (R. iii. 15). There was a dispute between the Bishop and the citizens *de lege agraria*, by which was meant, either a dispute concerning tithes due to him as Bishop, or a dispute about rents due to him as Count. There was a party in the city favourable to Charles, and this apparently included Arnulf, a natural son of Lothaire, for the latter was later charged by Gerbert with having betrayed his Bishop (G. 217). This Arnulf, ' born first from a noble lady,' had been notary to his father after the promotion of Asceline to the bishopric of Laon, but he was a cleric of the Church of Rheims.

It was spring, and the time when vineyards were all in bloom (R. iv. 11). The forces of Lorraine, hiding in the neighbouring vineyards, waited for the signal from the city. News of their whereabouts was sent to their friends in the city, and they were told to enter at once. Approaching the city, they were immediately challenged by the sentries, who threw stones, but to the challenge there came at once the answer, ' We are citizens,' from the traitors. The doors were opened, and the soldiers of Charles entered at once and secured possession. It was night, and, as they sounded their trumpets and uttered their cries, the affrighted citizens rushed from their houses and sought safety in flight, but the walls were now well guarded by adherents of the Carolings, and escape was rendered difficult, so that the Bishop himself, though he passed out of the city and descended the hill, was soon taken in the adjoining vineyards. Queen Emma and the nobility of the town were taken, but the rest of the inhabitants were allowed to return to their homes in peace whilst Charles prepared for further military operations by strengthening the defence. Towers were built, a patrol of 500 for night service was formed, food was brought in from Vermandois and wood from the forests, whilst war machines were constructed, and forges for preparing necessary weapons of iron.

Neither the Queen nor the Bishop could expect much pity from Charles, for (R. iv. 16) he believed that it was through her persuasion that he had been driven from his brother's Court, and had evidently taken his revenge by insinuating adulterous relations between the Queen and the Bishop. A letter from Emma is preserved (G. 119) in which she refers to herself as ' captive slave of most cruel enemies and afflicted with insults.' Gerbert implored Charles to treat his prisoners leniently. It appears that both the Empress Theophania, Hugh, and the Bishops had urged Charles to release them (G. 120, 128, 122). Hugh even suggested a meeting between his wife and the Empress at Sternay (G. 120) to discuss united efforts for their release, but all these efforts, for the time, at any rate, proved fruitless. Charles, though he refused to release his prisoners, sought to gain the Archbishop to his side, and in a letter to him referred evidently to some kindness he had previously shown to the Archbishop. Perhaps he had saved his life in the attack on Rheims made by Louis V. Adalberon acknowledged the letter, and professed that he was no enemy to the Carolings (G. 122. 10). ' Who was I to impose a king on the Franks by myself ? ' cried he in mock humility, which does no justice to the important part he took in the change of dynasty. He took the opportunity of warning Charles against certain of his friends, who were really deceivers, by whom he probably meant Counts Eudes and Herbert, who apparently for the time were in alliance with Charles. He expressed his fear of treachery and difficulty in writing, and begged that his nephew might be released from the hands of the Count. He roundly condemned Charles for his treatment of the Queen and the Bishop, and for his disloyalty to Hugh Capet. There was no weakening of his attachment to the cause of Hugh Capet. Charles at once perceived that his diplomatic efforts to break the power of Hugh, by drawing from him his most powerful adherent, had failed. The Archbishop continued his negotiations with the Counts, and secured the release of his nephew in the autumn of 988, probably through the intervention of Gibuin of Châlons and of his ambassador Renier (G. 127). Hugh meanwhile called a council at Compiègne, which confirmed immunities granted to St. Columba of Sens and Corbie. This council was attended by the Archbishops of Rheims, Sens, and Bourges, and numerous bishops, and whilst it was sitting the news of the fall of Laon arrived. The council at once issued anathemas against Charles and Arnulf, but without avail.

Hugh prepared for war, and besieged Laon in the summer of 988. It was a hot summer, and Gerbert, who was present, felt the heat intensely, and suffered from fever (G. 123). Adalberon was evidently present with the troops of Rheims (G. 121, 125). During August the besieged (R. iv. 23) made a sudden sortie, burnt the camp, and put to flight the besiegers, who retired hastily in some confusion. Gerbert described the disaster in his letter to Archbishop Egbert of Trèves (G. 121). He tried to make light of it, but admitted that at midday, whilst the soldiers were oppressed with wine and sleep, the townsmen made a sortie with all their forces, burnt the tents and all the apparatus of war. The siege was to be resumed on August 25, but we find later on that he complained of the perfidy of the soldiers, and asked for military reinforcements by September 20. Another letter (G. 125), referring to the perfidy of the soldiers, speaks of resuming the interrupted siege on October 18. It is certain that the disaster was very great, for Charles's extensive military preparations had made him immensely strong, both for offensive as well as defensive purposes. It is also clear that in the army of Hugh there was widespread discontent, and possibly considerable sympathy with the cause of Charles.

The siege was apparently resumed in October (R. iv. 17), but autumn days were now bringing with them bad weather, and eventually the approach of winter compelled the raising of the siege for the second and last time. Thus, with armies estimated by Richer as 8,000 and 6,000 respectively, Hugh had failed to take Rheims. Charles, whose careful preparations had been so strikingly justified, took the offensive, and, according to Sigebert of Gembloux (Migne 160), captured Montaigne and ravaged the districts around Soissons till Adalberon trembled for his safety at Rheims (R. iv. 25) and for the security of his city. The letters of Gerbert reveal his fears, his appeals for help to Lorraine, and his distrust of his own soldiery.

Meanwhile Asceline had been impatiently enduring his captivity, and there is a letter from Archbishop Adalberon (G. 136) in which the latter calls upon the former to bear his tribulation patiently. He promises to do all he can for him, and mentions a certain Anselm as a safe intermediary. Probably, therefore, it was through the scheming of this Anselm that, some time in the October of 988, Asceline escaped from the Tower of Laon by a rope let down from the window, and made his way quickly to the Court of Hugh, where he was well received.

Emma remained a prisoner some time longer. An appeal was made by Gerbert to her mother, the Empress Adelaide, on her behalf (G. 128), asking for her intervention with Charles. It is not known whether the Empress Adelaide responded, but probably she did, for, at the end of the year, Emma was released. In a pathetic letter she wrote, ' I have neither companions of my own speech nor domestics ' (G. 147), but she was evidently free and residing at Dijon, in the territory of Duke Henry of Burgundy. So the curtain falls at length on the scene of her strange, varied, and, in the end, unfortunate life. She, formerly Queen, who once ordered thousands, now sought help from some holy priest, probably Bruno, and was enjoying the hospitality, meagre enough, of a Capetian duke.

About this time we have hints that Hugh Capet had difficulties from the side of Conrad, King of Burgundy. Conrad was uncle of Emma, and his wife sister of Lothaire. His sympathies were certainly with the Carolings, and so we hear of some conference on the confines of Burgundy, the Empire, and France for establishing peace between the kings. In these negotiations Adalberon of Rheims took some active part, and his confidants, Renier and Anselm, are mentioned as carrying messages (G. 138, 140, 141). Had this conference something to do with the release of Emma ? We do not know, but it may have resulted in strong pressure being brought to bear on Charles from the Empire, Burgundy, and Paris, in united strength.

The Archbishop Adalberon, wearied by many sorrows and anxieties, felt the approach of death (R. iv.). It is certain he was afraid of the progress of Charles. It is probable that he felt disappointment at the apparent desire of Hugh to adopt a policy independent of the Empire. He called the King to his bedside, but it was too late, and before the arrival of Hugh the Archbishop had passed away. Gerbert was evidently away at the time, for we have a letter written from Gerbert to Adalberon in which the former expressed anxiety at the silence of the latter, and asked for information (G. 149). The date of the death was January 23, 989. He had ruled the see nineteen years (Chr. Mouzon).

With all his faults, Adalberon was a prominent figure in the France of the tenth century. It is doubtful whether he could have preserved for long his confidence in Hugh, for he was from first to last a thorough Imperialist, who desired to see a Holy Roman Empire ruled by one chosen by the Church and people for merits, apart from any hereditary relation with previous sovereigns. For this splendid ideal he had schemed against and helped to dispossess the Carolings, but he must already have discovered that Hugh had no intention of being a subordinate prince of the Empire, but was prepared to continue the policy of Lothaire. Did he realize at last that instead of helping the Empire of the Othos he had helped to lay the foundations of a new State which, as the Kingdom of France, would be in constant rivalry with the Empire of Germany, and its bitterest foe ?

Adalberon's death led to complications. Gerbert had been closely attached to him, and, as *scholasticus* of Rheims, had increased the reputation of the see, and as secretary he had been led to expect the reversion of the see (G. 152). He had helped to give the crown to Hugh, and had some claim on the gratitude of the latter.

It was said that he ' deposed and made kings ' (G. 162), but gratitude had no place in the policy of those days. Hugh had other plans. He doubted Gerbert, for he knew his Imperialistic sympathies. Had not Gerbert taken the oath to Otho when appointed Abbot at Bobbio ? Further, Gerbert was of obscure birth, and Hugh, typical feudal lord, knew the value of a good birth and ancestry. Moreover, the see of Rheims had an important place in the politics of the time. Why not make a selection that would divide the Caroling interests ?

Arnulf, the cleric of Laon, nephew of Charles, son of Lothaire, approached Hugh and sought the appointment (R. iv. 25). He promised to leave Charles, and take a solemn oath to Hugh and surrender Laon. Adalberon of Verdun wrote (G. 154) a warning letter, but Hugh had already made up his mind. He wrote to the clergy and people of Rheims, recognizing in form at least their right of free election, but at the same time showing clearly his mind (R. iv. 26).

The story of the election as given by Richer is of special interest, because it shows to us the power of the King, his right of nomination, and his control of episcopal elections. The citizens promised fealty to him, and the King conceded to them the freedom of election and then returned to Paris. Then Arnulf visited the King, evidently with a full understanding as to whom was committed the real power, and urged his case. The King returned to Rheims, made known to them the desires of Arnulf, and, addressing the citizens at length, recommended them to choose him as their Archbishop. The citizens then replied, and expressed gratitude for the gift of free election conceded by the royal majesty. They admitted that Arnulf had approached them with many promises, but ' because we consider his character and disposition uncertain on account of his youth, we do not think our judgement sufficient for these things. Let both sides confer, and let each say what he thinks ; let those be present who persuade you,' &c.

The King approved of the suggested procedure, and the matter was then carefully reasoned out, with the result that the citizens said, ' Arnulf is worthy of election if he will keep faith ' ; so he was called before the King, and, having given every satisfaction, he was led to the Monastery of St. Rémy, where Hugh made a statement in the presence of the assembled bishops and princes (R. iv. 28) : ' Louis, son of Lothaire, died ; but had he lived or had issue, that issue would have had a right to the throne ; but, because he had no issue, I have been chosen by the desire of all princes and barons. But this man, about whom there is discussion, is the sole surviving son of Lothaire, and, lest the name of so great a man be forgotten, you ask that he be endowed with the honour of this dignity. If, therefore, he promise loyally to guard the city and to communicate in no way with our enemies, I shall not be reluctant to concede to him the episcopacy in conformity with your wishes, provided that he be bound to me by the authority of an oath taken in accordance with the decision of wise men.'

The King then asked that Arnulf should sign a declaration (R. iv. 29) containing a curse on himself if he were to break the oath, the declaration to be in duplicate, so that the King might possess one copy and the Archbishop the other. Arnulf readily agreed, and signed the following declaration : ' I, Arnulf, by grace of God Archbishop of Rheims, promise unbroken faith to Kings of the Franks, Hugh and Robert, also to give counsel to them and aid in all things according to ability and knowledge, and not to be disloyal to them by knowingly giving counsel or aid to their enemies. It is in the presence of the Divine Majesty, of the blessed Saints, and of the whole Church, that I make these promises. If I observe them, I shall obtain the reward of eternal life ; if I break them, which God forbid, then let all blessings be changed to curses, let my days be reduced, let another take my bishopric, let my friends turn from me and become my enemies. I subscribe this a witness either to my salvation or ruin, and beg my brothers and sons to subscribe in turn.' This solemn oath was followed by the Eucharist (R. iv. 30), a course of action, however, which was opposed by some, who, realizing the weakness of human nature, feared lest the sacrament of blessing might be turned into a means of judgement. Arnulf went so far as to say that bishops would be absolved from allegiance to him if he broke his word.

Thus Arnulf, Lothaire's son, became Archbishop of the principal see of France, and chancellor to the rival house of the Capetian kings. He was bound by tremendous oaths, and weighted by terrible curses of spiritual penalty in case of failure. It was a dangerous and difficult situation for a young man with the blood of the Carolings coursing in his veins.

The election of Arnulf was nominally made by bishops, clergy, and people (G. 155), but this election shows us also clearly the power of the King, whilst at the same time indicating that the powers of the citizens of such a city as Rheims were by no means negligible, and had to be respected, at any rate in name and form. Why did Hugh thus substitute

Arnulf for Gerbert ? Was it a feeling of respect for the only surviving son of Lothaire, or a belated feeling of penitence for having assumed the crown whilst Charles was still alive ? Rather, from what we know of his life, we should imagine it was an endeavour on his part to break up the unity of the Carolings. He had already befriended Emma. If now he could bind Lothaire's son to him, he might seriously divide the Carolings, and thereby weaken the cause of Charles. It was an astute move, but it was also a very risky one ; and the fact that Hugh took the trouble to place Arnulf under most solemn oaths showed that he recognized the nature of the risk. He had to learn later that ties of blood relationship may be stronger than the ties of a religious sanction.

Arnulf had evidently been elected by March 989, but it was not long before he began to work in the interests of Charles. Rheims was delivered to Charles in the August of the same year. Charles came in the night to the gates of the city (R. iv. 32). According to Richer, it was carefully arranged so that Arnulf should appear as an unwilling participator in the affair.

Manasses, Count of Rethel, and one Roger, vassals of the Church, were won over, and Robert, maternal uncle of Arnulf, a former lord, took an active part in what followed. One Adalger (R. iv. 34), a presbyter, alleged that he was approached by Dudo, one of Charles's vassals, and induced actually to open the gates of the city, assurances having been given to him that such was the desire of the Archbishop, and that he would be well supported in case of trouble. The forces of Charles then entered the city. Arnulf, with Count Guy of Soissons, Bishop Bruno of Langres and Count Gilbert of Roucy (a brother of Bruno), who were with him in the city, and had pledged themselves to Hugh for the good faith of Arnulf, were forced to surrender and sent to Laon, whilst Soissons as well as Rheims now passed into the hands of Charles. The Counts Roger and Manasses appear to have sacked the cathedral and pillaged the city, and this became a subject of bitter complaint at a later stage.

Meanwhile Arnulf now took the oath to Charles and returned to Rheims, and the Counts soon obtained their freedom after giving solemn oaths of obedience. The prospects for Charles were exceedingly good, for he was now the proud

possessor of Laon, Rheims, Soissons, and his armies triumphant on the field of battle. At first Arnulf launched an
anathema against the robbers of the Church, and called upon
his Bishops to do the same, but it was later noticed that even
in this anathema he did not so much refer to the wrongs of the
people and clergy as to the material possessions of the see
which were damaged. Suspicions of double dealing were
soon abroad, and before long the robbers were absolved without
satisfaction having been offered, and the absolution was given
by the Archbishop acting alone, which was against the expressed
demands of Canon Law, which stated that the Archbishop
in such a case must act with his clergy.

At the same time Arnulf drew towards Germany, following
the Adalberon tradition, guided by Gerbert, who, though
obviously disappointed at not being elected to the archbishopric, nevertheless chose to remain in the service of Arnulf as
scholasticus and secretary. Arnulf wrote to Egbert (G. 157)
expressing his intention of following in the footsteps of Adalberon, and he also approached Theophania (G. 160), then at
Rome, with a view to securing the pallium through her
patronage. He intended to visit Rome in person, but was
forbidden by Hugh, who feared this revival of Imperial friendship with the influential see of Rheims. Hugh was steadily
drawing away from his earlier friendship with the Empire.
Whatever may have been the promises which Hugh made
to Adalberon in order to secure his powerful support, Hugh
had no more intention of becoming a mere creature or vassal
of the Empire than Lothaire or Louis V.

The Bishops were now summoned to Senlis. At first they
endeavoured to distinguish between Arnulf and the invaders
of his see, but suspicion grew that Arnulf had more to do with
the betrayal of Rheims than he himself admitted. Arnulf
was thrice summoned to appear, but did not respond. Guy,
Bishop of Soissons, obtained an interview with him at Chavignon, near Laon, and summoned him to attend in the name
of the bishops, but Arnulf said he could not go without the
protection of Eudes and Herbert. Guy offered his own father
and brother as hostages, but Arnulf at last admitted that he
had taken the oath to Charles and could not therefore return
to Hugh. When he heard this, Guy broke out into indignant
protest.

Arnulf was reminded that he had sworn fealty to Hugh before he took this oath to Charles, and a safe journey to the royal Court was promised if he would answer the summons ; but he definitely refused, and the treason therefore seemed to stand out as a clearly proved fact.   Meanwhile, Gerbert had remained with Arnulf, and wrote in his name to Egbert of Trèves, pleading his difficulties, and the alternative of either submitting to Charles or enduring punishment (G. 169), and he asked for an interview, which Egbert did not grant.   Gerbert belonged at this stage to Charles's party, and a letter written to Asceline, Bishop of Laon (G. 164), is most interesting. Asceline, now at the Court of Hugh, had published a terrible anathema against the diocese of Laon, pronouncing a curse on any one who should try to usurp his functions, even to baptize children or bury the dead.   Gerbert wrote a letter of protest in which he said : ' The brother of Lothaire, divine Augustus, heir of the throne, has been chased from the kingdom and his rivals have been created interreges.   By what right has the legitimate heir been disinherited and deprived of the crown ?   And, because he has returned into the dwellings of his fathers, by what decrees of Pontiffs of Rome have you forbidden children to be baptized ?   But these are of little importance compared with accusations against you, written by priests of the Lord, that you are full of crimes.   Put not your hope in Seine and Loire, for you will gain nothing.'   The Seine and Loire represent the district ruled by Hugh Capet, with whom Asceline had taken refuge.   Gerbert at this stage was an out-and-out supporter of Charles and his hereditary claims, and very emphatic in his references to the character of Asceline.   On the whole, it is not a pleasing incident in the life of Gerbert, for he appears as an opportunist, taking the side most favourable.

This learned grammarian and philosopher was certainly not without convictions and principles, but he was no martyr, and was not prepared to risk his head either for Hugh or Charles.   However, it is only fair to add that Gerbert had been treated with gross ingratitude by both Hugh and the Empress Theophania, and that, further, in spite of this, after a short period he returned with many expressions of sorrow and penitence to the policy of the one man he really loved, his former patron Adalberon of Rheims.   But for wellnigh eight

months he remained at Rheims, writing in the names of Arnulf
and Charles, as if fully convinced of the essential justice of the
hereditary claims of Charles.

But within the year Gerbert had turned back to Hugh.
Apparently he was at the King's Court by March or April 990.
Bruno had succeeded in obtaining release, though efforts to
interest the Pope in his case had proved fruitless. Gerbert
sought an interview with him at Roucy (171), and was restored
into favour at Court. Possibly new promises had been made
to him, including the reversion of the see of Rheims (171).
His letters to Egbert (G. 172) had already shown his real
mind, and there is another letter to Egbert, written after his
return, in which he speaks of himself as having been an ' organ
of the devil ' and having been the ' chief of criminals.'

He soon entered into the confidence of the King. Two
letters (G. 174, 175), which seem to have been written to
Queen Matilda of Burgundy in an endeavour to establish
peaceful relations with that kingdom, and a letter to Rothad
of Cambrai inviting him to hand in the anathema against the
spoilers of Rheims, were apparently written by him in the
name of the King. Conrad and his wife were united by blood
ties to the Carolings, and had resented the arrival of the new
dynasty. It is probable that the various mysterious references
to conferences for making peace between kings really related
to this feud between Conrad and Hugh Capet, which had
existed from the beginning of the reign, and had caused anxiety
to Adalberon before his death. The guilt of Arnulf may have
been first suggested by the return of Gerbert, for Gerbert had
been in his confidence, and may have learned much. At the
same time, it must not be forgotten that the evidence of
Gerbert was the evidence of an interested party. Steps were,
however, now taken to bring the matter before the Pope in
order that the method of procedure ordered in the False
Decretals might be followed. A statement of the case was
prepared. ' The clergy and people have been reduced to
captivity. Arnulf pretends he is the sport of the enemy, but,
if so, why has he forced chevaliers and burgesses to perjure
themselves ? Why has he gathered troops against us ? If
captive, why does he refuse to be released ? If he is free, why
is he not with us ? Called to the Court, why does he refuse
to come ? Summoned by Archbishop and Bishop, he says

he owes nothing to them. It is then your duty, successor of the apostles, to decide the fate of this new Judas. If not, there is fear that the name of the Lord may be blasphemed by us ; that we, excited by just resentment and by your silence, may take in hand the ruin of the town and devastation of the whole province. You will be without excuse before God, your judge, if you give no reply or judgement to our request.' This letter containing this solemn threat, as well as an earnest appeal, was received at first with some favour ; but Herbert, the emissary of Charles, was already at Rome, and by magnificent presents won the ear of the Pope. The ambassadors of Hugh, left waiting for three days before the Pope's gate, returned to France in disgust. Hugh, realizing that no help was forthcoming from Rome, dominated by the Imperial interest or the interests of Crescentius, and so unfriendly to him, determined to fulfil his threats, and renew the war. Gerbert broke definitely with Arnulf in a letter in which he asked him to protect his houses and friends and the churches which he had obtained by legitimate donation, according to the custom of the diocese (G. 178).

Hugh led an army of 6,000 men into the Rheims district, burning and ravaging to such an extent that there was not left even a hut of peasants grown childish with age (R. iv. 17), and harvests were destroyed, showing that this savage, quite in-effective attack on inoffensive peasantry was made in or about September 990. Charles advanced to meet Hugh with 4,000 men (R. iv. 39), invoking divine help that the few might be protected from the many. Arnulf accompanied Charles with his contingent from Rheims, exhorting the army to stand firm, and promising victory if they did, ' because of divine help.' Hugh, with his superior forces, advanced in three columns ; but, when battle seemed inevitable, he, according to Richer, felt the sting of a conscience which rebuked him for having spoiled Charles of his rights and for having trans-ferred the kingdom to himself (R. iv. 39)—an unlikely excuse in view of later events, and hardly to be reconciled with his harsh treatment of the peasantry in the country round Rheims. Rather we may suppose that courage was not a strong feature of Hugh's character. Hugh trusted rather to diplomacy, and found it easier to destroy the cabins of the unarmed than to meet the armed though inferior forces of his rival.

Charles returned to Laon, Hugh apparently to Paris (R. iv. 39). Eudes, who had been friendly to Charles but was never reliable, always seeking his own advancement, promised to deliver Laon to the King if the latter would pledge Dreux to him. The King surrendered Dreux, but Eudes did not deliver Laon, and it was doubtful whether he ever intended to do so ; but help came from another quarter.

Asceline, ever false, now entered again on the stage, and took his accustomed place in a sordid, intriguing world as arch-traitor and deceiver. He approached Arnulf, and offered to reconcile him to the King, provided he in his turn would reconcile him to Charles, and thus bring him once more into possession of his see, which he was anxious to recover. Arnulf fell into the trap. He and Asceline vowed eternal friendship, and embraced and exchanged the kiss of peace. Arnulf sought out Charles and told him of the new situation, magnified the ability of Asceline, witnessed to his friendliness, and became surety for his faith. Charles listened, and agreed at last to receive Asceline and grant to him the bishopric again. Asceline met Arnulf and Charles at an appointed place, and they discussed the basis of a lasting peace, and how much glory and honour a reconciliation would produce. They swore friendship mutually, and Asceline then proceeded to Hugh and revealed all that had been done. The King professed satisfaction, and agreed, as his part of the bargain, to receive Arnulf and to accept his protests of innocence in the matter of the betrayal of the city. Asceline and Arnulf then visited the King, and the reconciliation seemed complete. Hugh refused to listen to Arnulf's excuse, and professed to believe that Arnulf had only acted under compulsion and as an unwilling actor in the scene. Further, he stated that he would be quite satisfied for Charles to hold the cities he possessed, provided that he held them from the King. Arnulf promised everything, and the interview terminated satisfactorily, the Archbishop being promoted to the seat on the King's right hand at the King's table, whilst Asceline sat on the left.

The tale is soon told, for we have it in all its ghastly detail in the contemporary pages of Richer (R. iv. 44). Asceline returned to Laon with those who had been exiled with him, and was received by Charles, who, however, sought assurances of his loyalty.

After asserting his belief that God's hand was in all these events, he added, introducing relics, ' Holy things are here ; place your right hand upon them ; without exception swear loyalty against all men.'   Asceline did not fear to place his hands over the sacred relics and swear his loyalty, whilst he himself deliberated about the city defences, consulted about all city matters, and learnt all the city secrets.   Then, suspected by none, he began to plot to betray the city, and, in order to increase confidence, offered to take the most solemn oaths on his lips.

So they sat down to supper in the best of spirits.   Charles took a golden vessel, into which he broke bread mixed with wine.   ' Since you have sanctified palms according to the decrees of the Fathers to-day, and have consecrated the people with holy blessings and have brought the Eucharist to us, I, paying no attention to those who suggest that you ought not to be trusted, since the day of the Passion of our Lord Jesus Christ draws near, hold out to you a vessel worthy of your dignity, with wine and bread broken.   Drink this potion as a sign of having preserved faith.   If indeed it is not in your heart to preserve faith, do not drink, lest you bring back the horrible form of traitor Judas.'   He replied : ' I receive the vessel and freely drink the potion.'   Charles then asked that he should add : ' I pledge faith.'   He drank, using these words : ' I promise faith ; if I break it, let me die with Judas.'

Night drew on, and they retired to rest.   Whilst Charles and Arnulf slept, Asceline removed their swords and hid them. He then sent the attendant to fetch one of his own men, promising to mind the gate.   He had a sword hidden beneath his coat.   When his own friends arrived he immediately opened to them.   Charles and Arnulf, wakening, sought their swords as they leapt from their beds, but of course found them not. When they asked the reason for this interruption, they received the answer from Asceline : ' You recently seized this citadel from me and compelled me to go away into exile, now you are expelled by changing fortune.   I remained free as regards my person, but you will fall into the power of another.' ' I am amazed, Bishop,' replied Charles, ' that you should be so little mindful of the supper of yesterday.   Does not reverence for God restrain you?   Is the obligation of the Sacrament nothing ? '

Saying this, he threw himself on the enemy, but it was in vain. Totally unarmed as he was, he fought furiously, but was soon overpowered, and thrown on the bed and secured.

Both Charles and Arnulf were shut up in the Tower, closely guarded with bolts and bars. The cries of the women and children roused the city, terrifying the citizens. The friends of Charles, taken by surprise, sought refuge in flight, and this they scarcely effected, because Asceline had already taken charge of the city and given orders that his opponents should be seized. One of Charles's sons, a boy of two, called Charles, was, however, safely carried out of the city by a faithful servant before the measures taken by Asceline had been completed. The boy was probably taken to his brother in Lorraine, but evidently he died young, as nothing more is heard of him ; but Charles of Lorraine, his young wife Adelaide, of humble parentage, a son, Louis, and two daughters were all taken.

Asceline sent messages to Hugh at Senlis, and he, quite willing to benefit by consummate treachery, hastened to the city, and, having demanded and obtained oaths of allegiance from the citizens, returned to Senlis with his captives (R. iv. 48). Here he discussed with his princes and vassals the fate of these captives. Some said, ' Put them on oath never to take up arms for retaking the kingdom, and then let them go when you receive hostages.' Others said, ' Let them be kept in confinement until it shall appear whether Charles has a strong following in the State or not, and if he has, his person will then prove to be an asset in bargaining.' So Charles, his wife, and son, and daughters Gerberge and Adelaide, together with Arnulf, were imprisoned in the royal city of Orleans, and Charles's reign was at an end. Sigebert of Gembloux says he died in 991, but the actual date remains uncertain. He seems to have been alive in 992, but probably died in prison.

If Charles had survived long, it is difficult to believe that his claim would not have been heard from time to time, and, moreover, his son Louis was put forth as the Caroling heir by Eudes and Asceline at a latter date. The eldest son, Otho, born before 985 by the first wife of Charles, a daughter of Herbert of Vermandois, had apparently remained in Lorraine and succeeded to the duchy, according to the express statement of Sigebert of Gembloux. He was devoted to the Emperor Otho, whom he accompanied into Italy, and from whom he

F

may have received the possessions of Bishop Thierry of Metz
at St. Trond, and apparently survived till 1012, when
Godfrey, son of Godfrey of Verdun, succeeded him, as he
died without issue.

The story told in later writings that Louis and Charles were
both born in captivity is certainly not true, as they were both
alive before the captivity of their father. The younger Charles
escaped, and may have been taken to his brother in Lorraine
or to the Emperor for safety, but Louis remained in captivity.
He had been in Arnulf's mind as a possible King of the Franks,
and later became the tool of Asceline in some fresh treachery
he meditated. What is certain is that Louis was delivered
to the tender mercies of Asceline, who kept him as prisoner at
Laon. The date or place of his death is uncertain, but in 999
Robert was engaged in an effort to take Laon from Asceline
for some fresh act of treachery, and it is possible Louis was
alive at that time and was again being made the tool of the
prelate's ambitious purposes. One daughter was certainly
married to Count Lambert of Hainault, who was killed in
battle in 1015 in an attempt to take possession of the duchy of
Lorraine, which apparently he regarded as his rightful possession through his wife Gerberge on the death of his brother-
in-law Otho. Gerberge seems to have brought to him, as
dowry, Brussels and Louvain (Gesta abbatum Trundonensium).
Later historians speak of the second daughter as married to a
Count of Namur, and try to trace thus a connexion between
the later Capetians and Carolings by marriage of Philip II.
to one of her descendants ; but there is no contemporary
evidence, and even the name Hermengarde differs from the
name Adelaide, which Richer gives to the second daughter
of Charles.

Thus the Capetians held undisputed possession. Treachery
had prevailed against valour. None can read the story without
sympathy with this last brave and unfortunate defender of the
Caroling inheritance. He had many faults. His action at
Cambrai in 976, his letter to Thierry of Metz (G. 32), his violent
attacks on Queen Emma, his early alliance with the Empire
against his brother, show a nature full of faults, but much of
our information about him comes from prejudiced sources,
and it is obvious he had provocations. He had, at any rate
in these latter days, shown resource, courage, and energy. If

Richer is to be believed, he possessed also religious sentiments, for he went to battle relying upon divine help, and expressed his confidence that God was with him in the events of life. With inferior numbers he made headway against Hugh, supported by powerful ecclesiastics and feudatories, and it is doubtful whether Hugh would ever have overcome him by force of arms. The chances of Charles's recovering his inheritance had been by no means desperate. His former alliance with the Empire, his fierce, relentless persecution of Emma, had compromised his position with many old supporters of his house, but one may easily forget these failures, and pity the misfortunes of the last reigning scion of a great house. He had some place in the affection of the people at Rheims, Sens, and Laon, and his administration at Laon and Rheims suggests some degree of organizing ability, whilst his defence of Laon proved him to have military qualities as well. His marriage with a lady of lower grade would not weaken his reputation in the modern world, though it gave a handle to his enemies in those days. It is safe to assume that he was not the monster he has been painted in some quarters, but a by no means unworthy representative of his family. Possibly his greatest fault was that he was unfortunate, and the success of his rival has led to the dishonouring of his name.

IV

THE GALLICAN CHURCH AND ROME

Note

A.A.   = Aimon Vita Abbonis.
A.C.R.= Acta Concilii Remensis ad Sanctum Basolum.
E.   = Eudes Vita Burchardi.
G.   = Gerbert's Letters.
G.P.A.= Gesta Pontificum Autissiodorensium.
R.   = Richer.

IT now remains for us to trace the relations between Hugh and Arnulf. The last heir of the Carolings was in prison, and Hugh Capet might well have thought that his victory was complete, but if he thought so, he was greatly mistaken. A great conflict developed, which was at the same time an extraordinarily interesting assertion of ancient Gallican rights, and a challenge to the Papacy, now strengthened by claims contained in the False Decretals. The imprisonment of Arnulf on charges of treason meant that steps had to be taken to deal with his position as metropolitan, and, if a case could be made for deposition, to provide a new prelate for a see of such great importance.

The capture of Arnulf and Charles was effected on Palm Sunday 991. The celebrated Synod of St. Basil, near Rheims, followed in June 991. An elaborate argument of Lairs would put the council as late as June 993. The theory is ingenious, but Lot has clearly shown that this cannot be accepted. (See his *Studies on the Reign of Hugh Capet*, page 249, &c.).

This important synod was held at Verzy, in the Church of St. Basil, some two and a half miles from the city of Rheims, and there were two sessions, on June 17 and 18. Gerbert edited the Acts of the Synod, and a summary of the proceedings of the council is found in Richer. The figures seem sketched from life. The bishops have their individual characteristics, and are clearly represented in their differing attitudes to the subjects of debate. It is hardly likely that Gerbert would dare to fabricate such a public writing as this, in the days when so many of the bishops taking part were alive and active. We may conclude that his narrative, on the whole, is reliable in regard to main facts, though we may still allow for bias in describing the proceedings. The synod was not really an assembly of all the bishops and abbots of the Gallican Church. The bishops of the Rheims Province were of necessity present, Asceline of Laon, Heriveus of Beauvais, Gotesmann of Amiens, Rathbod of Noyon, Eudes of Senlis, and Guy of Soissons. In addition, we find the Archbishop Dagobert of Bourges, Archbishop Seguin of Sens, with his bishops, Arnulf of Orleans and Herbert of Auxerre, and Bishops Milo of Maçon, Walter of Autun, and Bruno of Langres from the Lyons province. It is noticeable, however, that there was an entire absence of Lorraine and Burgundian bishops, who would probably be more friendly to Arnulf. The bishops present are all from sees under royal influence, and Richer's statement that those who would not come had to give proof of their fidelity, and the ominous appearance of the King and his friends at the close of the proceedings, sufficiently prove the strength of the royal power in the background. A decision unfavourable to Arnulf was a foregone conclusion in an assembly so obviously controlled by the King. There is evidence that the bishops feared the royal power, and dreaded an actual intervention, and to this extent the synod was certainly not without a decided bias. Yet, on the whole, the care taken to secure evidence, and the judicial bearing of the president and secretary, suggest an honest attempt to find out the merits of the case without ruining the young Archbishop or offending the King.

A study of some of those present at the synod will be advisable. The president was Seguin of Sens. Gerbert, in his defence of this council, declares that Seguin presided as a representative of the Pope, and certainly some such primacy had been conceded to Sens in 876 by Pope John VIII. The tradition had survived, for Odoran in his Chronicle calls Seguin Archbishop and Primate of Gaul, and Gerbert, even after his accession as Pope, calls Liotric the successor of Seguin by some high-sounding title. However, it was little more than a debating point, for the Primacy was not recognized by the Pope contemporary with the synod, nor by the Archbishop of Sens himself. A later tradition that Seguin actively opposed Hugh is not true, but there is reason to believe that he had some sympathy with both Charles and Arnulf. He himself had been recommended by Lothaire, and delayed some time to take the oath to Hugh, whilst the historians of Sens (Hugh of Fleury, &c., Migne 163) call Hugh the usurper, and speak highly of Arnulf's character. Perhaps, therefore, he was peculiarly fitted to preside over such a meeting. In the writings of Odoran and Clarus he is represented as a true pastor, a hater of simony and a patron of monks. He completed the Church of St. Peter, which Anastasius had begun, and restored the churches of St. Peter of Milum and the Mother Church of St. Stephen, which he loaded with gifts after a solemn dedication. He was a keen searcher after relics, and secured an arm of Pope Leo and a finger of St. Ebbo. He was particularly generous to the Abbey of St. Peter, and gave high honour to the Abbot Rainard. In the Translation of St. Savivian (Migne 137) it is stated that he once prostrated himself before the brethren, begging indulgence for his faults, whilst promising to return all things to the Abbey with the exception of a small portion for necessary uses. This humility and love of the monks made a great impression on the city. His epitaph tells us he was ' tender for the honour of religion ' and calls him ' excellent.' We may conclude that he was a serious lover of justice, an earnest, sincere prelate of the better type. Yet he figures in Aimon's life of Abbo as an opponent of the monks in the Synod of St. Denis, over which he presided. At the close of this synod he was actually attacked and received injury from the mob. There is, moreover, a trace of weakness in his nature, and he was among the first of the prelates to yield to the demands of the Papacy. Dagobert of Bourges is not so well known, but his contribution to the debate showed considerable shrewdness and sympathy. He took his part in the Peace Movement of Aquitaine.

Bruno of Langres was one of the noblest prelates of the period. Nominated by his uncle Lothaire when only twenty-four, he nevertheless showed himself a true pastor, a zealous promoter of reform, and a lover of the saintly monks of Cluny. He took a leading part in inaugurating the reforms connected with the name of William of Dijon. His policy was a substitution of monks for the seculars, and, in the religious foundations he sought to introduce the ideals of St. Benedict in their original purity. Born of Caroling blood, he had readily agreed to the election of his cousin Arnulf, and had evidently offered himself to the King as surety for his faith. The failure of Arnulf, his own imprisonment at the hands of Charles, and the despicable attitude of the Pope to the messengers who, seeking for his papal intervention, were simply asked as to how much money they could supply, had burnt into his soul, and his attitude throughout was one of righteous indignation. He was well in the counsels of the King, and had much to do with the bringing back of Gerbert to the King. However, as years went on, something of the old Caroling feeling may have accounted for his opposition to Robert, when the latter sought the conquest of Burgundy. He is described as 'perfect and profuse in charity, holy in conversation, terrible to criminals, but a father to clerics, monks, widows and orphans, one who gave attention to adornment of character rather than the status of the person, who tempered the censure of authority with a spirit of humility, who honoured those who lived well, and was venerated by all. He protected Burgundy as long as he lived as patron, and defended it not with shield or lance but with the counsels of prudence.' (Chronicle of St. Benignus, Migne 160.)

Arnulf of Orleans was a somewhat different type. He was a close personal friend of Hugh. He was one of his companions to Italy when Hugh sought the help of Otho against the menaces of Lothaire. An instance of his ready wit is supplied by Richer (iii. 85). The Emperor, passing out of the room, had purposely let his sword slip. Hugh would have stooped to pick it up, and thus, following the Emperor, would have given the impression of feudal homage, but Arnulf boldly seized the weapon and carried it before his lord. His reputation as scholar and counsellor stood very high ; Gerbert speaks of him as 'a man brilliant in eloquence and wisdom, beyond all Bishops of Gaul,' and (A.C.R. i.) explains that this was the reason why he was appointed secretary to the conference. This judgement, which, standing alone might be considered biassed, as Arnulf was to the last Gerbert's most faithful friend, is supported by the evidence of one hostile to him. Aimon (A. 7) is constrained to admit in his

life of Abbo, even whilst condemning his attitude towards
his hero, that he was ' excellent in morals,' and, in the Miracles
of Benedict (i. 19) he describes him as ' serving ecclesiastical
rules in knowledge, and otherwise wholly good.' R. Glaber
writes that he was ' very noble, wise, and very rich ' (i. 20).
He further describes how he rebuilt a church after the fire,
and how, when workmen found money supposed to have
been placed there by Evertius, he gave it to the church. His
speeches show that he possessed a knowledge of church history
and canon law. His attack on Rome constituted an episode
of extraordinary interest, and he was capable of moral indignation. True he was a close friend of the King, and a courtier ;
but he could resist Burchard at the Synod on a matter of
priestly privilege, in defence of the secrets of the confessional
(A.C.R. 52). He stood out to the last a fearless exponent
of the principles he upheld so boldly at Rheims, when Seguin
and the rest of the episcopacy had bowed to the storm. He
possessed, therefore, courage and principle, but he was no
friend of the monks, and was constantly involved in disputes
with the monks of Fleury. ' He did not love Fleury,' says
Aimon, and he was roundly accused of encouraging violent
personal attacks on Abbo. To him the monks were intruders,
and their claim for privileges and immunities against the
diocesan bishop was an attack on the ancient episcopal order,
which he was prepared to defend against Pope and monks,
and, if need be, possibly against the King himself.

Walter of Autun seems to have been a friend of the monks,
and he loved Cluny, and gave generously to the monks there,
because in his opinion the ' brothers flourished in the nobility
of former days, worthily upholding the standard of their
order.'

Heriveus of Beauvais was a correspondent of Gerbert
(G. 200), but Eudes of Senlis, Milo of Mâcon, Gotesmann of
Amiens, and Rathbod of Noyon are little known to us except
in so far as they impress us by their contribution to the discussion.

There are two remaining prelates of whose lives we know
much, who are thoroughly secular, with no religious sentiment
whatever, and morally false, viz., Asceline of Laon and Herbert
of Auxerre. Asceline's career has already been followed,
and it is one long series of crimes and betrayals ; yet he was

not without scholarship. He had pride of noble birth and a lofty contempt for plebeian monks. On the whole, his position in the episcopate was a standing disgrace to the Church which tolerated him. It was nothing less than a scandal that the arch-traitor who had betrayed Arnulf to Hugh should have been a judge in such a trial as this. Whatever guilt rested on Arnulf, he was innocent in comparison with the crimes of the Bishop of Laon. He entered history accused of adultery with the Queen, the wife of his benefactor, and at the last we have a letter from Gerbert, then Pope Sylvester, condemning him for some fresh treason against Robert and Archbishop Arnulf. Yet he was clever and astute enough to hold his see until his death. Dudo dedicated his *History of the Normans* to his name, and his own *Satirical Poem* and *Song* (Migne 141) witness to a certain literary ability and power of satire. A prelate, dangerous, clever, false, he held his bishopric for over forty years and died in peace ; but let it be noted that, though present at the synod, there is no reference to his having taken part in the discussion. Perhaps, even in this false and cruel life, there was just conscience enough to close his lips. Yet he signed the judgement of the man he had betrayed.

Herbert of Auxerre was present, but took no part in the debate. He was a thoroughly secular prelate, and owed his promotion simply to the fact that Auxerre was in the King's nomination, and that he, a natural son of Hugh the Great, was therefore half-brother of Hugh Capet and Henry of Burgundy. He was handsome in appearance, but an unworthy bishop (see G. P. A. i. 47, Migne 138). He gave episcopal estates to soldiers, as if these estates were his own private property, built castles which became centres of disorder, and spent much time in hunting, for he had a passion for the chase. This thoroughly secular prelate far more resembled a feudal baron in his manner of life than a pastor of souls, and his presence at the synod is an indication of that feudal peril from which the reformers like Bruno sought to deliver the Church.

The defence was undertaken by Abbo, Abbot of Fleury, John, *scholasticus* of Auxerre, and Ramnulf, Abbot of Sens. No representative of the Church of Rheims spoke in the defence of, and none spoke against, the Archbishop. We may imagine that, had there been any opposition in the Church, such convenient enmity would have been utilized, but possibly fear of the King and a new Archbishop would at the same time interfere with any wish to defend the accused.   There is reason to believe that Arnulf was not unpopular with a large proportion of the clergy and people of Rheims, for Gerbert had to face active opposition to his claims when he was elected afterwards.

Of Abbo we shall write later, and need not anticipate what will be there stated ; but at the Council of Rheims Abbo fulfilled a consistent rôle in identifying his interests with those of the Papacy.   In a letter to the Canons of St. Martin (Ep. 5) he said : ' The Roman Church has this privilege over all churches that, just as the key-bearer of the kingdom of heaven has obtained high rank and apostolic place, so the same Roman Church assigns authority to all its members, so that he who contradicts the Roman Church . . . becomes reckoned among the adversaries of Christ.'   He probably had little sympathy with Archbishop Arnulf, but he knew that Papal protection was needed if he was to be able to resist the episcopate, and a common interest drew Pope and abbot together.

Ramnulf of Sens may be the Abbot of St. Peter Le Vif and nephew of Seguin, or the Abbot of Sens, to whom Gerbert wrote many letters (G. 116, 167, 170.)   John, the *scholasticus* of Auxerre, and formerly one of Gerbert's students, became bishop of that see later, being raised to that high position because of his singular piety and unusual scholarship.   He was, like Gerbert, of obscure birth and of comparatively poor family, and his election was opposed by the nobility, but King Robert favoured the appointment when the city populace asked for him (G.P.A. i. 48).   These three men were the protagonists on behalf of Arnulf, or rather on behalf of the claim of the Papacy to intervene in the affairs of the Gallican Church.

One prominent layman appeared later in the synod, and seems to have come forward as a mouthpiece of the King. Burchard, Count of Vendôme, is an interesting, and in some respects a very significant, figure in the history of those times. He was a son of one Burchard, a petty Count of Vendôme and Tours.   The young Burchard was brought up at the Court of Hugh the Great, Duke of France, from boyhood, and was intimately associated with the son of the Duke, afterwards

Hugh Capet. He succeeded his father as Burchard II. His vast estates by the Loire are given in detail by his biographer, Eudes of St. Maur (see Coll. of Texts).

Hugh married him to Elizabeth, the young widow of the Count of Corbie, and this brought to him the county. Their son Renard became later Chancellor of France and Bishop of Paris. Hugh gave to his friend also Milum, which commanded the navigation of the Seine, where he had a viscount presiding in his absence.

Both as vassal and friend he frequented the Court, and was at St. Denis in March 987. Indeed, between 978 and 983 he appears rarely to have visited Vendôme. In 980 he accompanied Hugh on his expedition to Flanders, and was one of those who carried the relics of St. Valerie. He was present with Hugh and Arnulf, Bishop of Orleans, in Italy in 981, when Hugh sought the alliance with the Emperor against Lothaire, and he was with Hugh at Senlis in the same year. When Hugh became King, he gave to the faithful Burchard the county of Paris, but he is called ' royal Count,' and his position was apparently far more that of an official than a vassal of the King. It is significant that ever afterwards a viscount is found in Paris instead of a count, the title of count evidently being included in the royal title. Burchard held high position as an intimate courtier, or ' palatine,' for he is said to have commanded troops and concluded peace for the King, and also to have carried ' wax tapers before the King ' (E. ii. 9).

His close relationship with the King, his comparatively humble origin, his presence in the palace as trusted adviser, his royal sympathies, all tended to emphasize the palatine at the expense of the vassal, and to make of him a royal official rather than a semi-independent feudatory. In such men, bound by interest and real sympathy with the monarchy, we detect the beginnings of the royal Court which will later supplant the feudal lords and minister to the needs of absolute monarchy. His relation with Maiolus and Cluny and his position as ' advocate ' to Du Fosse are dealt with elsewhere. He had great sympathy with the Reform Movements, and loved Cluny. He accompanied Hugh to the funeral of Maiolus at Savigny in 994, and took an important part in the war which Robert, with Normans and Angevins, waged against Eudes of Chartres, who sought to take Milum from Burchard.

The traitor Walter and his wife were both hung for delivering the city to Eudes, and, in a great battle at Orsay, Burchard completely routed Eudes. He was with Robert in 1005, at the sieges of Sens and Avallon. He then made known his desires, and divided his inheritance. The county of Paris was suppressed. Vendôme and Milum went to his son, Bishop Renard of Paris. Manger, who had married the daughter of Aimon, the late count, received Corbie, and his step-son Theobald had already obtained the Abbey of St. Maur du Fosse. His daughter Elizabeth married Fulk of Anjou, and met a tragic death by fire. Falling ill, the Count retired to the monastery of St. Maur and performed the duties of a novice. He gave great gifts to the monastery, precious ornaments and vases for use in the sacred ministrations, a copy of the Gospels wrought in gold and silver, and he died there on February 26, 1007, his wife dying shortly afterwards. In 1860 their bones were discovered in the crypt. He was a great benefactor to the monks of St. Peter of Milum. St. Valerie, St. Guennaud, Notre Dame of Paris, and St. Maur du Fosse owed much to him, but especially the last, for which there was a special decree that whosoever of the faithful should wish to give part of their possessions to Du Fosse should have free right to do so without considering living heirs. He is described as the restorer of monks and a faithful defender of churches.

The Council of Rheims opened with a statement of the case from Arnulf of Orleans, who asked for freedom of investigation. In the middle of the wars and tumults, it was reported, the city of Rheims had been delivered by treason to the enemy, then pillaged and devastated, whilst the holy places were profaned by soldiers. The instigator was loudly stated to be the Archbishop himself. By this fact sacerdotal dignity was brought into question, and the whole order had become the butt of insults. Now for the sake of religion, and because of the desire of the most sincere Lord Hugh, the matter must be thoroughly investigated, otherwise it would be said that bishops could sin with impunity, and thus all the bishops would be involved in the treason of one. The justice of episcopal law was in question, so he concluded by asking for a fair trial, so that nothing should be done contrary to divine and human laws.

Seguin, as president, then declared that the question of treason should not be raised unless it were agreed that, in case of guilt, the King's mercy should be sought. This declaration was challenged by Dagobert, Archbishop of Bourges, who in a few shrewd words of severe logical import, opposed the trial for treason. Such a question lay outside the province of the Church. If Archbishop Arnulf were condemned, the Church might be involved in a death penalty, whilst if he were acquitted, the bishops might have to violate their consciences. To avoid such a dilemma let the Church leave the treason charge well alone.

Heriveus of Beauvais, however, pointed out that such action would precipitate royal intervention, and a summons of the case to a secular court, and such would be a grave threat to episcopal privilege. Bruno followed with a personal attack on Archbishop Arnulf. He had been a hostage for the good faith of Arnulf, and he had suffered imprisonment in the betrayal of the city along with his brother, and he felt keenly a sense of personal grievance against his cousin. He did not doubt Arnulf was guilty of treason.

Gotesmann of Amiens admitted all this might prove treason, but he asked Bruno if he were in favour of an appeal for indulgence, as it was not right that those who were to be authors of salvation should be responsible for shedding blood. Bruno followed by stating that he put the claims of Christ's blood before the claims of his own blood, though he did feel intensely the claims of blood in one joined so closely to him as the son of his uncle Lothaire. However, discussion should proceed, and they must not be afraid to shed blood if necessary, though he did not think there would be any difficulty in appealing to the pity of the King. He, however, associated himself with Heriveus in seeking to avoid the danger to the whole episcopal order which would be incurred by refusing judgement, and concluded by asking that the presbyter be brought in. The synod at once agreed.

At this stage Rathbod, the Bishop of Noyon, asked for the reading of the actual oath which Arnulf had taken, as it had been stated by certain bishops of Lorraine that the oath was not authentic. The oath was then read by the decision of the synod. The Bishop of Orleans pointed out that in this oath Arnulf really had condemned himself. Adalger, the presbyter, then gave evidence, and he described how Dudo, a soldier of Charles, approached him with a view to his opening the city gates. When he had expressed surprise at being singled out for such a purpose, Dudo had extolled his prudence and ability. He, however, refused to act unless he heard from the lips of the Archbishop that it was in accordance with his wishes. This assurance was given, with the promise of help from Count Manasses, Count Roger, and Robert, uncle of the Archbishop. The presbyter proceeded to state that he actually received the keys from the hands of the Archbishop, and offered to prove his statement by submitting to hot-iron or boiling-water tests. He concluded by saying that, on giving evidence, he had barely escaped the sword of Richard, the Archbishop's brother.

Eudes of Senlis intervened, not, apparently, to hurry judgement, as Richer puts it, but rather to point out that he had received, through Guy of Soissons, a certain anathema against the ' brigands ' who had taken away the ' movables ' and ' *biens* ' of the church. The reading of this anathema roused the wrath of Walter of Autun, who noted that he who condemned the guilty for taking only material possessions was silent about the captivity of the clergy and the wrongs of the suffering populace. The Archbishop had forbidden the robbers to take gold and silver, but had not demanded from them the food and drink which the poor needed, and which was their portion. ' He is a butcher of the poor, a patron of brigands. He submits to feigned captivity to secure the real captivity of many, and he does not refuse communion to the sacrilegious ; it is because he knows himself to be the instigator of the attack, &c.' Guy of Soissons, who had frequently interviewed Arnulf, asked, in a more moderate tone, why, if the Archbishop's guilt was so clearly proved in his own writings, he had not been condemned at Senlis. Then, at his request, the declaration of the bishops of Rheims province (issued at Senlis), which condemned Adalger for betraying Arnulf without attributing any guilt to the latter, was read.

The president now indignantly intervened. Apparently he saw an opportunity of avoiding the treason charge by dealing with the whole question as a purely ecclesiastical offence. He asked a series of leading questions. ' Was this written with the knowledge of Archbishop Arnulf ? ' ' Yes.' ' Has he

separated these invaders of the see from communion?'
'No.' 'Then I am astonished at his audacity. He excom-
municates the ravishers, and yet without public penance for
a public offence, and without any restitution of stolen goods,
he absolves them. It is impossible to be satisfied with secret
penance, for it is written that "he who sins publicly must
repent publicly."' Bishops were not to absolve unless there
had been public penance and satisfaction, but how could there
be either penance or satisfaction, seeing that none of the
captives had been released at the time? 'Has he absolved?
If in secret it is of no effect, and in any case would require the
presence of the clergy to make it valid,' and he proceeded to
quote the twenty-third canon of the Council of Carthage in
support of this contention. 'Then he has acted against the
canons, and is open to canonical judgement.'

If Seguin thought that by this method he would escape the
treason charge, and quickly secure deposition, he was mistaken. Arnulf of Orleans called the attention of the synod
to the presence of clergy of Rheims and certain abbots, who
had a perfect right to urge anything they chose in his defence.
'We desire not the ruin of our brother, and no one will take as
personal anything said by way of defence.' The invitation
was at once responded to by Abbo, Ramnulf, and John, who
were thereupon conjured by a solemn appeal to the name of the
Holy Trinity to speak the truth. None of the Rheims clergy
appear to have taken part in the case for the defence, but the
defence brought forward many volumes of the Decretals. The
synod did not know these were False Decretals of pseudo-
Isidore and the most astonishing and successful forgery of
history. The decretal most frequently quoted was one
ascribed to Pope Damasus demanding that the deposition of a
bishop must receive the *consent* of Rome. All but the first
two decretals of the total of eighteen were sent by the
Lorraine clergy through the hands of Rathbod of Noyon.

Gerbert puts the case for the defence thus: (1) that he be
restored to the see, and not asked to defend himself until
restored; (2) that there be a legal summons; (3) that it be
referred to Rome; (4) that the accused and accuser, witnesses
and judges, all be called and set apart in one great synod; (5)
that all be done in accordance with the canons.

The answers given to these various pleas were as follows:

(1) Adalger was not the enemy of Arnulf, but carried out his duty through religious zeal.   (2) Summons was given through proper channels, and had been repeated through twelve months, not six months only.   (3) It was impossible to re-establish him in his see, because he had despised the calls, and according to the Council of Carthage, even if re-established, he would have no more right to make himself heard.   (4) His captivity was neither unique nor against canons, e.g. the cases of Hildeman of Soissons and Ebbo of Rheims were prece-dents.   (5) The case had been carried to Rome eleven months before, in letters from Hugh the King and the bishops, which were then read.   The letter of the bishops charged Arnulf with betraying first Laon and his bishop, and then Rheims with the clergy and people, and noted his refusal to answer to sum-monses.   ' Several churches are without pastors, people perish without priestly blessing and confirmation, human and divine laws are despised, whilst tyranny increases.'   They quoted Matt. xxv. 25, and asked for Roman judgement against Arnulf.   The letter of the King, given earlier, was a strong presentation of the royal case.   When the synod was informed that eleven months had elapsed without reply, and that the delegation had been insulted at Rome, it agreed that Rome could no longer blame the synod for taking action.   The synod then quoted from other decisions of certain African Councils in the times of Popes Zosimus, Boniface, and Celestine, held in the presence of Augustine, which seemed to give the precedents for such action.

Arnulf of Orleans followed in a great speech.   The speech, as given, included different statements made during the discussion.   ' We prefer to collect into one so that a continuous speech may be more useful for the studious reader ' (A.C.R. 28), says Gerbert, and much of what is thus given would not be given publicly, but only to those who judged with him, viz. the higher clergy.   But the speech as recorded here, and we have no reason to doubt that the contents were substantially as recorded, is an extraordinarily vigorous assertion of Gallican claims, and apparently coincides with views held by Gerbert himself.   ' We estimate, very reverend Father, that in memory of St. Peter the Roman Church ought to be ever honoured, and we dare not pretend to withstand the decrees of Roman pontiffs, saving only the authority of Nicaea, which the Roman

Church has always reverenced.   We assert that sacred canons
put forth in divers times and places, but always under divine
inspiration, have eternal authority, and we believe that all
ought to observe them.   A double question faces us.   Is the
silence of Rome, or a new decretal, able to weaken the canons or
decretals of earlier Popes ?   If silence has this virtue, canons
and decretals are all annulled necessarily by the caprice of
Popes.   If a new decree has this power, what advantage is
there in making laws, where everything is therefore submitted
to the caprice of one ?   You see, if one admits these two
premises, we put the state of the Church of God in grievous
peril. . . . Shall we attack the privileges of the Bishop of
Rome ?   Certainly not.   For if he is recommended by his
knowledge and virtue, there will be no need for doubting his
silence nor a new constitution.   If he is under the influence of
ignorance, fear, or of cupidity, if he is controlled by circumstances, as he seems to be in these days, for tyrants are master
of Rome, his silence and his decrees will be still less feared,
for one who to a certain extent is an enemy of law is not able
to weaken the laws.   " O lamentable Rome, you who have
revealed to our ancestors the brilliant light of the Fathers ! " '
He quoted Leo, Gelasius, Gregory, and Innocent, and said it
was good for the Universal Church to trust itself to such, and
yet, even then, these privileges were contested by the African
Church.   Then he reviewed the present situation.   There was
Octavius plunged in debauchery, who, having conspired against
the Emperor Otho and having been driven out by the Emperor
and replaced by Leo VIII, re-entered Rome, mutilated the
Deacon John, and committed many murders.   Then there
was Benedict V, chosen by the Romans and exiled by Leo
VIII.   Then there was Boniface VII, a frightful monster of
more than human wickedness, red with the blood of his pre-
decessor, who was put to death by his successor, Peter, Bishop
of Pavia.   ' Is it to such monsters, void of knowledge both
human and divine, that innumerable bishops of God throughout the world, distinguished by their knowledge and virtue,
shall be legally obedient ?   Whose is the fault ?   Surely partly
ours, because, in election, sufficient attention has not been
paid to character.   What is this man seated on a throne,
resplendent in purple and gold vestments ?   If he lack charity
and is puffed up only by knowledge, he is Antichrist, seated

G

in the temple of God, wishing to make people believe he is
God ; but if there is neither charity nor knowledge, he is a
statue, an idol in the temple of God. To interrogate such is
to consult marble. To whom, then, turn we for counsel ?
The gospel advises patience before cutting down. Let us
be patient and seek nourishment from the divine Word where
we can obtain it. Belgium and Germany contain eminent
and pious bishops, and, if the dissensions of the princes did
not prevent it, one would rather appeal to such than to the
city which sells its blessings for weight of gold. If, as Gelasius
says, the Roman Church is judge of all Churches and submits
to the judgement of none, so that no one is able to call in
question its decisions, we have established at Rome one whose
judgements are never able to be reformed. The African
Council said : " Is it admissible that God inspires with the
true spirit, and gives justice to only one, and refuses it to
innumerable bishops assembled in council ? " According to
report, there is no one at Rome who studies letters. How
dare one of these clerics pronounce on that of which he is
totally ignorant ? Ignorance is to be tolerated in other prelates, but not in the pontiff of Rome, who has to decide on
faith, life, morals, and ecclesiastical discipline. Even Peter
was rebuked by Paul, who, though inferior in dignity, was
nevertheless superior in knowledge ; and so it ought to be with
Rome, for even Gregory held that, if any bishop be without
reproach, humility exacts that he and the Bishop of Rome be
equal. Supposing there were bishops to-day at Rome like
Damasus, have we acted against his decree ? He said, indeed,
that episcopal affairs ought to be deferred to the Holy See,
so that the Holy See should have power to examine and pronounce, but this has been done both by kings and bishops in
this case. We have only taken the matter up when hope
of judgement from Rome has passed away. The Roman
Church has been consulted, but it has kept silence. Those
whose interests are at stake have been compelled to provide
for the necessities of the Church.' He appealed to a canon
of the Council of Sardica, and, whilst admitting that Damasus'
decree includes the reservation to Rome of the final judgement,
added : ' We do not contest Damasus, but we allege the writings
of Gregory ; thus Gregory does not support vice, but he sup-
presses it. Do we not encourage vice by keeping silence ?

What ought we to do when kings accuse one of our colleagues of treason ? What if they find that we trifle with frivolous discussions, long detours, tortuous subtleties ? Do you believe they will be able to obtain from Rome an appearance of justice for the price of money ? The guilty will not make the mistake of offering to the Romans some bits of gold and silver for absolution.' He then quoted the case of Egidius in the time of Childeric, condemned by the bishops and imprisoned without one word of protest from Gregory, and the case of Ebbo, whose deposition by the Gallic episcopate was actually confirmed by Pope Sergius. ' Do we wish to criticize Damasus ? In doubtful cases, and those which by their importance demand a superior tribunal, we shall have recourse to a Universal Council or to Damasus, though this latter appeal was forbidden by the African Councils ; but in self-evident affairs, which do not require an appeal to Rome, we appeal to provincial or co-provincial councils, conforming to Canon xiv. of the Council of Antioch.' He claimed that the Synod of Rheims could be called Universal because several provinces were represented, but he quoted Hincmar as illustrating the fact that the canons of Nicaea and other assemblies allowed judgement by such provincial councils, and only provided for an appeal to Rome in case of difficulty in reaching a decision. Again, the Councils of Africa were quoted forbidding appeals to transmarine authority. Yet Damasus said, ' to hold a council without the approbation of the Roman see is not catholic, but what if the barbarians forbid communication with Rome, or if Rome is under barbarian domination ? During this time must there be no council, even if that implies a risk to royal authority ? Further, the Council of Nicaea orders that two councils be held in the year, and says not a word about the authority of the Bishop of Rome in reference to this. In memory of the Apostles, and following the customs of our ancestors, we honour the Church of Rome more than the African Church, and whether she be worthy or not, we will ask counsel if the state of the country permit, as indeed we have done. Her response will be either just or unjust. If just, the peace and unity of the Church will be preserved ; if unjust, we listen to the voice of the Apostles, who said, " Whoever announce to us other than we have received, let them be anathema." O misery of the time, depriving us of the patronage of such a Church! In what town may we find a refuge, when the sovereign of the nations is deprived of all human and divine aid. Alexandria, Antioch, Constantinople, Spain, have escaped from her laws, the approach of Antichrist is imminent, since his supporters have occupied Gaul; the mystery of iniquity prepares itself, the name of God is dishonoured by perjurers, the observance of the laws of the Church is disdained by highest priests.' Arnulf quoted in conclusion Augustine and the judgement of Pelagius by twelve bishops, in the absence of Roman guidance. Rome had failed in its duty, so the Gallican Church had to act.

Such is the great contribution to the history of Gallicanism. We notice how hampered Arnulf was by the False Decretals, which he dared not deny; but there was throughout the address an appeal to reason and moral judgement, to Church History and Canon Law, which really undermined the Papal authority. Nevertheless, the contradiction remains. If Nicaea, Sardica, Gregory, and the African Councils are to be followed, there is no place for Damasus, for the Forged Decretals demand not only that Rome be informed, but that Rome's consent be obtained.

This speech seems to have convinced all of the validity of the council. Even the defence admitted that they had studied too lightly the facts of history (if we trust Gerbert's statements), and the council proceeded to business. Arnulf of Orleans mildly pointed out the many benefits the Archbishop had received from the King, and the poor return he had made. To this, Arnulf the Archbishop reiterated his defence, that he had kept faith, and that it was because of this he had been imprisoned, and when faced with the evidence of the presbyter, he denied it point-blank, asserting that the evidence of a presbyter ought not to be preferred to his own.

Adalger stated that his testimony was not forced evidence, but a witness freely made in order that he might clear himself of the guilt of treason. Arnulf then proceeded to say that he had never heard of an archbishop being treated so harshly, that he was in the hands of enemies, and was being denied the support of monks and clergy. No wonder, then, that in this state of isolation he was unable to frame satisfactory replies. The obvious reply was that abbots and the clergy of Rheims had been summoned, but had not chosen to speak.

Then Guy of Soissons intervened, and an interesting dialogue followed. ' Why did you refuse to reply to the many summonses of the bishops and the King ? ' ' I had been denounced to the King and feared to approach him.' ' It is not true, for when I met you in the neighbourhood of Laon, at Chavignon, in the presence of faithful witnesses, clergy, and laity, I invited you three times to a conference with your brethren.   Under the binding obligation of the Divine Name, according to canonical authority, I advised you to preserve all the oaths which you had promised to the King, and you were not able to deny that you were guilty of perjury because of the cirograph which you had subscribed and made others to subscribe. When you replied you were not able to go without guides, like Eudes and Herbert, I promised that I and my father and Count Walter would be guides, so that without danger to life or limb or fear of captivity, you might return to your own place. At the same time I was ready to give security by oath, and when you then pretended that you had been captured by Charles and given oaths and hostages to him, and thus were not able to go without his licence, I asked which oath ought to be preferred, the one to the King, or the one to an armed enemy ? For there were three oaths sworn which cannot be overlooked. You have sworn that you would never withdraw from fidelity to your Lord, and that, if intercepted by the enemy, you would return at the first opportunity ; and, in this case, I promised you, if there were only a few with you, I would supply a force of the best soldiers.   Further, all your citizens have sworn to retain the city for the King, yet you have opened its gates.'   He concluded by saying that Arnulf had released bishops from subjection to him if he were at any time to withdraw from the faith promised in the cirograph.

Arnulf, having listened to this recital, blushed, and was silent.   Renier, a confidant of his, was then called, and stated that, in a conversation by the Aisne, Arnulf had said that he loved Louis, son of Charles, beyond all others, and that ' if I wished to please him, I should work for his safety.'   Then followed a threat that, if Arnulf would not confess, he would openly proclaim the scandal of the treason.

Certain abbots then suggested that Arnulf be given an opportunity to retire in order to consider his reply, and, this privilege being granted, he proceeded to the crypt of the

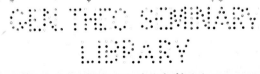

church, accompanied by certain bishops whom he chose as advisers, Seguin, Arnulf of Orleans, Bruno, and Gotesmann. In their absence the council proceeded to discuss Arnulf's relations with the Empress Theophania in opposition to Hugh, the presence of his troops with Charles, and his treason. A great number of canons were also examined, drawn from the Council of Toledo, condemning bishops who had broken their oath of loyalty to the king.

Further proceedings were interrupted by a message from the bishops, asking their colleagues to meet them in the crypt. Meanwhile there had been much deliberation in the crypt. The bishops had seen a resemblance between this case and the case of Apiarius, a priest of Carthage, who had been condemned by African bishops against the wishes of the Pope. The analogy was not a true one, for Apiarius was only a presbyter, whilst Arnulf was a metropolitan bishop, but it seemed to give the bishops a handle to work with. Moreover, the sensational news with which the bishops greeted their colleagues was that Arnulf, touched by God, had fallen at their feet with tears ; had, to their consternation, confessed the incredible faults charged to him ; and had asked to be relieved of episcopal functions, for which he believed himself unworthy. The nine bishops, who had recently arrived, warned him not to swear falsely from fear, and promised to re-establish him on the episcopal throne if he were innocent, in spite of the kings. Arnulf, however, was utterly broken now ; arguments failed him, and he simply confessed his fault, whilst thanking them for their consideration.

They called in thirty of the most religious clergy and abbots to advise them, and these, under vow of secrecy, also received the confession. They regarded themselves, nevertheless, as judges, as well as counsellors chosen by Arnulf. This confusion of functions enabled the Bishop to justify immediate action, and to rule out a reference to Rome by appealing to African precedents, which regarded judgement by specially chosen judges as final.

The synod proceeded to discuss methods of procedure. Various precedents were considered which proved that the law now called for deprivation, but the question still remained how deprivation was to be carried out. The Council of Toledo showed that deprivation might be effected by the removal

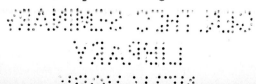

in succession of the insignia of office, annulum, baculum, and the pallium ; but there arose another difficulty, for the pallium had been given by Rome.   Could it be taken away without Rome's permission ?   The council ruled, however, that, as Arnulf had not appealed to Rome, but had confessed voluntarily, as they claimed, before specially-chosen judges, and as Rome had refused to break silence, the pallium could be removed without prejudice to Roman authority.   The cases of Paternus, Archbishop of Bruga, Ebbo and Egidius, Archbishops of Rheims, were quoted, and it was decided that the garments of the Archbishop should not be rent, lest episcopal dignity suffer in the eyes of the people.

There was still the question of how to make known the faults of the Archbishop without revealing the nature of those faults, for his deposition would need justifying to the people. It was decided that an act of deposition should be prepared by the council, signed by the Archbishop and attested by his living voice, which statement would contain the information that this deposition had not been extorted, but that, on the contrary, he was involved in crimes, and could not continue to approach holy altars.   The synod held that, if such acts of abdication could be prepared in cases of physical weakness, they could most certainly be prepared in cases of moral weakness.   A quotation from the Council of Antioch (xiv.) and a judgement of Pope Gregory provided the necessary precedents.

The problem was acute, and the discussion was adjourned till the following day.   Some felt pity for the youth of the Archbishop ; some felt sympathy with the race he represented ; but there was a sense of shame and fear which disturbed the clergy, for the guilt of Arnulf seemed to bring scandal on the whole episcopate in the eyes of the people.   Yet a public explanation of the deposition would be demanded.

The situation was not rendered easier by the arrival of the kings themselves with their courtiers, including Count Burchard. The kings thanked the bishops for their loyalty, but asked for full particulars of the discussion of the previous day. The arrival of the lay element gave a sinister meaning to the trial.   Political, not ecclesiastical, considerations were involved here.   Arnulf of Orleans represented the council, and caustically suggested that, if it was their duty to consider the royal interests, it was also their duty to give all their time to the

safety of their brother. He proceeded to describe the proceedings of the previous day, including the story of Arnulf's
confession in the crypt before many abbots and clergy, and
finished by stating that Arnulf himself would expose the
whole affair to the public eye, as his own witness and judge.
The Archbishop was then introduced before the people, and
there was a great silence. Arnulf of Orleans put the question :
' Do you see the faces turned to you ? Why do you not speak
for yourself ? ' He only poured forth confused words, and
Arnulf of Orleans asked : ' Are you still in the same mood
as that in which we left you yesterday evening ? ' ' Yes.'
' Do you wish to abdicate from the honours of the priesthood
which you have abused ? ' ' You have said so.' Then
Burchard, interfering, and watching carefully for the interests
of the King, asked : ' What meant the words " You have
said so " ? Let him express himself clearly, and confess
openly, lest he go on to pretend that the bishops have covered
him with imaginary crimes, and go back on his avowals.'
Arnulf replied : ' I say openly and acknowledge that I have
failed in fidelity to the King. I only ask that you will refer
to Arnulf of Orleans, who will speak for me. I beg him, since
he knows all which concerns me, to express my case in your
presence.' Arnulf at once replied with some sternness :
' He is by nature taciturn ; he has hesitated to avow publicly
what he has confided to our good faith and to our discretion,
under the guarantee of Christ. Let it suffice to you to know
that he has confessed publicly that he has not at all preserved
the oaths given to the kings and that he has acted openly
against his profession of faith and what he had signed in the
cirograph.' Burchard said : ' It is not enough unless he
publicly acknowledge, or deny publicly, that he has acted as a
traitor, so that a free opportunity of succeeding him may be
given to another.' Arnulf of Orleans was roused, and replied :
' Surely you will not be the equal of priests, to whom alone
entire confession is due. If a vassal of the King was accused
of a stated crime, if he should deny having committed this
crime, but recognize himself guilty, so as not to be able to
hold a domain or fief, and ask only the favour of life—if, say I,
this domain or benefice were offered to you by the munificence
of the King, would you refuse to receive it ? What does it
matter if the guilty party be punished, particularly for murder

and adultery, &c. ?   Let it suffice you to know that Arnulf
has uncovered his sins in confession, that he declares himself
unworthy of the priesthood in the face of the kings, and in
the presence of the Church he avows himself unworthy of
the honours of the age.   It matters little that it be for such
or such a fault that he is degraded.'

Then he turned to Arnulf.   ' What have you to say to
what I speak in your name ? '   ' I accept it, and make mine
your words.'   ' Then throw yourself at the feet of the masters
you have so gravely offended, avow your faults, and beg for
your life.'   The miserable Caroling then threw himself in
the form of a cross before the kings of the rival house, and
begged most humbly for his life.   The bishops were moved to
pity by this picture of abject, helpless impotence.   Dagobert
particularly begged for his life, and offered to go surety for his
safety if delivered to his control.   Hugh was not willing to do
this, but he gave promise of his life—unless guilty of some
fresh offence—to the Archbishop.

There then followed degradation.   Arnulf expressed himself
as willing to undergo degradation according to the precedent
of Ebbo of Rheims, and then he read to the council :   ' I,
Arnulf, formerly Archbishop of Rheims, recognizing my weakness and the weight of my sins, have established as judges of
my faults the following witnesses, my confessors—Seguin, the
Archbishop, Dagobert, Arnulf, Gotesmann, Heriveus, Rathbod,
Walter, Bruno, Milo, Adalberon, Eudes, Guy, Herbert.   I
have made to them a full, entire confession, and, to obtain
the remedy of penance and the safety of my soul, have resolved
to abdicate the office and the episcopal ministry, of which I
recognize myself unworthy, and to which I am rendered a
stranger by reason of the sins which were charged to me
publicly.   These I have confessed in detail in such a way that
they declare there is reason to substitute and consecrate in
my place another prelate, who may be fit to direct and serve
worthily this Church over which I have presided, until now,
unworthily, and to this I agree.'   They said to him in turn :
' Cease from your office, according to your subscription and
profession.'   Then he absolved clergy and people from their
allegiance to him.   Then Adalger was introduced, and fell at
the feet of the kings, asking to be deprived of Communion.
In spite of the fact that the bishops had used his evidence,

and that on their showing he had acted under orders, he was very sternly treated. ' Did you open the gates ? ' ' I opened them.' ' You entered the temple of God as an enemy.' ' I am not able to deny it.' Walter of Autun said : ' Since your bishop has been punished for ordering it, you will be punished for obeying and carrying through the orders, and will pay the penalty due.' Bruno was very severe. ' You have ruined a young man by bad counsels, and should you sing whilst he laments ? How could I cease from groaning if I saw you exempted from all chastisement—you, who have caused the misfortune to my uncle's son ? ' The presbyter chose to be deposed rather than to bear the perpetual anathema, which was the alternative offered, and the degradation of Adalger closed the proceedings.

The election of Gerbert followed inevitably. Adhemar, Helgaud, and R. Glaber all declare that his appointment was the work of Hugh, the King, as also do hostile writers like Hugh of Fleury, &c. There was no other name which could be put forward. Gerbert had played his cards well, and was now in favour with the Capetians. In the *Act of Election*, which he himself edited, he is described as prudent in character and open to good advice. ' We elect Gerbert, whose life and manners we have known from boyhood, whose zeal in divine and human affairs we have experienced, and by whose counsel and teaching we are instructed.' But it is noticeable that in this *Act* a significant distinction is drawn between the ' Voice of God ' and the ' Voice of the People.' The election is by bishops, with the favour of Hugh and Robert, and the assent of those ' who are of God among the clergy and people,' and it is distinctly stated that it is not permitted to the crowd to elect the priest. This may be taken as a clear indication that Arnulf was popular with many of the clergy and laity in Rheims, and that Gerbert's election was due to kings and bishops rather than to the free choice of the clergy and people of Rheims.

Gerbert was very conscious of this latent hostility, to which he often referred, and, indeed, it was the consciousness of this lack of sympathy which led eventually to his abandonment of Gaul and Gallicanism. For the present, however, he was at the height of his ambition, the defender of the liberties of the Gallican Church, and swayed vast political and religious power in the interests of the Capetian kings.

But the Synod of Rheims did not close the discussion.   In fact, it was only just beginning.   Pope John XV sent legates to inquire into the matter further, and by these legates—Leo, Abbot of St. Boniface, and Dominicus, Abbot of St. Sabeanus —a council was summoned to meet in Aachen, a city lying outside the Capetian sovereignty, but conveniently near the border-line.   It was apparently only attended by German prelates, and proceeded to condemn the decisions taken at Rheims (Annals of Cologne and Corbie, letter of Leo).   A letter (G. 196) from Gerbert to Abbot Leo seems to have been written about this time, for Gerbert, very anxious to retain the favour of so influential a dignitary, speaks of him in flattering terms, and expresses himself as ' happy in the friend-ship of such a man.'   Gerbert followed this up with a letter to the Pope in which he defended himself from the charge of betraying Arnulf, and expressed his sorrow that his withdrawal from the society of Arnulf had been so understood.

The calling of a Council at Aachen was sufficient indication that the Papacy was at enmity with the Capetian kings, who were now cited to Rome.

The reply of the kings was not a direct refusal, but was couched in diplomatic terms.   Hugh was prepared to meet the Pope in France, and, if this was impossible, he was even prepared to go outside his own territory, provided that the meeting be at Grenoble, which lay, significantly enough, on the French side of the Alps, where, on the confines of Italy and Gaul, the priests of Rome were wont to meet the kings of France.   This letter (G. 188), sent by the Archdeacon of Rheims, protested the King's ignorance of any action against the Apostolic See, but, as probably was expected, the Pope declined to cross the Alps, and the interview therefore never took place.

The Capetian kings called a council at Chelles, over which Robert himself presided, and the Archbishops of Sens, Tours, and Bourges were present.   Richer has described this synod (R. iv. 89), which was held in 993.   Gerbert took the place in this synod which Arnulf of Orleans took in the Synod of Rheims, for to him ' was committed the explanation of all the business which had to be discussed.'   Extracts from the judgements of the Fathers, bearing on the state of the Church, were published, and counsels of unity advanced.   It was agreed that they should all be of one heart and soul, and, if any tyrant were to arise in any Church, they were to act together, and issue decrees in unity. If anything were suggested by the Roman Pontiff contrary to the decrees of the Fathers, such suggestions or decisions were to be regarded as null and void, for the Apostle had said, ' Avoid completely the man who is a heretic, dissenting from the Church.' The substitution of Gerbert for Arnulf at Rheims was confirmed, with the judgement that ' what had been done in a provincial synod ought not rashly to be undone.' This synod thus committed itself to a clear statement of the superiority of a council and of the ancient canons over the judgements of the Papacy, and even ventured to attribute heresy to the Roman see, thus advancing the strongest claims possible for the principles of Gallicanism.

This synod was probably an answer to the Synod of St. Denis (991), where there had been a controversy between monks and bishops about tithes. The bishops laid the monastery under an interdict, and Gerbert refused to celebrate the sacraments there even when asked to by the kings. In a letter to Arnulf of Orleans (190) he refers to some agreement similar to that made at Chelles, and this same letter shows that the Pope had spoken on behalf of the monks. It is significant that Arnulf of Orleans and Archembald of Tours, who was prominent at Chelles, were both in controversy, with the monks of Fleury and St. Martin respectively.

For some time the matter rested there, for the German Emperor was actively engaged in wars with the Slavs, whilst the Papacy lay powerless in the grip of Crescentius, the Roman senator. But in 995 Pope John moved again, and sent Abbot Leo once more to act in conjunction with the German bishops (R. iv. 95). The Capetian kings were notified concerning the calling of another synod. The place chosen was Mouzon, in the diocese of Rheims, but in German territory. Hugh and Robert had at first temporized, but finally refused either to go themselves or to allow the bishops to go. ' If this concerns the affairs of Gaul, why should not the synod be held on Gallic soil ? ' was the substance of their contention, for French bishops were not to be ruled by German bishops. We thus trace another step in the growing estrangement between Capetians and Imperialists. Richer tells us that a new plot formed by Asceline was mixed up with this summons. The intention of Asceline was to make Otho King of France, with Eudes of Chartres as Duke of France, whilst he himself was to receive promotion to the archbishopric of Rheims.

Otho apparently was to remain with a force at Metz, whilst the unsuspecting Hugh was to be called to Mouzon; and it is also evident that Asceline was prepared to make use of Louis, who had been delivered to him for safe keeping. Hugh scented conspiracy, and demanded that Louis and Laon be returned to him. When Asceline refused, he denounced the bishop for his treason. One of Asceline's vassals offered to prove his master's innocence by fighting a duel on his behalf, but the offer was ridiculed by Count Landri of Nevers, who suggested that he had better ask his lord first whether the charges were true or not. Asceline forbade his servant to engage in the duel, thereby admitting his own guilt. The Bishop apparently yielded to the threats of the King. He was imprisoned by the King, and his soldiers bound to the King by oath.

The truth of such a conspiracy might easily be confirmed by what we know of the characters of both Asceline and Eudes, for both these men were thoroughly unprincipled schemers, and consumed with ambition. The references to young Louis and to Count Landri are likely enough to be true, for, in the satirical poem of Asceline, the Count appears as his personal enemy. With reference to Eudes, we may recollect that he had married Bertha, daughter of Conrad of Burgundy, and, through her, might think he had some claim on the Carolingian and Burgundian inheritance. He had favoured the Carolings, and acted as jailer for Lothaire's prisoners of Lorraine, and had shown considerable hostility to Hugh, even to supporting the claims of Charles, and forcibly seizing Milan in 991, from which he was only evicted by the united forces of Normans, French, and Angevins. At the time of his death in 996 he was still at war with the kings, having been in arms against the royal forces allied with the forces of Anjou under Fulk. That such a man should have plotted with Asceline and the Emperor against his sovereign for the purpose of increasing his own power is both possible and probable.

The Synod of Mouzon was held in June 995. The legate, Abbot Leo, presided. Heymon of Verdun introduced the subject of debate because he knew the language of the district, and other prelates included Notker of Liège, Liudolph of Trèves, Bishops of Lorraine, who were favourable to the claims of Arnulf and Charles, Suger of Münster, and some abbots. Count Godfrey, as Advocate of the Church and principal magnate, attended among the laity ; whilst Gerbert, braving the opposition of the kings, attended, and sought an opportunity for defending himself. It will be at once seen that the council was not sufficiently strong in numbers or influence to settle the question. Heymon spoke in French, stating at once the Papal case. It had come to the ears of the Pope that the metropolitan city of Rheims, against all law and right, had been deprived of its own pastor. He, the Pope, had suggested more than once that a council called by his authority should condemn so great a crime and restore the see. Heymon pointed out that, after some delay, Abbot Leo had been sent to act in the Pope's name, and proceeded to read the bull of John XV constituting the council. The bull was addressed to all the bishops of Gaul.

Then Gerbert spoke, delivered his speech to Leo, received from him the Papal letter, and sat down. Gerbert's speech was a thorough defence of his attitude towards Arnulf and the Pope, and of his acceptance of the archbishopric. He had been designated by Adalberon as his successor, but Arnulf had been introduced through simonistic influences. He had remained faithful to Arnulf until he had learnt of his apostasy and falsehood, and then he had left him without in any way desiring his office. Arnulf, ' demon in human form,' had been rightly judged seditious and rebellious, and deprived of office according to the precedents of the African Councils, and he, Gerbert, had been asked to take his bishopric by the assembled bishops. He had long delayed to accept the office, and protested, in the presence of the Lord and the Bishop, that his conscience was clear in all these matters. He proceeded to answer various charges. He had never betrayed Arnulf, having, in fact, never taken an oath to him. He had remained in Rheims simply because he had been told to do so by Adalberon, his patron, but, having been robbed, he had scarcely escaped from the swords of the robbers. Then he left the apostate. Moreover, he had never sought the imprisonment of Arnulf, but had, on the contrary, actually approached the kings in the presence of the faithful, and begged his liberty. To the charge that he had pervaded the see, he made answer that Arnulf was the real pervader who had polluted and violated the Church, and, if one were to concede that the Church was really his own, he had prostituted his betrothed.   The Apostolic See had been consulted, and sentence delayed eighteen months to secure the decision of Rome.   Gerbert proceeded to quote Scripture (Matt. v. 29, xviii. 17) in order to justify the action taken by the Synod at Rheims.   The brother who had not heeded the call of the Church must be treated as a publican and sinner. Arnulf, in fact, had not been judged in deference to the Apostolic See, but he had judged himself, and to have absolved him in such circumstances would have meant the incurring of guilt as one accessory to the crime.   He concluded with an earnest appeal for consideration, and such action by the Synod as would bring strength to the Church of Rheims and every other Church.

The Bishops then withdrew to consult with Count Godfrey. It was agreed that the monk John should be sent to the King, and that another synod should be called to meet at Rheims that July.   This would be in full accord with the desires of Gerbert, who, in a letter to Notker of Liège, signified his earnest desire for such a council to be held (G. 193).   In that letter he referred to a third summons to these hostile prelates, by which he no doubt meant that this second Council of Rheims should count as in the true order of succession with the first council and the Synod of Chelles.   He no doubt believed that a synod held on French soil would substantiate his claim and entirely justify his policy, and so, in this sense, Gerbert had secured a triumph at Mouzon ; but when the council had finished its deliberations, and was about to disperse, Gerbert received a message from Abbot Leo calling upon him to abstain from divine offices until that council met.   Gerbert refused to obey the call, saying, in the presence of Leo, that it was not in the power of any person to remove the faithful from Communion unless he had been convicted, or had confessed, or had refused a summons to a council, on each of which counts he was obviously innocent.   Liudolph suggested that, lest he gave occasion for stumbling to the weaker brethren, he should abstain from the celebration of Mass until the next synod.   To this he agreed, and the synod thereupon concluded its proceedings.

It would seem that, as a result of this synod, Gerbert issued the *Acts of the Council of St. Basil, near Rheims,* his letter to Wilderode of Strasburg (G. 217), and his letter to Notker of Liège (193), which together constituted his apologia for undertaking the archbishopric of Rheims after the deposition of Arnulf.   The legate replied in a strong letter, which, however, did not allude to Gerbert as author by name.   Two accusations—of ignorance and venality—brought against the Roman See, were rebutted by scoffing references to Plato and Virgil, and by referring to the bribes paid as presents, given by grateful and loyal Churches.   The heresy of Arnulf of Orleans was worse than that of Arius.   Rome had been grievously insulted. ' It is clear you have separated yourself from her.'   He tried to refute the statement that Africa and Spain and the East had withdrawn from Rome, by giving instances of reverence shown by these Churches to the Papal See.   The delay at Rome could be accounted for by the power of the tyrant Crescentius, and he concluded by a defence of Arnulf, enfeebled by captivity, condemned by a single witness, and menaced by soldiers.   Arnulf had only confessed after a threefold denial, and when threatened with death.   ' Ask pardon to save your life' meant, ' If you do not own the crime, you shall die.'   The reply was not without its sting, especially in regard to the treatment of Arnulf the Archbishop, but the attempted defence of the ignorant and corrupt Papacy would mean little to those who knew the facts.   To compare the Pope, receiving bribes, with Jesus, receiving gifts from the Magi, was of course absurd, approaching blasphemy, but probably was not seriously meant ; and, though he might be right in contending that the Roman Church was venerated and honoured, this certainly did not mean that the East was prepared to accept the Roman claims and submit to them.

The letter of Leo was, however, in accord with the new claims which were now being advanced by the Papacy, as a result of the widespread acceptance of the False Decretals. The modern student cannot but stand aghast at the immense contrast afforded by the claims, largely admitted by Western Christendom in the tenth century, and the utterly contemptible character of the adventurers who occupied the see.   Peter's throne was not occupied by men of Peter's character, but to that age it was still Peter's throne, and had authority as such.

The synod gathered at Rheims apparently in July, 995, and it would appear that the acts of a council called Causeium (Migne 139) represent the acts of this synod, which was presided over by the Abbot Leo.   Richer, having stated that the synod was to be held at Rheims, mentions Senlis as the place of meeting; but he may have confused the council with a previous Council of Senlis by a slip of memory or pen, for the history of the Franks of Sens distinctly states that the synod assembled at Rheims, and this is borne out by a statement of Abbo's in a letter to Abbot Leo (Ep. 15).   In his defence, Gerbert reiterated the facts about Arnulf, but he was not so harsh in his references to the Roman See as at Mouzon.   He admitted that the tyranny of Crescentius created difficulties for Rome, but this led him to ask why all the members of the Church should be weakened because the mother and head of all the churches happened to be oppressed by tyrants, and he proceeded once more to quote African and Gallican precedents. It is permitted to do good even without the authority of the Apostolic See, and it is always good to withdraw from a criminal. He used the old argument that the Archbishop of Sens had special prerogative as Papal legate, that Seguin presided in that capacity over the first Synod of Rheims, and he compared the eighteen months' delay over Arnulf's case with the two months' delay in the case of the African Councils. 'Who will be guilty if the betrayer of his country is absolved as innocent?'   'Laws are useless, if it is lawful to none to give judgement except the one whom Crescentius controls, who in absolving or punishing is influenced by a bribe.' If the decrees of Gregory, Leo, Zosimus, and African Councils are to be considered valid, they who suggest that Arnulf has been irregularly deposed are to be blamed and despised.   Arnulf, in fact, betook himself to judges elected by himself, and asked from them, after confession, the form of penance.   He concluded by appealing to the Pope to support in his own interests the judgement of the Universal Church, otherwise the Papal See would lose moral influence with the people.

The reply of Leo to this appeal seems to have created some impression, for Abbo, in a letter to the Abbot, 996 (Ep. 15), refers to the fact that at Rheims his mouth in torrents of eloquence distilled the honey of Holy Scripture. 'I am constrained to proclaim everywhere that you were indeed the

H

thunder of the Holy Ghost.' But apparently no decision was taken. The report of a condemnation of Gerbert, contained in the Chronicles of Sens (Hugh of Fleury), must be discounted. The council met on French soil, and the bishops were in full force, and a condemnation of the royal nominee would be unlikely. Then there is the silence of Richer, who simply tells us that the matter was discussed. The visits of Gerbert to Rome, and the need of further councils, would be difficult to explain had a final decision been reached at Rheims. A new council certainly met at Ingleheim on February 5, 996, but again separated without settling the difficult situation. We only know of the meeting of such a council by a brief note in Richer and some slight reference in the Annals, which, however, place it as early as 994. Gerbert visited Rome in the company of the Emperor Otho III. in the middle of 996. This was the beginning of a strong friendship, for the Emperor, young, earnest, and a lover of studies, became strongly drawn to the scholar, and ties were formed never to be broken. Letters (G. 213-17) seem to have been written during this tour in Italy. The Pope died before they reached Rome. Otho nominated his cousin, who, as Gregory V., crowned him in Rome in May. Gerbert was present, and wrote in the name of the Emperor to the Empress Adelaide. The real purpose of Gerbert's journey to Rome was, however, to restate his case to the Pope and secure favour. The appointment of a new Pope closely related to the Emperor, now Gerbert's friend and patron, might have been expected to help the prospects of Gerbert, but this was not so. The case of Cambrai illustrates the position. Erlwin had been chosen bishop. In view of the quarrel between the rival archbishops at Rheims, he sought consecration from Rome, and this was granted by the new Pope, together with certain privileges for the Cambrai Church, in which Papal letter Arnulf is called the Archbishop and Gerbert the 'invader of the see.' It is therefore certain that in May 996 Gerbert was not recognized as Archbishop at Rome, even by Otho's nominee. Still, Gerbert, returning to his own see, maintained his position at Rheims till the death of Hugh Capet, which robbed him of a good friend (October 24, 996).

The succession of Robert changed the situation unfavourably for Gerbert. The new King had been a pupil of Gerbert, and had hitherto accepted and actively supported his father's ecclesiastical policy, and, in fact, had presided in person over the Council of Chelles, which had asserted so strongly the Gallican claims. Nevertheless, there were factors in the situation making for a change of policy. He loved the monks, and, according to Helgaud, was himself devoted to pious works, alms-giving, and psalm-singing, whilst he had literary and artistic tastes which also drew him towards the monks. Abbo of Fleury had considerable influence over him, and brought him to consider the case of Arnulf of Rheims from another point of view, and probably fixed in him a desire for reconciliation with the Papacy. But there was, after all, another and more mundane reason. Helgaud, amid his glowing tributes to the piety of King Robert, has to break off to acknowledge that his hero had sinned like David. He had married Susanne, widow of Arnulf of Flanders, but he repudiated her in 991 on the ground of disparity in age, and, on the death of Eudes of Chartres in 996, sought to obtain his widow Bertha for wife. This marriage was declared null by the Church, on the ground that Robert and Bertha were cousins. It was probably opposed by the old King because of the enmity between him, the house of Chartres, and the Carolings of Burgundy, for Bertha, daughter of Matilda of Burgundy, was of Caroling descent. Gerbert himself opposed the marriage, perhaps in the interests of the King, but also, no doubt, in the interests of Church law ; and, if the latter reason predominated, it should be noted as an instance of real principle, for his opposition to Robert's marriage with Bertha cost him the King's friendship. It is at least certain that, before the death of Hugh and before Gerbert's visit to Rome, Bertha, wishing to marry Robert, consulted Gerbert, and was resisted by him. Now Robert's one hope of retaining Bertha was in securing Papal sanction, so he sought friendship with Pope Gregory, and appears to have been willing, if necessary, to throw over Gerbert and reinstate Arnulf, if by so doing he could receive Papal sanction for a marriage with Bertha. This defection of the King was a great factor in the settlement of this dispute concerning the archbishopric of Rheims.

On the death of Hugh, Robert celebrated his marriage with Bertha, and Archembald of Tours performed the ceremony. He had not waited for Papal sanction, and his purpose now was,

by a surrender on the Rheims issue, to secure that belated
sanction.

Meanwhile Pope Gregory V summoned the French clergy,
who refused to attend. At a council held at Pavia, a bull of
excommunication was issued against all the clergy who had
taken part in the Council of St. Basil, and especially against
Asceline, who had betrayed his Archbishop. At the same time
Robert was summoned to Rome, because of his marriage
without the Pope's consent within the prohibited degrees, and
threatened with excommunication unless satisfaction were
immediately rendered. There was a general panic in France.
The clergy and soldiers of Rheims refused to eat with Gerbert
(G. 181) and take the sacrament with him, and he was
treated with contempt. The bishops, including Seguin
of Sens, hastened to make their peace with Rome, and
refused to administer the sacred offices, to baptize and
bury.

Gerbert wrote a strong letter to Seguin (G. 192, 203) urging
him to resist the bull. Gerbert asserted once more the great
principle of the Gallican Church Movement. He quoted against
Rome the words, ' It is God that justifieth,' and words of our
Lord concerning sin against a brother, which in the last resort
demanded that the sinner be treated as a publican. ' Are you
able to teach that the judgements of Rome are greater than the
judgements of God ? The Bishop of Rome is the first prince of
apostles, but it is necessary to " obey God rather than man."
If any announce to you other than what you received, even if
it be an angel from heaven, let him be anathema. I say if the
Roman Bishop has sinned against a brother, and, after he had
been admonished, has refused to hear the Church, the Roman
bishop is by precept of God to be considered a publican and
sinner. The higher the grade, the greater the sin. He is not
able to separate us from the Communion of the Church, since
even presbyters, unless confessed or convicted, ought not to be
so separated, especially when the apostle says, " Who can
separate us from the love of Christ ? " What greater separation
is there than separation from the body of the Son of God, who
is for our sins daily sacrificed ? . . .'

Again he referred to the corruption of Rome and the priesthood. He quoted Gregory to the effect that judgement not
placed in writing is no judgement, and Leo to the effect that

the privileges of Peter are not held where envy obtains. He appealed in an important passage to the common law of the Catholic Church, which rests on the Gospels, the apostles, prophets, canons inspired of God, and decrees of Holy See not contrary to them. He concluded by stating that a confession of sins which are no sins was equivalent to homicide and the slaying of one's soul.

This letter was the last great defence of Gallicanism by Gerbert, and in it he approached the Protestant standpoint and appealed to the apostolic and prophetic writings for the Church law. He threw the Decretals to the winds, and placed God above the Man, the Church above the Pope, and the Bible above the Decretals; but it was his last great effort, and it failed. Seguin yielded to the threats of Rome, and put into operation the Papal mandates and subjected his province to the anathemas. Robert the King approached Abbo, and endeavoured to placate the angry Pope by meeting him on the Rheims issue. Gerbert perceived his work was done, and that, in the midst of an angry and threatening people, with the Bishops timidly submitting, and the King increasingly hostile, his life was in danger. Meanwhile Abbot Leo, who probably brought the decisions of Pavia, had apparently given Robert some hope that the Pope would meet him on the marriage question, and he was the more eager to sacrifice Gerbert to his passion (G. 181). Rumours of the impending release of Arnulf reached Gerbert in Rheims, and suggestions were put forward by way of compromise that Gibuin, the nephew of Gibuin of Chalons, should take the see of Rheims, thus dispossessing Gerbert as well as Arnulf. Gerbert attended a Synod of St. Denis in March 997. At this council the Bishops took up the case of Archembald of Tours, who was in controversy with the monks of St. Martin supported by Abbo, and the monks charged with rebellion were summoned to present their case at Chelles in May (G. 207, 209). Before the next council came due, Gerbert had abandoned France, for in April he was with the Emperor, who gave him the monastery of Sassbach (G. 183), and from henceforth he was the constant and loyal supporter of the Imperial cause.

In April he wrote to the Empress Adelaide complaining of his sicknesses and advancing age. ' Pleurisy seizes my sides, my ears tingle, my eyes dilate, my whole body is pricked with stinging pain, and for a whole year I have been in bed from sickness ' (G. 208). He had probably been asked to excommunicate someone in the Imperial part of the diocese, and so excused his attendance on grounds of ill health, but his condition was evidently miserable and unhappy by reason of the enmity of King and people. About the same time he wrote to Arnulf (210), commending to his protection himself and his possessions. These were the last letters which he wrote before his departure.

Queen Adelaide, holding some high and influential position in the kingdom of her son, ordered his return, threatening to confiscate his possessions if he did not obey. Gerbert replied in a letter in which he reviewed the situation and said farewell (181). He hinted at dangers to his life in France. He expressed his regret that he should have to leave the Queen and the King, of whom he had such memories, and stated that his only consolation was the friendship, favour, and generosity of Otho, whose desire for friendship with Adelaide and Robert, a fellow-pupil, was so strong. Having received the government of the province of Rheims by the judgement of bishops, he would not quit it without their judgement, so he would go to Rome for a synod there, and would await patiently its decisions. He showed that he was aware of the efforts being made to release Arnulf and to substitute Gibuin, and wrote bitterly of his treatment by soldiers and clergy, and the contempt shown to him in the accepting of the edict of excommunication by the Bishops. The letter concludes with a clause hinting at a possible return, if the Roman Synod be deferred.

A letter written to Adalberon of Verdun (211), rejoicing in liberation from unjust persecution, reveals his true mind. He never returned to France, for he remained at Sassbach during the summer of 997, whilst Otho was engaged in his wars with the Slavs, and wrote from there many letters (219, 220, 182, 157). Then he accompanied Otho to Italy at the end of the year. In the letters from Sassbach he denies the rumour that Arnulf had already been released, but in a letter to Heriveus (184) of Beauvais says, ' I fear not the return of Arnulf, but, if it happens, I shall be glad to be released from Ur of the Chaldees.' A letter written later in the year shows that someone had been trying to break the friendship between Otho and Gerbert, and he protested his great services to

Otho I and Otho II, and showed what troubles his past services had brought to him. Otho replied by emphasizing his delight in Gerbert's friendship, and paid glowing tribute to Gerbert's scholarship, from which he hoped still to benefit. ' We wish you to provoke our Greek subtilty and abhor our Saxon rusticity.' Gerbert retorted by new professions of obedience and flattering reference to a man ' Greek in race, Roman in Empire, seeking, as if by hereditary right, treasures of Greek and Roman wisdom for himself.' So did the attachment between Gerbert and Otho deepen.

Meanwhile Abbo had visited Rome on behalf of Robert. He returned with the pallium for Arnulf, with privileges placing Fleury outside the interdict now reigning in the rest of the land, but he brought back no dispensation for Robert's marriage with Bertha. Robert was duped, and realized that he had sacrificed Gerbert and Gallicanism for naught. Abbo's letter (Ep. 1) to the Pope says : ' I fear not the animosity of the King whilst I have preserved faith sworn to you. I added nothing, changed nothing. Arnulf of Rheims has been released from prison. I offered to him the pallium as from your hands. I persuade you to teach Arnulf how to converse with his clergy, and how to draw the Church from errors and restore lost property to St. Mary's. The evil Arnulf and Gerbert did has been avenged. I have never heard of anything worse than to have rendered the noblest Church of Gaul abject and vile, and to have denied its rights. Now bring help by your unbroken authority ; bring it back to the former state in which Adalberon left it,' &c. He implied that Robert had promised obedience, but the King still clung to Bertha, whom he seems ardently to have loved.

This letter shows the order of the events. Abbo had visited Italy, and discovered the Pope at Spoleto, to which place he had fled from the presence of Crescentius in the September of 997. The Pope demanded the immediate release of Arnulf, and ordered Abbo to carry the pallium to him, reserving judgement to a later synod, but refusing tacitly the dispensation of the marriage. On his return in December with this information, Abbo encountered the animosity of the disappointed King, but by the February of 998 Arnulf had been definitely released and reinstated in the see of Rheims. Meanwhile, as Robert still refused to give up Bertha, there was issued from

Rome a bull decreeing seven years' penance for the King ; but
Robert continued to resist for three or four years.

Arnulf consecrated Boso to Sens in June 998, and also
subscribed a donation of Count Burchard in favour of
St. Valerie three months before. Yet it is noticeable that the
reinstatement of Arnulf was only conditional; as Richer
says : ' Pope Gregory permits to Arnulf the sacerdotal office
till he should acquire or lose legally the right of it.'

Meanwhile Gerbert, who, by attending the various synods,
had apparently escaped the anathemas hurled at the other
bishops, remained in the favour of Otho, who, using his influence
with Gregory, secured for him the vacant see of Ravenna. A
year later, on the nomination of Otho, he succeeded Gregory
as Pope Sylvester II. He died in 1003, but not before he had
granted a contemptuous pardon to Archbishop Arnulf.

By strange irony of fortune, the defender of Gallican liberties
had become a Pope in defence not of the national but of the
international ideal of the Holy Roman Empire. Two important
letters, written after his election as Pope, are preserved, and
bring him into relation once more, and finally, with the two
important figures of Archbishop Arnulf and Bishop Asceline.
The one to Arnulf is the closing of the controversy. ' It
belongs to the Apostolic See not only to consult about sins, but
also to lift up those who have lapsed, and to adorn those of
our number who have been deprived with restored dignity,
so that free power of loosing and absolving may belong to
St. Peter, and so that the glory and dignity of Rome may shine
on all sides. Because you, Arnulf of Rheims, had been deprived
of pontifical honour for certain excesses, and because your
abdication was without the consent of Rome, we have thought
well to help you, so that reparation may be accomplished by
the gift of Roman piety. For it is the highest privilege of
Peter, with which no felicity of mortals is able to compare, so
to absolve. We grant, therefore, through our privilege and
permission, that the staff and pallium be returned to you, that
you may perform the duties of the archiepiscopal office, and
enjoy in the accustomed ways all the distinctions which pertain
to the metropolitan church of Rheims in solemn celebrations,
so that you may obtain the blessing of the Kings of the Franks
and the Bishops subjected to you. You may undertake every
duty which your predecessors seem to have undertaken by our

apostolic authority. We think that no one in the synod should
oppose you by quoting any crime mentioned in your abdication, or should rage against you with words of unbecoming
nature relating to this, but let our authority protect you on all
sides, even if you are troubled by a guilty conscience. We
confirm and concede to the archbishopric, with all bishoprics
subject to it, monasteries, plebs, tithes, chapels, curtes, castles,
villas, &c.'

This letter is immensely significant. The Pope maintains
the justice of the charges urged against Arnulf. These excesses
are to be forgiven, but this fact alone is an admission of their
reality, and in a cutting phrase he refers the Archbishop to
his own conscience. It is clear that Sylvester does not alter the
opinion he entertained as Gerbert in regard to the guilt of
Arnulf. The free act of pardon is contemptuous, and stings
even whilst it pardons ; but it is the Papal privilege to pardon,
and the election without the consent of Rome is condemned
implicitly. The action of Gregory in reinstating Arnulf and
endowing him with the pallium was the annulling of the
Synod of Rheims, and the acceptance of the Papal claims over
the metropolitan see. Even whilst admitting the personal
guilt of Arnulf, Gerbert, as Pope Sylvester, does not withdraw
from the judgements of his predecessors. Arnulf, who had been
deposed by a Gallican Synod, is reinstated by the Roman
Pope without any further vote being taken at any Gallican
synod. Sylvester triumphs over Gerbert in this contemptuous
pardon of Arnulf, for the abdication without Rome's consent is
something which needs repairing, and can be repaired by the
favour of the Roman See. Whilst in reality Sylvester
withdraws from his earlier attitude, we cannot but admire
the skill and ingenuity which he shows when, in retreat from a
former position, he so masks his retreat as to assume the
dignified aspect of a gracious sovereign pardoning an offender.
Pope Sylvester may have triumphed over Gerbert, Archbishop
and defender of Gallican liberties ; but Gerbert, as Sylvester,
does effectually triumph over a former rival, who, though
pardoned, is nevertheless convicted.

Pope Sylvester also had further relations with Asceline,
the notorious Bishop of Laon, and the letter shows that
Asceline had once more been scheming, this time against the
King as well as against Archbishop Arnulf. Was it a new

attempt to support Louis, and substitute a Caroling for a Capetian? At any rate, it involved a war in which Robert, accompanied by Baldwin of Flanders, besieged Laon in 999. ' If faith allies mortals to God, perfidy equally allies them to the brute beasts. We greatly wonder that you, knowing this, should have abandoned your proper sphere, and perpetrated new and unheard-of crimes. There is a letter of King Robert and his priests, offered to our apostolic and Imperial hands, which accuses you in the presence of all clergy and people of these public crimes.' We gather from the letter that Asceline had been summoned to a synod at Compiègne, where the Archbishops of Tours and Rheims gathered with their bishops. Security was promised on oath. Asceline, fearing the severity of the synod, prayed for mercy, but was unable to answer the charges, nor to deny that he had offended the King. However, through the mediation of the synod he obtained the King's pardon for perjuries so often renewed. Hostages were then given, and Asceline promised to return Laon Castle, which apparently he still held. Some subtle intrigue against Arnulf appears. Asceline wished the Archbishop to visit the Castle evidently with the intention of securing his person there in confinement; but the fate of certain soldiers, already betrayed and held, revealed the fraud to the Archbishop, who thus escaped the repetition of a former betrayal. ' O Judas, reviving the betrayal of his Master, corrupting the pontifical glory without tears. Since you wished to betray the Archbishop, your master, you would not spare the King, if you could secure him. How often we have advised you in persuasive letters! We have longed for you to turn away from peril, but, since we are unable to turn you from the multitude of your sins, we call upon you to be present at Easter in Rome. We advise you to hasten to the synod to be held there. Therefore you should in no way transgress or postpone the acceptance of our summons, since, if you are present, you will be subjected to synodal authority, and will gain nothing by absence. There is no excuse about the difficulty of the way, since there are no ambushes waiting for you, and only bodily injury will afford excuse. But witnesses are to be sent who may help you, and reply to your accusers, and clear you from the laws.'

It is not known whether Asceline responded to this call. It is clear that there was conspiracy afloat, and that Robert and his clergy had appealed to the Pope against the arch-traitor ; but it is also clear that he escaped the just penalty of his treason, and soon passed into the royal favour again. He dedicated a poem to King Robert, was present at the crowning of Henry I, and enjoyed his bishopric till his death in A.D. 1031. Arnulf lived on at Rheims, and it was his hand that placed the crown on the head of Robert's son Hugh. He died in A.D. 1021.

V

THE MEANING OF THE GREAT DEBATE

Note
A.A.   = Aimon Vita Abbonis.
A.C.R. = Acta Concilii Remensis ad Sanctum Basolum.
E.   = Eudes Vita Burchardi.
G.   = Gerbert's Letters.
G.P.A. = Gesta Pontificum Autissiodorensium.
R.   = Richer.

IT is difficult, if not impossible, to unravel the complications
of the controversies. Throughout the dispute between Arnulf
and Gerbert there is appeal and counter-appeal to Canon
Law, and each side is able to quote precedents. The modern
student will be puzzled till he remembers that Canon Law had
not reached in the tenth century the stage of consistent
codification in the interests of the Papacy which it did reach
in the thirteenth century. There was general agreement
that the Scriptures were in some way the final authority in the
expression of Divine Law. Special acknowledgement was
made of the value of the teaching of the early Fathers, of the
decrees of certain Popes like Innocent I, Leo I, Gregory I,
and of the great Oecumenical Councils like Nicaea, Sardica,
Chalcedon. Universal Councils should have precedence over
Provincial Councils, and with certain exceptions, mentioned
above, later councils have precedence over earlier councils.
The character of the person, the nature of the dispute, the
place where the council was held, had all to be taken into
account. There was room here for much disagreement as to
the precise value attached to this council or that decree, and,
above all, it had not yet been decided what authority the Pope
had in reference to Canon Law (G. 217). His legislative and
dispensing powers were still challenged.

In spite of these difficulties, various issues do appear, arising one out of the other, until what was primarily a personal and dynastic issue between Capetian and Caroling became a great ecclesiastical issue between the authority of Rome on the one hand, and the Universal Church on the other, supported by reason, conscience, and the Scriptures. Let us, therefore, try to trace out these related issues :

I. There was obviously a *personal and dynastic* issue. The old conflict between the Capetian and Caroling, beginning with the struggle between Eudes and Charles the Simple in the ninth century, broke out once more, and finally, in the struggle between the descendant of Eudes, Hugh Capet, and the descendant of Charles, Arnulf. The endeavour to avoid the treason charge failed, and Arnulf was judged, or rather judged himself, of being unfaithful to the King. Hugh Capet's appearance at the council, the study of the precedents of the Toulouse Councils, the statements of some of the bishops, prove that treason was the charge. Hugh was determined, having destroyed Charles of Lorraine, effectually to break the Caroling power by humiliating and degrading Arnulf, Lothaire's son. This was the primary question in the mind of the King, and the debates in the council were overshadowed by the royal power.

Now the personality of Arnulf figures largely not because of any special personal characteristic, but because he was the representative of the Carolings, a proud but doomed dynasty. Certain facts about him seem clear in the story :

1. His appointment was entirely political. He had no spiritual qualifications. Hugh nominated him to divide the Caroling interest. He probably accepted the appointment in order to help that interest. In the mind of both the King and the Bishop the political or dynastic factor predominated, one of many indications of the perils which shadowed the Church and its moral life, when appointments to high office were given for political rather than religious reasons.

2. Arnulf was a man of secular mind, young and ambitious. He had pride of race without moral dignity, ambition without courage, and in his life there is enacted the tragedy of high birth separated from high character. He was the heir of great and heroic men, but possessed neither greatness nor heroism himself. His attitude at the council showed a weakness approaching imbecility. His contribution to the debate consisted mainly of passionate denials and humiliating avowals,

whilst a terrible fear of judgement undermined his case and injured his witness.   He appealed neither to the Pope nor to the pardon he had received from the King.

3. There can be little doubt that he was guilty of treason in the technical and literal sense of the term.   He had been willing to accept the pallium through the Empress Theophania, then at enmity with Hugh Capet.   He had certainly taken an oath to Hugh, and broken it by appearing as a supporter of his rival.

But there is something to be said on the other side :

(*a*) He was surrounded by deceit and intrigue.   He must have known something about the conspiracies against his father's government, for he had been his father's secretary and had some experience of the tortuous mind of Hugh Capet.   The atmosphere of that period was heavy with intrigue.   He probably knew that his own election arose out of political expediency, so he met plot with plot.   He was probably neither better nor worse than most of his contemporaries, but he was neither wise nor prudent enough for a supremely difficult situation.

(*b*) He was a Caroling, and it was difficult for him in the peculiar circumstances in which he was placed to forget the fact.   He seems to have had a special regard for his young cousin Louis.   The wrongs of his family, their sorrows and adversities, seemed to be his own, and he felt the call of the blood relationship.

(*c*) There is a certain mystery about the surrender of Rheims, and motives and intentions are difficult to define.   Hugh Capet was at one time prepared to negotiate with Charles on the understanding that the latter should be allowed to retain certain cities he had conquered under some formula of allegiance.   Some such compromise may have been in Arnulf's mind from the beginning.   The actual details of the surrender are obscure.   The Papal legate believed that Arnulf's confession was only made from fear of death.   The presbyter Adalger, the only witness called, was not treated with much consideration by the council, and Bruno's words seem to place large responsibility for the city's betrayal upon his shoulders.   Such treatment is difficult to understand if he were merely the dupe he claimed to be.   Arnulf's confession was made in secret, and full details would be known to few.   A comedy by which Arnulf was starved into surrender sounds rather like tragedy.

It is quite possible that Charles exceeded his brief, and that the Archbishop was compelled to travel much farther than he intended to go at that stage, and that he was only willing to surrender the city on conditions which were not fulfilled. The negotiations which opened between Hugh and Arnulf through the mediation of Asceline may have been in accord with the considered policy of Arnulf throughout. Such a view would explain some of the curious details in the situation referred to above. At any rate Arnulf appears to have had a strong following at Rheims, for Gerbert's election was certainly not by the unanimous judgement of the citizens, whilst at Sens a tradition favourable to Arnulf lingered a long time. There may have been something more than youth, or race, or misfortune to account for it. Gerbert's account, whilst true in bare fact, may have erred in the subtler delineation of motive, and it must never be forgotten that Gerbert's evidence is the evidence of a rival.

(*d*) Again, if the whole charge of treason in act and motive could be proved, it must be remembered that Arnulf had since then been received into favour by Hugh, and ultimately he was the victim of a treachery every whit as black as any treachery of which he had been guilty. Hugh surely had no moral right to urge a charge against Arnulf for crimes committed before that kiss of peace. No trace of any further betrayal on Arnulf's part is hinted at in the Council of Rheims, and little attention need be paid to a certain very vague reference in one of Gerbert's letters (217). There is in fact little to choose. If Arnulf had used his episcopate at Rheims for political purposes, Hugh had nominated him for political purposes. If Arnulf had betrayed Hugh, the latter had been a party to the betrayal of the former. Lose sight of the fact that Arnulf was a bishop and the issue is plain. By plot and counter-plot Capetian and Caroling contend once more, and the Capetian wins.

II. There was an issue involving the Gallican Church and Rome. The King wished to ruin Archbishop Arnulf, and this could be done according to custom by condemnation and deposition in a council of bishops. The question was whether this deposition also needed the consent, as well as the knowledge, of the Papacy. The King was quite willing to appeal to Rome, for he was moved by no hostility to the

Pope ; but he was determined to be, as far as possible, master in his own house, and when Rome remained silent he not only defended the rights of the bishop to depose, but urged them to do so. This produced a conflict between the Church and Rome.

A certain similarity, amid many differences, to the action of our Henry VIII could be noticed. Henry, for example, was not unfriendly to the Pope, but he had certain personal or political designs, and, when the Pope was unwilling or unable to meet his wishes for fear of the Emperor, Henry broke with the Pope and carried through the Anglican settlement. This was rendered possible by the close relation of the Church with the King, by a certain confidence which his strong personality inspired, and by the tradition of Anglican independence of Rome to which he could appeal. Now Hugh was able, when Rome remained silent to his appeal, to utilize for his purpose the earlier traditions of the Gallican Church, traditions of independence of Rome ; whilst the dependence of the Church on him and its confidence in him, made it all the easier for him to use the Church for his own ends. Thus out of the personal matter, there developed a real assertion of the Gallican Church as against Rome.

The question was, could the Gallican Church, represented by the bishops in council, deprive a metropolitan of his church and elect another in his place without the consent of Rome ? Throughout the Merovingian and early Carolingian period, the Pope's influence in Gaul was not strong. The deposition of Egidius in Merovingian times, and of Ebbo in Carolingian times, without any protest from the Pope, afforded useful precedents. Hincmar, whilst recognizing Rome as a court of appeal in the sense that, when appealed to, the Pope had the right to summon a synod presided over by his legate, which should be the final authority, had endeavoured strictly to limit this right by all kinds of restrictions, and thereby maintain this independence in the latter part of the ninth century. He left a mass of literature on the subject.

However, in the ninth century, the celebrated False Decretals were forged, probably by a cleric of Rheims called Wulfang. Originally issued for the purpose of defending the bishops against the metropolitan by allowing for an appeal to Rome, these decretals came to be a terrific power in the hands of the

Pope, who used them to claim right of interference in the bishoprics of Christendom. One decretal, attributed to Damasus, definitely declared that no deposition or election to a bishopric could take place without the consent of Rome. This claimed much more than the appellate jurisdiction allowed to Rome, for it placed the initiative in the hands of the Pope and gave him a power of veto. Thus Pope Nicolas humbled the powerful Hincmar. In the tenth century we read of frequent interventions. In the case of a disputed succession to Rheims, an appeal to Rome settled the question in favour of Artold (A.D. 948–52).

A Papal legate presided over the Council of Ingleheim when Louis IV declared his case against Hugh the Great ; Theobald, Bishop of Amiens, was deposed A.D. 975 by the intervention of Benedict VII ; Adalberon appealed to Rome for the confirmation of his reforms at Mouzon. We read of Papal intervention for the protection of Cluny, Vezelay, and other great monasteries, for the maintenance of the rights of the Archbishop of Tours over the Celtic Churches of Brittany, and for the confirmation of reforms at Noyon. Gregory V consecrated Erlwin to Cambrai without consulting either of the rivals to the see of Rheims.

In spite of these instances there remained the tradition of Gallican independence. The False Decretals were everywhere accepted as genuine, and therefore the claims of Damasus could not be definitely rejected, but there were many precedents to be quoted on the other side. Hincmar was a mine of information on this matter, and frequent use is made of the decisions of various Councils held in Gaul, and certain National Synods in Spain and Africa are freely quoted. The Council of Rheims was therefore an effort to recover lost ground, and to retain the rights of the Church threatened by the use of these false documents. The Gallican sentiment was the more easily exploited by the King because so many of the bishops were his nominees. Moreover, many of these bishops sprang from families deeply attached to the soil, and liable to local pressure. The fact that, by a curious irony of changed conditions, the Empress had taken up the cause of Arnulf, and that the Roman see was much under German influence, certainly gave strength to Gallicanism.

There is some reason to believe that a national consciousness

I

was slowly awakening in the heart of France. This had
nothing to do with the change of dynasty or the rivalry
between Caroling and Capetian, but many factors entered into
the situation. The growth of the French language, the feud
with Germany over Lorraine, the rivalry between Caroling
and Saxon followed by the rivalry between Capetian and
Saxon, the rise of a distinct epic connected with Charlemagne
or the great defence of Paris by Eudes, all tended in the direction of a national spirit. Probably it was strongest in the
circles, clerical and lay, in close touch with the King and his
Court, but it had a great deal to do with the rise of Gallicanism.

The King and his bishops resented the Papal claims when
they involved the accepting of the decisions of synods held on
German or Italian soil. The King claimed that French bishops
were quite as noble and powerful as, and even wiser than, the
German bishops (R. iv. 96), and forbade the bishops to attend
the synod at Mouzon. Hugh may have come to the throne as
the ally of Germany, but he did not propose to subordinate
either himself or his kingdom to the Empire. The Gallican
Church protested against government from beyond the Alps
or from beyond the Rhine.

III. This protest against Rome took on various aspects, and,
directed by Gerbert, passed far beyond merely national or
Gallican limits. Gerbert appealed from the Pope to the
Universal Church, Nicaea and Sardica appeared in the argument, and endeavour was made to show that the council at
Rheims expressed the mind of the Universal Church. The
words of Jesus in Matthew xviii. 17 were frequently quoted to
exalt the Church over the Papacy, and were applied to the
Pope as much as to any other bishop, and if Rome refused to
hear the Church she became thereby a Gentile and a publican.
In fact Gerbert had recovered the international setting. The
Universal Church, the Church of the Great Council, was set
over against the Pope and above him. His letter to Notker
(183) shows his desire to appeal to a council as universal as
possible, including bishops from Germany and Lorraine as
well as France, and Arnulf of Orleans had also hinted at the
same method (A.C.R. 28). The Church could sometimes find
voice in national and provincial councils, but the authority of
the Church did not depend upon its nationalism, but on the
fact that it was the ' Church of Christ throughout the world.'

The appeal was also carried to the Scriptures. The 'pro-phetic and evangelical writings' were uniquely valid. The words of Jesus are freely quoted, and represent the final authority, and in his appeal beyond Pope and even council, to the Bible and Jesus, to the 'Bone Jesu' who is the salvation of men (193, 217), Gerbert is approaching a Protestant stand-point. If Rome sins against the Church, Rome becomes an outcast. 'Ye must obey God rather than men,' said Peter, and Peter's successors must recognize the same truth. These quotations were highly significant. They struck at the founda-tion of all the Papal claims. The voice of the Pope might not be the voice of God, but of an erring man needing the discipline of the Church, the authority of the Word of God. That the Papacy saw the danger is obvious, for the representative of Rome regarded the whole movement as a heresy equal to that of Arius.

But there is more still. The Papal claims were examined in the light of reason, and the facts of the case were presented for consideration. If Rome is silent, must the Church do nothing? If Crescentius holds Rome in captivity, must therefore religion be allowed to decline? Damasus might issue decretals, but, if Rome is silent on appeal, must not someone else speak? Such questions as these represent an unmistakable appeal to the essential logic of facts. There is reason and argument and a challenge to the mind. In fact Gerbert finds a rational basis for his opinions.

But it is not just an appeal to bare logic or to the facts of the case. The conscience has claims, and these are introduced. Gerbert boldly stated that it did not require the authority of Popes to do right and renounce wrong, or to find out what is right and what is wrong. The dark crimes of the Popes are brought into the light of day, the cruelty, rapacity, corruption, debauchery and utter ignorance of the Roman Church are loudly condemned. The degradation of the Papal Court prompted Arnulf of Orleans to call it 'an idol, a pretence, or even Anti-Christ.' The sins of Rome have outraged the conscience of the age. The councils are alive to moral issues. Walter of Autun, denouncing the treatment of the poor, Bruno waxing eloquent over the treachery of the time, Arnulf denouncing the Pope, significantly show that the whole controversy had a moral aspect. The Pope stands condemned

before the bar of reason, conscience, history and Scripture, and
what began as a political and dynastic question becomes a
great Church crisis involving the nature of authority in the
Church.

Incidentally this opposition to Rome on the part of the
bishops is closely related to the persistent quarrel between the
monks and the bishops to which reference is made in another
chapter.   It is highly significant that Arnulf of Orleans,
champion of the episcopal interests, and Abbo, defender of
the monks and most powerful abbot of his time, are on
opposite sides.   Arnulf and Abbo were bitter rivals.   Abbo
knows that in taking sides with the Pope, he is defending
himself and the monasteries from the combined authority
of king and bishops.   The Synod of St. Denis was held the
same year as the Synod of St. Basil, and the relationship
between St. Denis and Chelles has already been referred to.

In spite of all that had been said, Gallicanism, as we may
term it, failed.   Rome won the case.   Arnulf was re-instated,
not by judgement of a council, but by the pardon of a Pope.
The question is asked, ' Why did a movement so promising
fail ? '   The reasons are not far to seek.

1. There was a great improvement in the moral character of
the Papacy.   Attacks upon immoral Popes had been a feature
of the protest, but no charge of that kind could be made against
the character of such Popes as Gregory V and Sylvester II, who
was none other than Gerbert himself.   A temporary reformation in the character of the Popes weakened the case against
the Papacy.

2. We must not forget the decretals.   They were everywhere
regarded as genuine.   Even Hincmar and Gerbert seem to have
accepted them.   If genuine, the Papal claim was substantiated.
They could not be reconciled with Nicaea and early councils,
but the Church had to face up to them.   It could not get
through them or round them, it dared not challenge them,
neither could it ignore them.   The decretals were certainly
false, but the very fact that they could obtain sway so easily,
is a proof of the attachment to the Roman see throughout
Western Christendom.   It was a superstitious age, credulous,
and for the most part, ignorant.   Rome was the great city, and
the Church was believed to be the Church of St. Peter.   Respect
for the Papacy was strengthened by the glamour of the name of

Rome, and by the tradition of its central place in the life of the ancient world.   Protests were frequently made by kings and bishops against the power of Rome, and these protests were often accompanied by national feeling as well as reasoned judgement, but Rome successfully resisted, and as a rule increased its influence, because it seemed to satisfy certain demands of mediaeval society.   It offered a visible embodiment of unity and authority which that disordered and largely illiterate world needed, whilst by its august name, its legends, associations with martyrs, apostles, and saints, it appealed to a certain mystical tendency which, with a crass materialism, curiously expressed the paradox of mediaeval life.   It must not be overlooked that the monks and lower clergy found in the False Decretals their protection from the tyranny of the baronage and the arrogance of an aristocratic episcopate. Though the French national spirit was slowly rising, it must further be remembered that there was a vast mass of oppressed and submerged humanity to whom the ' Voice beyond the Seas,' which spoke in the name of God and St. Peter, would sound like the voice of a deliverer from another world, whilst the remoteness of Rome, though it covered the shame and scandal of the Papacy, would add to the mystery and wonder of that voice.   The great monastic orders were international, and the Church itself through its diocesan system, inherited from Imperial days, was historically centred in Rome.

Thus the Roman claims, as expressed in the False Decretals, came out of, and were rooted deeply in, the needs, feelings, and traditions of mediaeval Europe.

3. Then Gerbert himself, the brain of the whole movement, to which he gave the benefit of his vast learning, was always at heart an Imperialist, and was drawn by secret inner ties of growing admiration to the Othos.   He had taken an oath to Otho II in the old Bobbio days, and considered himself bound by it.   His correspondence in the earlier days, when he wrote for Adalberon, and in the later days, when he wrote to Otho III, shows the true bent of his mind.   His ambitions, his interests, his historic knowledge, his disgust with Italian Popes, his feeling of displeasure at the ingratitude shown to him by the Empress Theophania, may have led him into the championship of the Gallican ideal ; but throughout all the debate, his attendance at conferences and synods outside

France, his letters to Popes and legates, and his visits to Rome, show the uncertainty of his inner mind and his eagerness for Papal support.   There was in fact an inner contradiction which gave him no rest.   He had felt the glamour of the Imperial and Roman ideal, and it may be truthfully said that the Gerbert of Rheims, scheming with Imperialists against Carolings, was truly and fully expressed in the Pope Sylvester II, united by common ties of sympathy with Otho III, in pursuit of a great ideal of a Holy Roman Empire and Holy Roman Church, as two aspects of some great world-system. For such a man, Gallicanism must ultimately prove too narrow a conception and too limiting an ideal.   Gerbert had defended brilliantly and ably the liberties of the Gallican Church, but his heart was with the Othos and his ideals were always more Imperial than national.   As we have seen, he defended Gallicanism by arguments drawn from the Church, the Bible, reason, and the conscience.   His was essentially an international and Imperialistic mind.   He anticipated Dante in his zeal for, and confidence in, the Empire, regarded not as a merely German power, but as a universal order.   When, therefore, broken in body, wearied in spirit, exasperated by the ingratitude of the King, by the coldness of the people, and the cowardice of the bishops, he sought the Imperial court, the feelings of satisfaction which find vent in his letters prove that he had at last found his true home.   But Gerbert was the brain of the movement, and his departure from France, following the death of Hugh Capet, ruined the cause.

The question may be asked, Why did he not continue to plead for the Universal Church against the Papacy ?   And it was a curious turn of events which turned the spokesman of anti-papal theory into a Pope.   Yet the inconsistency is not so great as it would appear.   It is true that Pope Sylvester could not speak as Gerbert had done, and his accession must have made impossible the incipient Protestantism which had emerged in the great debate.   Yet what Gerbert had really opposed was not the Papacy, as such, which would seem logically to have been as necessary in the Church as the Emperor was in the State, but its intolerable arrogance, its corruption, impurity, and ignorance.   This at least can be said, that when Gerbert became Pope, he carried to the Papal throne culture, purity of life, and a certain moderation in tone

had been divergent views on the question of peace with Eudes. Hugh having joined forces with Fulk of Anjou, Eudes, ill and despairing, sought a truce, which, however, Robert induced his father to refuse, though he was inclined to grant it. Eudes, the powerful Count, died before he received the royal reply. His death must have been a great relief to the Capetian House in one sense, yet in another sense, because it was followed by Robert's attachment to his widow, it introduced complications of a disastrous kind. Still, in spite of difficulties from feudatories and royal princes, Hugh held nominal supremacy over the whole Caroling dominion, and his authority was not challenged. He had married a sister of William IV of Aquitaine and Poitiers, and seems to have preserved unbroken peace with that important duchy. Burchard of Vendôme also proved to be a strong, faithful courtier and friend, but it is obvious that he was helped by the bitter rivalries of his powerful vassals. Thus the quarrel between Fulk of Anjou and Eudes of Chartres meant that Hugh, in resisting the one, could count upon the assistance of the other, and at one time Hugh marched at the head of an army of Normans and Angevins against Milum, which had been betrayed to Eudes. At another time the royal forces took the side of William of Aquitaine against an unruly but powerful vassal, Audebert, Count of Perigord, who had united with Fulk of Anjou to take Poitiers and Tours. Once more, the revolt of Asceline of Laon at once brought to the side of the King, Landri, Count of Nevers, a personal enemy of the bishop. At the same time, we must give due weight to the astute character of the King, who could so take advantage of these troubles as to strengthen the position of his family and dynasty.

It is true the personal character of Hugh largely escapes us, but there are certain factors to be noted. He had a reputation for piety, was a friend of the monks, and a supporter of the Reform movement associated with Cluny. He shared the popular passion for relics and reverenced holy places and the saints. He was ambitious, able, astute, and possibly gave considerable impetus to the national feeling by his attitude to Pope and Emperor in the Gallican controversy, but on the whole his character is not attractive, and wins neither admiration nor affection. In personal courage and military genius he compares unfavourably with his rival Charles, and his savage

raid on the Rheims district shows a nature singularly callous
and cold, if not actually cruel ; whilst his share in the base,
treasonable plans of Asceline and his intrigues against Lothaire
reveal a nature subtle, treacherous, and unscrupulous.   He
worked in the shade, practising the underhand methods of
tortuous diplomacy, and achieved his purpose by stratagem
rather than by open warfare.   Yet he must have had abilities
to an uncommon degree, for he secured his throne, overcame a
rival, suppressed rebellions, left the position intact for his son,
and founded the longest-lived dynasty in Europe.   Was it not
a Louis Capet who was placed on his trial in 1793 ?   With all
his faults it may at least be said that his influence was on the
side of a purer Church, that he did something at any rate to
stir up the glowing embers of a nationalism which could assert
itself against the ecclesiastical tyranny of Rome and the
dangerous challenge of a Caesar ; whilst the loyalty to his
person of such men as Count Burchard and Bishop Arnulf,
both men of culture and piety, must count to him for righteousness, for their loyalty to him was continuous and consistent.

The King's piety showed itself in the closing days of his life.
He sought the reformation of St. Denis from Maiolus of Cluny,
for, as Odilo says, he always received him with humble devotion and great honour.   Hearing of the saint's death he hastened
to his obsequies.   Syrus also informs us that he approached the
grave of Maiolus for help, in view of the seriousness of his
infirmity.   Two visits may here be referred to, or perhaps there
is some confusion in the immediate reason for this visit, but an
appreciation of Maiolus is at any rate suggested, and an
indication of some prolonged illness preceding his death.

According to Richer he died ' in the town of Hugh, his body
covered completely with pustules, killed by Jews.' The town of
Hugh may mean Paris, but probably Milum (Lot 185). We
may gather that his physical weakness had exposed him to the
ravages of small-pox, and that the case had been handled
badly by some Jewish physician, at any rate according to
popular belief.   The date of his death would be October 24,
996, according to the judgement of Lot.   There can be little
doubt that the alliance with the Church had strengthened the
position of the Capetians, as the break with the Church had
weakened the Carolings.

Hugh Capet had secured, in spite of his struggle with the

Papacy and the Empire, the support of the episcopate, represented by Arnulf of Orleans and Gerbert of Rheims, and the sympathy of great teachers or monks like Abbo and Maiolus. The secular and religious clergy, disagreeing among themselves, had nevertheless common loyalty to the first Capetian, and this, whilst in some sense suggestive of the tact and skill of the King, also goes far to explain the strength of the Capetian, maintained in spite of their apparent political weakness, in the midst of the great warlike feudatories.

This extraordinary tact and ingenuity, whereby Hugh held the loyalty and confidence of both bishop and monk, gave him a very strong position in his assertion of Gallican rights, and we can easily see how the succession of a king who took sides with the monks against the bishops, and for private reasons would abandon public interests, would seriously prejudice those rights. The death of such a king as Hugh was as serious as the defection of Gerbert, and ruined Gallicanism for the time.

5. One more important fact must not be overlooked in accounting for the victory of Rome over the Gallican Church.

In a later chapter we shall consider a Reform movement which consisted in a revival of Benedictine monasticism, and we shall learn that, by the curious irony of circumstances, the monks were allied to the Papacy. Both monks and the Pope were exposed to danger from kings and bishops, and represented an international principle, and for these reasons they were brought into a union of a very close nature in spite of great differences in their respective moral standards.

We shall learn that among the monks were found the saints of that age. In the sixteenth century moral passion and religious fervour characterized the great leaders of protest, Luther and Calvin. This constituted the real significance of the event in European history rightly called 'The Reformation,' but in the tenth century moral passion and religious fervour were associated with the monks, who were the allies of the Papacy. Gerbert and the bishops might have the best of the argument, but Fleury and Cluny possessed the tremendous asset of sanctity, enthusiasm, self-denial and purity, and when the reformers of the tenth century carried the weight of this witness to the side of Rome, the victory of Rome was assured. The witness of the holy life is always greater than an argument, and the saints who know God in experience will always command attention from a world that really needs and wants Him.

The monks in their Puritanism and mysticism had certain points of contact with later Protestantism, but in the actual circumstances of the tenth century they proved to be the stalwart defenders of the Papacy, and they therefore contributed to its victory.

VI

THE CHURCH AND ITS INNER LIFE

Note
A.   = Abbo.
A.C.R. = Acta Concilii Remensis.
B.   = Burchard.
G.   = Gerbert's Letters
R.   = Richer.
Rath. = Rathier.
R.G.   = Rudolph Glaber.
Th.   = Thietmar.

OUR purpose is to sketch the inner life of the Church. It is true that the Church had many faults, yet, in spite of the subtle influences of feudalism and the struggle with lawless barons, the moral and spiritual ideals were by no means lost, for men bowed before the law of God and reverenced the mysteries of the Holy Faith.

I. In regard to government, we shall see the immense influence of the lay power on elections and in the synods. Let it therefore suffice to say that government by bishops in synod was still the normal method. There are numerous references to synods in contemporary writings. There are diocesan synods, where the archbishop or bishop met the clergy of his diocese, priests and archdeacons. Thus Rathier tells us that he met his clergy twice a year, and adds that it is customary in such synods to amend anything contrary to Canons (Itin. 5). There are provincial synods, presided over by the metropolitan, such as the St. Magna Synod, which considered the charges against Asceline, Bishop of Laon, and the Synod of St. Mary, which discussed 'things useful to Holy Church,' confirmed reforms at Mouzon, and took steps to improve the discipline of diocesan monasteries by calling abbots into consultation. Archdeacons, presbyters, and sometimes abbots attend these

synods with the bishops.   Character and discipline are regarded
as fit subjects for such synods to discuss, as well as the honouring of relics, the arranging of Church festivals, and the
oversight of monasteries.   Flodoard tells us that many synods
were summoned at Rheims to take measures for protecting
Church lands from greedy nobles.   The Provincial Synods
were summoned twice a year, at Pentecost and in October,
according to the Canonist Burchard (i. 43 and 44).

Larger synods are held, for Richer tells us that thirteen
bishops from Sens and Rheims gathered on the death of
Artold, under the presidency of the Archbishop of Sens, to
elect his successor.   Thus the election of a metropolitan is a
fit subject for discussion by a synod.   This, however, introduces
the whole question of the relationship of the Papacy to the
Gallican Church, and has been dealt with separately.   The
Synod of St. Basil was attended by bishops from four provinces,
viz. Rheims, Bourges, Lyons, and Sens.   The Synod of Chelles
was attended by the Archbishops of Rheims, Tours, Sens,
and Bourges.   The Councils of St. Denis dealt with the vexed
question of the relation between bishops and monks, the
claim of monks to share tithes in general, and, in particular, the
claims of the monks of St. Martin to freedom from the control
of the Archbishop of Tours, and to enjoy their own monastic
bishop for episcopal rites, &c.   We shall see that various
synods at Laon and in the south dealt with the question of
peace and the needs of the peasantry.   Then we have the
Synods of Mouzon, Ingleheim (948), and the second Council of
Rheims (995), attended by French, Lorraine, and German
bishops.   In these larger synods we get a conception of a universal or international council, to which an appeal can be
made, and at which the Pope presides through a legate in
accordance with the decisions of the Council of Sardica.   These
larger councils were only to be summoned when there was
real necessity (B. i. 53).

II. It is certain the BISHOP held the first place in the government of the Church.   Asceline believed that the order of the
Kingdom of God was bound up with the maintenance of the
Bishop's authority.   Rathier, in his great work *Praeloquiorum*,
enormously exalts the Bishop's dignity.   The king must
venerate the Bishop because he is over the king, not the king
over him (iii. 4).   Christ is honoured in the Bishop.   The

structure of the Temple of God rests upon the Bishops, and they are pastors, doctors, pillars of the Church, lights of the world, stars of heaven, pupils of the eyes of the Lord, judges of both men and angels. Bishops are judged by God alone (iii. 9), and are more excellent than kings, because, though kings may designate them, they cannot ordain them, and they themselves are instituted by them (iv. 2). Gerbert, in his book *De Informatione Episcoporum*, declares in similar language that there is no honour equal to that of the Bishops, whilst Bishop Thierry of Metz applies to himself the words, ' Who touches me, touches the pupil of my eye,' and claims that he possesses the sword of the Spirit. The prerogatives of the Bishop are very many. He administers public penance in conjunction with his clergy (Rathier's Synodica). He represented the highest order of the ministry, and through him it was believed that grace was handed down from generation to generation in apostolic succession. To him were committed the rights of ordination and confirmation. ' He imposed the hand ; God gave the grace through him,' said Gerbert. In the order of the Bishops consisted the unity of the Church, so much so that a bad Bishop was to be reverenced because of his office (R. Con. xx.). Nevertheless, his character should correspond with his calling. Hunting, fowling, secular games, drunkenness, immorality, are strictly forbidden, as well as marriage and secular dress. Gerbert and Abbo believed that the higher the office the greater would be the sin of the one who held it unworthily, and both writers (*De Inform. Ep.* and Epistle to G.) state that he must fulfil the calling of a bishop as described in the Pastoral Epistles. As pastor of the flock and teacher, he should show a good example and teach by his life. If he represents Christ, he should lead the life of Christ and be able to lead the people to Christ. Arnulf of Orleans claims he should possess gravity of manner, merits, knowledge of things heavenly and divine (A.C.R. 28). Abbo, Rathier, and Gerbert are at one in emphasizing the importance of character, but on obedience to the Bishop depends the well-being of the Church.

Nevertheless, the Bishop's power was by no means absolute. He was nominally elected by the clergy and people of the city, and thus Hugh addressed the citizens of Rheims concerning the election of Arnulf. Gerbert's address at the same election reads : ' We who are called Bishops of the Province of Rheims, with all clergy of divers orders, with the acclamation of the people, and the consent of orthodox kings, elect for us ' (G. 155).   In the case of his own election (179), similar language is used, with one interesting qualification, introduced probably to justify Gerbert's election in spite of opposition : ' By the assent of those who are of God among the clergy and the people.'   Flodoard describes Rorico of Laon and Hadulf of Noyon as having been elected by the inhabitants of their respective cities.   In practice the power of the people may have been slight, but in theory it was still held that the Bishop was elected by the people as their representative.   Laymen and sometimes women attended synods, and though generally the local magnate would be the lay representative, there is obviously some survival here of the ancient view that the laity had some share in the government of the Church.

The episcopacy was constitutional in the sense that the Bishop was bound by the constitution of the Church as expressed in Canon Law.   He was expected to call his clergy into consultation in the legislative work of the synod and the disciplinary work of the diocese (R. iv. 5. ; A.C.R. 15).   He was to exercise his power through the synod in conjunction with the clergy.   In financial matters, for example, his authority was strictly limited by Canon Law.   It was always recognized that the Bishop was the financial authority, but at an early stage it was laid down that he should divide Church funds between himself, his clergy, the poor, with a fourth portion for the repair of the fabric (Abbo, Canon 35 ; Rathier, Synodica 14).   This provision was intended to prevent the abuse of episcopal control whereby the Bishop might claim all for himself or alienate to an outsider (Canon 25, 35).   The development of the parish system and the building of rural churches rather complicated the financial situation.   In France the parish priest was allowed two-thirds of the offering placed on the altar (Canon 27) ; the remaining third might go to the Bishop, but, if he did not require it, it was to be used locally for church repairs.   All returns from vineyards, property, and fields were to be administered by the Bishop (A., Canon 27).

The Bishop's authority was, as we shall presently see, seriously limited by the power of the king and the local magnates, but it was also challenged by the monks.   There was much controversy, in which Abbo took a leading part. Originally it was understood that the Bishop was the final authority over the monasteries in his diocese. He could alone administer ordination and confirmation, and he had the right to visit the monastery, and in conjunction with other Bishops, to depose the unworthy abbot and to exercise a general oversight. Thus the monastery of Lobbes applied to Bishops of Liège and Cambrai for their consent to the election of a new abbot (G.P.C. i. 101), whilst the Bishops exercised discipline over Fulvand, Abbot of St. Vevasti (i. 107, 115). Bruno of Langres, Liudolf of Noyon, Adalberon of Rheims, Adalberon of Metz, and other Bishops exercised authority in their dioceses.

This episcopal oversight was resented by the larger monasteries like Fleury, Cluny, and Vezelay, which secured Papal bulls and royal diplomas giving them protection from the local Bishops. By these ' immunities ' the Bishop's right of entry, though not denied, was modified. He was forbidden to stay long, to burden unduly the monastery by lavish entertainment, and he was not allowed to interfere with the free election of the abbot, to infringe upon the abbot's discipline, or to remove charters or possessions of the monastery (A. Canon 15). St. Martin of Tours claimed that its own monastic Bishop should exercise episcopal rites instead of the Archbishop of Tours, and was supported by Abbo and Gregory V. There was also a disagreement on the question of tithes. A large number of country churches were served from the monasteries through vicars. Abbo and his party maintained that, when it was stated that the finances were in the hands of the Bishop, it meant that he was to administer them in the interests of the people ; and, further, ' those who serve day and night in the Church ' ought to benefit from the gifts of those they serve (Ep. to G.). The council of St. Denis, 991, dealt with this matter, and feeling was so keen that the Council broke up in disorder. The monks further objected to the hasty use of excommunication by the Bishop, maintaining that the Bishop should not excommunicate for merely personal considerations, but only in accordance with the regular course of justice prescribed by law, and then in consultation with his clergy or neighbouring Bishop (Canon 36). The Bishops maintained that their ancient rights were threatened by monastic

K

interference. They contended that the order of the Church depended on their authority, and that the growing power of the monasteries would make diocesan government impossible and produce general anarchy.

In estimating the rights and wrongs of this controversy, we must remember that the monastic movement, backed by the Papacy, was introducing into the Church life a new element threatening the ancient order. On the other hand, it is fairly certain that at that particular time the noblest life of the Church was discovered in these reformed monasteries like Cluny, Gorz, and Fleury, whilst the half-feudalized, highly-born Bishop, like Asceline, compares unfavourably with the highly-disciplined, ascetic, and earnest monk, often of low birth, whom he so sharply criticizes. Abbo placed the monk above the cleric, whilst the reforming movement of the tenth century took the form of substituting the monastic for the secular life in the Church. The decadence of the monasteries came in its turn, but in the tenth century the monks were less engrossed in purely secular affairs than the average cleric. Thus, from the moral and spiritual point of view, the Church gained by these ' immunities.' It was necessary for the candidate for episcopal office to pass through the various stages of the ministry by the consecration of Bishops. We have to distinguish between the election by people, clergy, and king, and the consecration which could only be effected by at least three neighbouring Bishops—(B. i. 27.) But, whilst the Bishop had his own special authority, it must not be forgotten that his was only the highest order, and that beneath him there were presbyters and deacons whose spiritual functions were jealously guarded, and, lower still, sub-deacons, acolytes, exorcists, doorkeepers, readers, singers, all of whom had clearly defined duties. The distinction between clergy and laity was firmly held. Those who fought and worked were distinguished from those who prayed. To Abbo and Asceline this is the divine order of things.

The PRESBYTER, the second order of ministry, could administer baptism, hear private confessions, appoint private penance, and celebrate the mystery of the Eucharist. To him was committed power of binding and loosing. He also was supposed to have the power of bringing the real presence of Christ on to the altar, and ' great must be the one to whom the

Lord gives the power of handling Himself,' said Asceline. And this mysterious power, which he claimed to share with the bishop as the mediator between God and man, gave him tremendous influence in that superstitious age. At any rate, he witnessed to a world other than feudal, and feudal lords trembled at his judgements.

The pastorate of Presbyters in town and country was due to the increase in the number of churches in the dioceses. Presbyters were ordained and consecrated by the Bishop of the diocese, but, in appointing clergy to the various churches, the Bishop's power was limited by the more or less open claim of the patron, who had provided the building, to appoint whom he liked (Abbo, Canon 11). The Presbyters attended the synod with the Bishops, and formed a body of opinion which they could consult. They had a right of appeal to the Metropolitan (Canon 47) against their Bishop, who was forbidden to degrade without the judgement of the synod (Canon 12). Bishops and Presbyters, in holding the pastoral office, were to be educated in order that they might teach the people. Rathier (Synodica) insisted that the Creed, the Lord's Prayer, Bible, and the ' Services ' should be learnt so that they could be used and taught to the people. It was always laid down by the Canon Law (B. ii. 58–63) that the pastoral office included preaching, and Abbo was very urgent in this respect (Ep. to G.). Cluny gave a new impetus to preaching, but it is probable that the higher clergy were too much involved in secular duties, and the humbler clergy too ignorant, to be able to do justice to the demand.

The DEACONS had important duties. They dispensed alms, served in the preparation of the Mass, but were not allowed to offer the sacrifice of the altar. They came, however, into close contact with the Bishop in their subordinate capacity, and the Archdeacon often presided over the Bishop's disciplinary Court. The Deacon was consecrated by the Bishop, and the symbol of consecration was the presentation of the Gospels, whilst to the Presbyter was given the chalice and paten. The staff and crosier were given to the Bishop on his consecration, and the presenting by lay hands gave rise to the great controversy concerning investiture.

It was believed that these ministries were only valid in the CHURCH, from which the minister received his charge, and in

which he exercised it.   By the Church was meant, not the
fellowship of love and loyalty of the earliest days, but the
visible organization, with its ordained clergy, its graded orders,
its ordered services and worship, its sacraments, its Canon Law,
and its apostolic succession handed down through the line of
Bishops, and its mediating priesthood.   Inside the Church there
were both good and bad, but outside the Church, so ordered,
there was no salvation, for it claimed to declare the Word of
Life and provide the channels of grace (Dip. xxxiv.).   It was
the spouse of Jesus Christ, Catholic and Apostolic, the Church
redeemed by the blood of Christ—' Christ's Church, not even
Peter's,' according to Abbo ; ' the Holy Mother of all,' in the
opinion of Bruno.   ' There is one Catholic Church, whether at
Rome, Jerusalem, or Alexandria,' said Rathier (*Prae. Loq.*
iii. 5).   ' Outside the Church there is no remission of sins,'
wrote Gerbert (180).   To be cut off from the Communion of
the Church was to be cut off from the means of grace, and for
schism there was reserved the judgements of hell.   Hence the
tremendous seriousness of excommunication and anathemas,
and the terrific power of the priest, who could excommunicate
and curse the impenitent.   Outside the Church meant outside
the salvation obtained through baptism and penance and
priestly mediation.

The Church made tremendous claims.   It claimed to rule
life as a whole, to preserve contact with the past through its
historic episcopate, and with the whole world through its
international organization.   It claimed to possess the Holy
Spirit, and to enshrine the Christian experience of all ages and
all lands.

These claims are great, but the difficulty arises, not from
the vast claim, but from the nature of the Church which made
the claim.

The Church of the Middle Ages was only half Christian.
Pagan elements were there.   The Institution was emphasized
at the expense of the Fellowship.   The ethical ideal had been
compromised to meet the feudal age, and, whilst the ethical
entrance was too wide, the doctrinal entrance was far too
narrow, and intellectual beliefs received more attention than
moral character.   The Church had, moreover, surrendered too
much of its responsibility and privilege to a sacerdotal caste
in the Church.

The Christian Church has a right to exercise moral authority and leadership so long as it is the Church of Christians who do really possess the Holy Ghost because they possess the Spirit of Jesus, who are in loyal fellowship with one another because they are loyal to their Lord.   Only the Church that does His will can learn His mind and authoritatively declare it.

Nevertheless, the mediaeval Church did well to witness to the fact that the individual Christian is not, and cannot be, an isolated factor.   He is related to the past by many ties, as he is also related to the present.   He shares in a wider life, the social life of the City of God, the Kingdom of Heaven, and only by corporate effort in a Fellowship of Love can Christianity receive adequate expression.

III.   A word must be said on the subject of the *Celibacy of the Clergy*.   It was a burning question.   From the fourth century onwards it had been declared repeatedly by the Roman see that the three orders should be celibate, and various councils of the sixth and seventh centuries had striven to make celibacy compulsory.   However, concubinage and the marriage of clergy continued, especially in Italy, by those accepting the teaching of St. Ambrose of Milan, and the efforts of Chrodegang to impose celibacy on the Cathedral Canons failed.   In the tenth century the new reform movement endeavoured to replace ' seculars '—married clergy—by ' regulars,' or celibates. This movement, connected with the name of Dunstan in England, was represented in France by Adalberon of Rheims, Bruno of Langres, &c.   Nevertheless, celibacy was more an ideal than a reality.   Rathier acknowledged the existence of married clergy in Italy, and distinguished between married clergy and clergy living with concubines, both of which he condemned.   A letter from Pope Leo VI (Migne 132) to the bishops of France and Germany says : ' It is lamentable that priests of God publicly marry and put forward their sons.' Ordericus, in his History (v. 12, Migne 163), says : ' In Neustria, after the arrival of the Normans, the chastity of the clergy was weakened to such an extent that not only presbyters but bishops freely used the dwellings of concubines, and openly took pride in a large family of sons and daughters.'   He also refers to Robert, Archbishop of Rouen, who married like a layman, and by his wife Gerlina had three sons.   Between 950 and 1027 a grandfather, father, and son occupied the see of

Rennes in succession, and these marriages seem to have been quite regular ones, and recognized as such by the people. They might have proved safeguards against clerical immorality, but the Church authorities and the King himself saw the pressing danger of hereditary succession in the sees. The new reform movement connected with Cluny and Fleury was very hostile to what it considered the lower ideal of married clergy. Abbo fulminated against the married clergy, and placed the monk far above the cleric because of his celibacy. We may revolt against this aspect of the reforming movement, which opened a door to terrible abuses ; but there is little doubt that the celibate ideal, which ultimately triumphed under Pope Gregory VII, saved the Church from feudalism, for it set the clergy in a place apart.

IV. In regard to DOCTRINE, the confession adopted by Gerbert (G. 180) contained the clear statement of the orthodoxy of the Church in relation to the creeds adopted at the great councils. Gerbert believed in the Holy Trinity, the Incarnation in the Second Person, the true divinity and humanity of Jesus. He believed in original sin, and the salvation which is mediated through baptism and penance but cannot be obtained outside the Church. The Church did not deny the grace of God available for man because of the death of Christ, but too often thought of it as a Mysterious Force rather than as a Personal Attitude, and limited it to the sacramental and priestly order in the Church. Faith also lost its personal character, and became an assent to certain doctrines (B. ii. 62). Outside this order there remained God's judgements, which were for the impenitent, viz. the eternal fires of hell. There was no clearly-defined theory concerning the Atonement, though reference was made to Christ's death for us. It is indicated by writers of this period (Rathier and Odilo) that Jesus bore the punishment for the sins of men, but there is little teaching concerning the relationship between the death of Christ and the forgiveness of sins, mediated through the Church and sacraments. Nevertheless, the Cross was the central fact of salvation, and everything depends ultimately upon some mysterious and undefined service which Christ rendered there.

There were traces of heresy in this period. The view popularly held that people expected the end of the world in A.D. 1000 is not borne out by a study of the literature of the

period. Abbo implies that he opposed certain millenarian
theories about the coming of the end of the world in his earlier
years—perhaps about A.D. 970—and R. Glaber makes some
reference to similar theories that were abroad about A.D. 1030,
but that is all. The development in church building in the
eleventh century (R.G. iii. 4) can be attributed to the revival of
religion, associated with Cluny and other religious houses,
rather than to a belief in a new lease of life associated with a
new century.

In the early part of the eleventh century heresy appeared at
Arras, A.D. 1025; Orleans, A.D. 1022 ; Châlons, A.D. 1042 ; and
a terrible precedent was created by King Robert, when distinguished scholars of Orleans were burnt at the stake as heretics.
R. Glaber says that the heresy was introduced by a woman
from Italy (iii. 8), and says that it consisted of a denial of the
Old Testament, the Incarnation, the worship of the Virgin
Mary, relics, and the one Creator. He implies also that these
heretics rejected the sacraments, the eating of flesh, and second
marriages. The information comes from sources biased against
the heretics, but we may conclude that it was similar to the
Paulician heresy of the East. It evidently was of a dualistic
character, anti-clerical, ascetic, puritan, and associated with
Communistic ideas. It may be that it was brought into the
West by some pilgrims who had had contact with such ideas
in journeying to the holy places, but it is significant that the
heresy appeared in the north and central portions of France
and among the scholars of an important centre of culture like
Orleans. One cannot resist the conclusion that it had some
connexion with the new intellectual movement associated with
Gerbert, who, through his various students, had profoundly
influenced the intellectual life of northern France. Arnulf, the
Bishop of Orleans, for example, was a close friend of Gerbert,
and led the opposition to Rome in the celebrated Council of
St. Basil, Rheims. The free and spacious genius of Gerbert,
curiously devoid of theological prejudices, would be a likely
cause of an intellectual ferment in the schools.

There is no direct reference to heresy of this kind in the
tenth century, unless Havet is right in concluding that a certain
Walo (G. 29), summoned to a council at Vaudaumont for
having preferred human things to divine things and despised
synods (A.D. 984), was a Catharist, the name usually given to

these heresies. Gerbert, however, in the confession above quoted, emphasizes the Incarnation and the one Creator, and significantly declares that he himself believed in the receiving of flesh, second marriages, the resurrection of the body, and the authority of the Old Testament, whilst he held that the Devil became evil through will and not by fate. These seem to be unmistakable references to this heresy, from which Gerbert seemed anxious to separate himself. His passion for inquiry and his intellectual freedom had possibly exposed him to suspicion. One clear case of heresy in the year A.D. 1000 is referred to by R. Glaber. A certain peasant named Lietard (R.G. ii. 11) sent away his wife, broke the crucifix, protested against tithes, and said discretion was to be used in regard to the use and interpretation of Scripture. He was cautioned by the neighbouring Bishop (Gibuin of Châlons) and threatened with spiritual penalties. In his despair he drowned himself in a well.

The presence of heresy shows that there is an undercurrent of hostility to the clergy and the creeds, and that the Church is intellectually alive.

V. We must now turn to the SACRAMENTS. There was considerable difference of opinion in regard to the number and value of the sacraments, and no final decision had been taken by the end of the tenth century, and it was not till the four-teenth century that the seven sacraments were definitely accepted by the Church. This was a transition period, and different views on both the Eucharist and penance were competing for acceptance.

Baptism had an important place in Church life. We see by Gerbert's confession that it was believed to wash away the stain of original sin, and was thus administered in earliest infancy. Rathier said that all sins were destroyed by baptism (Conf. 42), and pointed out that, if infant baptism were neglected, children dying without it would be in great danger (Prae. iv. 20). Fulbert of Chartres said (Ep. 5) that the pollu-tion of birth was washed away in baptism, whilst William of Dijon referred to it as the recovery of angelic blessedness lost by our first parents. Fulbert was very anxious to show that the priest was the minister, not the author, of baptism, the author and source of grace being God. The special times for baptism were Easter and Pentecost, and in the article of death

(Rathier's *Synodica*) ; but the coming in of the heathen and
the urgency of infant baptism meant that the clergy baptized
all the year round.   Baptism was only valid in the Church,
was administered in the name of Trinity, and could not
be repeated.

Confirmation formed originally part of the same rite, but with
the lapse of years became so far distinguished from it as to form
a separate sacrament.   In the early days the Bishop presided
over the ceremony with his clergy, but, as the numbers to be
baptized grew, the Bishop found baptism to be too fatiguing
a process, and thus left it to his clergy, whilst he confirmed their
act by touching the forehead of the candidate (B. iv. 69.)   This
rite, known as chrism, was postponed for years at a later stage,
the confirmation of tiny children being regarded as an
anachronism.   Chrism could only be administered once, like
baptism, and was one of the special functions of the Bishop ;
thus in Flodoard's Additions we read how Asceline, newly-
appointed Bishop of Laon, administered chrism in the ecclesiastical manner, and, in his letter to his clergy (G. 98), the same
Bishop associated it with the episcopal blessing.

The *Eucharist* had mysterious, undefinable effects which
only added to its marvellous influence.   Partaking of this
sacrament would remove the stain of venial sin following
baptism.   Abbo believed that it could illuminate the spirit
and consume the crimes of the body, but those in wilful sin
were told to stay away until they had satisfied in penance,
for, if taken in known sin, it became a source of condemnation.
The case of Judas Iscariot was frequently quoted in this
connexion.   Unlike baptism and confirmation, this sacrament
could be repeated, and many earnest teachers encouraged the
faithful to frequent Communion.   Carolingian councils had
urged a weekly Communion.   Rathier held that four times a
year was at least necessary (*Synodica*).

This sacrament included the celebration of the Mass by the
priest, which was the Sacrament of the Sacrifice of Calvary,
and the Eucharist, which was the Sacrament of the Body and
Blood.   The former part was a dramatic representation of
Calvary.   Abbo says : ' The Lord again suffers for us in His
holy mystery,' whilst Gerbert speaks of ' the Body and Blood
offered daily for our safety ' (G. 192).   Originally intended as
a reminder of a sacrifice offered once for all, it came to be

regarded as a frequent repetition of our Lord's sacrifice. As the priest consecrated, the Holy Spirit worked miraculously on the altar. The Body and Blood were then offered to the faithful, and the recipient believed that, in receiving the Elements, he was receiving Christ, and in Him true life. As Gerbert put it, ' Through this mystery the true life is lived ' (208).

Now all this presupposed the real presence of Jesus in the Elements. Two opposing views of the Real Presence were still contending for mastery. Ratramnus had said that the bread and wine were to be called the Body and Blood in a figurative sense. Christ was not present in substance, but in power, and there was no change in the Elements. Paschase Radbert taught the Body of Christ was actually present by the transfer of the bread and wine into the actual Body and Blood, born of the Virgin, through the miraculous working of the Holy Spirit in conjunction with the priestly acts of consecration. He avoided gross materialism by introducing the necessity of faith. The doctrine, though not the word, of transubstantiation is present. The more spiritual view still had its adherents, and was apparently taught by Elfric in England about 990. A mediate view was put forward by an anonymous writer of the tenth century. By some this is attributed to Heriger of Lobbes, who is known to have written a book entitled *Concerning the Body and Blood of Christ.* By some it has been attributed to Gerbert. His name is associated with it in an early codex. The style of the book, the acquaintance with the Fathers, the use of a certain type of dialectics, and a certain medical knowledge shown by the writer, would all harmonize with Gerbert's authorship. In any case, it represented a certain body of opinion in Western Europe. It was an attempt to bridge the gulf between Radbert and Ratramnus, and various Fathers are quoted. It is a laboured but unconvincing effort. The author himself holds that Christ took three bodies—the actual body of the Virgin, the sacramental body on the altar, the mystic body of the Church,—the second being intermediary between the other two, which it unites. The writer avoids the extreme positions, and in this way affirms the real presence of Jesus on the altar. The body of Christ, ascended on high, is communicated through the sacramental body on the altar to form the mystical body of the Church.   The presence of Jesus provided a basis of unity for these three types of bodies.   The receiving of the sacramental body introduces a certain virtue which will resuscitate the body in the day of resurrection.   The result is mainly spiritual, for it produces fellowship and character when there is faith in the recipient and a withdrawal from sin on his part.

In spite of these attempts, the views of Radbert gained ground.   Rathier strongly advocated them.   Fulbert taught that the bread was ' transferred into the substance of the Body of the Lord,' and rejected the view that the sacrament was only an empty mystery.   There were various reasons for the triumph of transubstantiation :   (1) The materialistic conception of the age ;   (2) The use of the term ' Body and Blood of Christ ' without the word ' Sacrament ' ;   (3) Sacerdotal interest, for there was tremendous influence in the claim to handle the Body of the Lord on the Table ;   (4) The use of the term ' mystery,' and the splendid and awe-inspiring ritual accompanying it.

The Mass was above the disciplinary régime, and rather the supreme privilege offered by the Church.   The Church thought in terms of material substance rather than spiritual personality, and therefore looked for the Real Presence as the Body of the Lord on the altar rather than the Spirit of the Lord in the heart. There was a real confusion between the material and spiritual aspects of the sacraments, between the symbol and that which it symbolized.   Nevertheless, it must be said that, in spite of superstition and abuse, it did concentrate attention on Christ crucified as the ultimate ground of all salvation, and gave Calvary its central place.   A religious craving for fellowship through pardon was focused there.

As the Eucharist was not a method for dealing with post-baptismal sin, and as baptism could not be repeated, some other way of escape had to be provided for sinners.   These were the days when legal and feudal conceptions, derived from the study of Roman law and feudal customs, together with superstition and fear, survivals of pagan days, had obscured the gracious Fatherliness of God, and emphasized His retributive justice, His personal honour, or His arbitrary will, whilst theological dogma had obscured to some extent the historical Jesus.   The onrush of half-unconverted tribes into the Church, its mass baptisms and forced conversions, and the widening of the door to include all baptized in infancy, had reduced the spiritual vitality, and made it easy for external factors like law and dogma to triumph over inner factors of faith and love.

Hence also the necessity of some method of external discipline to take the place of inner loyalty and love to a Saviour, known intimately and loved greatly. This produced *Penance*, which has a history. In the earlier days, public penance was used for public sins, and the person so convicted was excommunicated by the bishop, and only reconciled to the Church when certain forms of penance were completed with every sign of inner penitence. For private sins a man was left to his own conscience and encouraged to seek help from experienced believers. This disciplinary system weakened when the ethical intensity of the Church declined. In the seventh century the Irish monks introduced a system of private penance and confession. The sinner confessed his sin, and the monks prescribed a rule of penance—a kind of tariff by which certain penalties were attached to certain crimes ; and absolution followed, not as a priestly act, but as the working out of self-acting laws of the penitentiary. Boniface, in the eighth century, tried to join the older discipline on to the Irish custom by introducing once more absolution by the mouth of the priest. Efforts were made in France to restore public penance for public sins in Carolingian times. Abbo says, ' Who commits mortal sin after baptism, let him satisfy with public penance ' (Canon 43). In his Apology he says : ' Public charges are not to be satisfied with private indulgence, nor private charges with public indulgence.' Gerbert says : ' He who sins secretly is to be punished secretly, he who sins publicly should be punished publicly ' (Letters 217). Seguin's charge against Archbishop Arnulf is that he has absolved public sinners without public penance (A.C.R. 15). Rathier distinguished between public penance, to be administered by the bishop, and secret penance, to be dealt with by the parish priest (Syn. 15). Nevertheless, these efforts to revive the ancient discipline failed. Confession, with private penance and priestly reconciliation, completely overwhelmed the ancient system in England, and gained ground everywhere on the Continent. It was believed that the fear of public exposure hindered many from confessing or accepting discipline, so in the supposed interests of the timid penitent the ancient discipline was relaxed (B. xix. 159). Thietmar in Germany, Rathier in Lorraine and Italy, and Fulbert in France, witnessed repeatedly to the triumph of this system. Penance was maintained as a discipline of obedience, including prayer, fastings, almsgiving, pilgrimages, and in penance post-baptismal sins were supposed to be washed away. But the rigidity of penance was modified in certain ways : (1) Confession rose in value as an essential to salvation and a meritorious act in itself. (2) The priest had discretion in the laying down of discipline, which he could modify both as regards the time and method (B. xix. 31). The absolution which used to come at the close of the penance might now follow very quickly the act of confession. (3) Almsgiving became increasingly prominent as a remedy for sin, as is seen by a glance at the royal charters and certain canons in the collections of Regino and Burchard (B. xix. 20). In the tenth century confession could still be made to a layman if necessary (Th. viii. 10). It was not yet compulsory, though highly desirable.

On the general question two points might be noticed. (1) The priestly absolution was declaratory (B. xi. 20, xix. 45) ; Fulbert asserts that it is Christ who pardons alone. Gerbert emphatically declares that, unless the priest's binding and loosing corresponds with Christ's wish and the real state of the penitent's soul, it is useless. Bruno, discoursing with his friends, calls upon them to confess to each other, in order that Christ may be their advocate with God. It is noticeable that Rathier's *Confessional* is directed first of all to God, and only then to the saints and the priests who read his writings. He declares that his hope is in God, that Jesus is the Saviour, that penitence and confession need for their efficacy the mercy of God, and that it is the mercy of God which absolves sinners. (2) Moreover, the writers of the period are all equally emphatic that a change of attitude on the part of the sinner and a real desire for amendment alone give value to the confession. Rathier says : ' What is the good of confession unless you leave behind the sins confessed ? ' (Conf. 12, Sermon iii. 2). There must be real conversion from the heart, fasting from vice as well as food, a real intention to do better, shown by charity and good works.

It is certain that an effort was made to bring in the grace of God and to preserve the inwardness and ethical character of salvation, but this endeavour was vitiated by the conception of grace as a kind of force proceeding from a God rather remote, operating only through certain narrow channels, and through priestly hands, rather than the actual loving attitude of God to men.   It was also weakened by the emphasis placed upon external act and rite as giving merit.

Some information concerning the administration of public penance for public sins is provided by the canons of Burchard (B. i. 90 and 91) and the writings of Rathier (It. 6).   This discipline was apparently controlled by the bishop in synodal courts, which were held in various parishes as he toured the diocese. The archpresbyter and the archdeacon preceded the bishop by a few days, and called the people together to the bishop's court for the confession or judgement of public crime.   Minor sentences were dealt with in conjunction with the parish priests, and graver offences were held over until the bishop arrived, such as drunkenness, adultery, and perjury.   The clergy as well as the laity were summoned to these courts to receive judgement.   Great care was taken to ensure a fair trial.   Witnesses from the district were called, who had to give evidence on oath.   The witnesses, the judges, the accused, and the accusers were to be clearly differentiated.   No witness or accuser would be tolerated who on investigation was found to be biased against the accused.   The accused had the right of defence.   Definite charges must be preferred in writing (G. 217), and false accusations were punishable.   The Church tolerated the ' ordeal,' and the accused was allowed to submit himself to what was called the ' Judgement of God,' in the form of ordeal of fire or water.   Adalger of Rheims offered to submit himself to the ordeal of boiling water or red-hot iron.   The Church, however, relied increasingly on the testimony of chosen witnesses and careful investigation in the open court. The bishop co-operated with his clergy, and was guided by the recognized procedure of Canon Law, which bore the impress of Roman jurisprudence and would compare favourably with the rougher judgement of the feudal courts.

It should be noted that the penitential system included

'larger excommunication' or the 'anathema,' which Abbo describes as 'the condemnation of eternal death.' A case of this kind is found in the anathema pronounced by the clergy of Rheims upon the robbers of the Church : 'Let the sons become orphans, the wives widows, let them be ejected from their habitation, let their days be few, let usurers seize all their substance, let another receive their authority.' Many immunities conclude with threats of terrible curses, such as sharing eternal fire with the devil and his angels, as the penalty of violation. The anathema was the judgement on those who refused the penance appointed, and declined to satisfy the Church order. It was supposed to signify the surrender of the person involved to eternal doom, and must therefore only be pronounced by the bishop in consultation with other bishops (Abbo, Canon 36). The anathema was closely associated with the 'interdict,' which meant that the excommunication was made to apply, not only to the guilty party, but to the community to which he belonged. Asceline placed his diocese under an interdict which prevented baptisms, confirmation, masses, and Christian burials (G. 164), and the Pope placed the sees of France under one at Pavia in 997. We find Gerbert strongly condemning such interdicts, though he seems to have been a party to one in the case of St. Denis and its monastery. Meanwhile, the claim to pronounce such a doom upon the impenitent was liable to great abuse, and in the hands of secular bishops was highly dangerous. It was, in fact, a logical development of the power of excommunication, when the tendency was to identify the visible Church with the Kingdom of God.

In conclusion we may state that the penitentiary stood for an ethical interest, and implied salvation by works, tending to a legal and external view of morality. On the other hand, the confessional stood for a religious interest, and implied salvation by mediated grace, but tended to put the priest in the place of God and to weaken the claims of morality. Both systems need never have arisen had the Church remained faithful to the New Testament conception of God as Father, and to the New Testament conception of grace and faith. There was an obvious confusion throughout between the sinner's relation to the Church as an institution, and of the sinner's relation to God, personal and inward, also a confusion between the

priest who declares the grace of God and the God whose
character it is.

We read of *Extreme Unction* in these days.   The Empresses
Adelaide and Matilda were anointed with holy oil.   This
anointing which was originally regarded as a healing in the sense
of James's Epistle, was now thought to secure the remission
of sins in the article of death.   It seems to have been already
attached to the rites for the dying, and, with the Eucharist and
last confession, formed the viaticum.   Prayers, the use of the
holy water, and signing with the Cross, entered into these last
rites, but Extreme Unction was not yet regarded as a sacrament.
Thietmar refers to these customs (Th. vii. 10, xxxvi. 4).

VI. PRAYERS FOR THE DEAD were a feature of popular
religious life.   The Empress Adelaide asked prayer for her
departed son, and for herself after death.   The epitaphs of
Sens—and they are typical of others—conclude each panegyric
with a prayer for the continued well-being of the person in
question.   William of Aquitaine, when he founded Cluny, had
specially asked that he might always enjoy the prayers of these
saints, and many followed his example.   Rathier refers to
Masses for the living and the dead, and such Masses entered
largely into the religious life of Cluny.   Prayers for the dead
implied a doctrine of purgatory which was in a very undeveloped
form, though associated with highly-coloured descriptions of
a place of fire, and associated, sometimes in legend, with
volcanoes like Etna.   But the custom also expressed a sense
of the union between the Church Militant and Triumphant,
and testified to the interest connecting the two worlds.

Prayers were not only offered on behalf of the dead, but they
were offered to certain of the departed, and the invocation of
saints was a popular form of worship.   One manifestation of
this worship was THE VENERATION OF VISIBLE AND TANGIBLE
RELICS of the saint, such as the bones themselves or certain
garments and personal possessions.

The literature of the period shows the enormous interest
taken in relics.   Thierry, Bishop of Metz, was a most earnest
collector of them, and he travelled in Italy seeking new relics
for his church.   The book called *The Discovery of Relics*
mentions the bones of Elpidius, a bishop, which had a white
colour and a fragrant odour, the blood of St. Stephen in a
crystal vase, the hair of St. Peter and his chains; and such

relics were given by the Pope to the Emperor to secure his favour, by which we learn that relics were actually used for reconciling enmities. Even Bruno, in spite of his learning, was a seeker after relics. He collected them that he might ' increase the glory of God ' and secure ' patrons for his own soul's welfare.' Kings and princes are equally affected by the prevailing fashion, and Adalberon of Rheims calls upon Lothaire and Emma to be present at the translation of the relics of St. Thierry, discovered at Rheims. This translation was carried out in the presence of soldiers, the great of the land, bishops and abbots, whilst the King himself carried the sacred relics (*Miracles of St. Thierry*).

Another interesting case is that of the translations of St. Valerie and St. Riquier. The Count of Flanders had bought the body of St. Valerie from Erchambald, a cleric of the monastery, in 948, and he had taken the body of St. Riquier from Centule in 952. Both bodies were then transferred to St. Bertin, August 29, 952. In 980, however, Hugh took Montreuil by surprise from Arnulf the Young, and, as a price of peace, extorted the bodies of the saints. The translation which followed was a great ceremony, and the people gathered in crowds from Ponthieu and all the country situated near the Seine and Somme. The relics of Valerie were conveyed in silver vessels by Count Burchard and Orland, Count of Vimieu, and it was said that the waters of the Somme parted to give them passage. Having replaced the relics of Valerie, Hugh recrossed the river on January 3, and in the morning rejoined his servants, who then carried the relics of Riquier on foot to Centule, within a league of the Abbey. Hugh alighted from his horse, and with bare feet carried the sacred shrine on his shoulders to the altar. The reformation of the Abbey was then carried out by Enguerrand of Corbie. The story was told that Valerie had appeared in a dream to Hugh and promised that his descendants would sit on the throne for seven generations, if he restored his relics to their former station. An historic fact lies behind these legends. Evidently Hugh felt compelled by religious and political motives to humble Arnulf by reclaiming from him the relics which his grandfather had stolen. Intense popular enthusiasm accompanied these translations, which were effected to the sorrow of Flanders and the joy of France.

L

Relics were believed to work miracles. St. Riquier made trampled earth to produce richly, the relics of St. Benedict frequently brought healing to those who touched them, whilst a blind man was healed by the tooth of St. Ursmar. When Arnulf of Orleans allowed his people to invade the vineyards of Fleury, the monks carried with them the bones of St. Maurus and St. Frangentius, and the invaders were powerless. Sick men were healed by the relics of St. Benedict, and candles were mysteriously lit in spite of wind and rain by these relics, detained at Cluny. Adhemar tells us (iii. 35, 36) that the relics of St. Martial of Limoges, carried round in time of plague, caused the plague to cease.

We thus learn (1) that princes and bishops joined in celebrating these translations ; (2) that cultured prelates as well as ignorant crowds enthusiastically reverenced them ; (3) that relics were popularly believed to heal the sick and protect the Church ; (4) that they were the cause of feuds between princes, were related to the diplomacy of the times, and entered into many a treaty.

It is certain that there was a vast amount of fraud in connexion with the veneration of relics. R. Glaber (iv. 3) gives us an interesting account of a man who was actually a dealer in relics and made a living by trading on the credulity of the people. This man, a peasant, took bones from a grave, and called himself Stephen, Peter, and John, in turns, and sold these bones to a shrine as the bones of St. Justus. A significant feature of the story is that the country people continued to believe in him, and that a local magnate, Manfred, built a church for the bones, and miracles were supposed to take place there.

Now this worship of relics was (1) a kind of animism. The spirit of the dead man would be popularly supposed to be in the relic just as, according to Glaber, spirits were supposed to dwell in trees and stones. This rude primitive animism hung like a miasma over the religious life of the age. (2) It was also a form of idolatry. The idol was originally a symbol, and remained so for the theologian, but the bane of religion has always been the confusion in the popular mind between that symbolized and the symbol. Man, finding it difficult to live by faith in the unseen, sought a material expression, and found it in the bones of the saint, which, originally venerated for their associations with the saint, were now venerated as in some way the saint himself. We must not forget, however, that respect for good men was the origin of this veneration for relics. The bones of Benedict were treasured because Benedict himself was a saint. The worship of relics was therefore closely associated with the adoration of saints. (3) The worship of relics was greatly assisted by the grossly materialistic views of the resurrection. Dust which some day would be a resurrection body was sacred indeed.

The first among the saints was the Virgin Mary. Fulbert of Chartres and Odilo of Cluny taught that the conception of Jesus left Mary spotless, and they proclaimed the value of her intercession (Sermon 5). There was a great and growing reverence for the Holy, Blessed, Immaculate Mother of God, as she was termed. Lothaire invoked her patronage, Maiolus offered prayers to her, William of Dijon was given by his mother to her protection, and the large number of churches dedicated to her sufficiently attest her place in the affections of the people. Mariolatry was in the air, though the doctrine that the Virgin was free from original sin was not yet present. The reverence for the Virgin Mary and such saints as St. Faith must have uplifted the standard of womanhood and helped to give the weaker sex that important place which they did occupy in the Middle Ages.

The Virgin Mary was only the first of the saints, and her invocation is only one special form of a general custom. Rathier has much to say about the invocation of saints. Bruno gathered relics of saints that he might enjoy their patronage, and built churches to their honour. In confirming the possession of a monastery, Lothaire associated saints with the Virgin Mary. The literature of the period gives the saints such power and influence that we are tempted to see in the local saint a revival of the ancient local deity, and thus in saint worship a revival of a former idolatry. Christ recedes into the mists created by dogma and ritual, whilst the saint comes into view as the one immediately able by his intercession to help the people. These saints are sometimes vindictive, at other times kindly ; but they defend their own people and places, and, like the ancient gods, are interested in the warfare of the times, whilst men fight with the name of the saint upon their lips.

The miracle literature, such as *The Miracles of St. Faith*, has an interest; but let us give special attention to Aimon's *Miracles of St. Benedict*, the work of a contemporary hand, and select from it a few illustrations. A soldier named Arnulf squandered the monastic possession which he controlled as a beneficiary, and as a penalty took fruit which choked him. A man who placed a sword on the altar of St. Benedict was killed by a knife which he used at dinner. Herbert, to whom Abbot Richard conceded a benefice, seized what belonged to the monastery, was struck by St. Benedict, and died by the way. Romuald, a citizen of Chartres, endeavoured to take a field belonging to the monastery for feeding his pigs, and died of fever. A man, who ate oats belonging to a peasant widow on the monastic lands, fell over a precipice and was killed (i. 14). The cry of Benedict (ii. 5) echoed through the mountains when Otherius sought to recover monastic possession from one Adhemar, and the latter was of course vanquished. A soldier (ii. 8) who forced his way into a monastery against the wish of the prior, drank to excess the wine of the monastery, fired his straw bed, and perished in the flames. These stories reveal the anger of Benedict against those injuring his people and possessions, but he delivered a poor man swept away in a sudden overflow of the Loire (ii. 9), delivered (ii. 6) a horse from a well into which it had fallen, miraculously provided a boat (i. 18) for a man seeking to cross the river, and healed those who called upon his name. The saint was the helper of the poor and needy, and was honoured by those he healed and comforted. On the whole the influence of the local saints would be a restraining one in lawless times, and the poor benefited by the magic of the saint's name. Nevertheless, the fact remains that the worship of saints was a kind of revived polytheism, and a widespread substitution of miracle and magic for character.

The worship of saints and their relics led inevitably to the honouring of their shrines. The local shrine where the relics were placed became as important as the temples of local deities in pagan days. The law of association applied on a big scale. Special localities became important because they had borne the impress of the saint's body or because his spirit was in some way associated with the place. It was believed that at certain places people could be specially blessed and healed by contact with the saint. Thus there grew up the habit of making pilgrimages to these sacred places, and the pilgrim began to figure largely in the records as a person for whom the Church must make provision. These men and women, travelling from shrine to shrine, were lodged with honour at the monasteries as they passed by. Fleury and St. Riquier, containing the relics of Benedict and Riquier, became famous in this connexion. Other centres were St. Martin of Tours and St. Denis of Paris.

But the pilgrim went farther afield. Rome was famous because it possessed the graves of St. Peter and St. Paul, and many other apostles and martyrs. There was a constant going to and fro of bishops, abbots, and laymen along the road leading to Rome, seeking not only the patronage of the Pope, but the inspiration of holy places.

But the pilgrim went farther still. Jerusalem had a sacredness all its own because of its association with the earthly life of our Lord. In the tenth century the tolerant rule of the Saracens opened the country to pilgrims. In a letter written by Abbo to Abbot Bernard, we gather that the latter wished to visit Jerusalem because his father, Hugh, had done so years before, fulfilling a vow of penance. Other pilgrims to the East in this period were an abbot of St. Aubin of Angers, 988, and Count Godfrey of Verdun, 997. Before the conversion of the Hungarians the journey was often made by sea, and was attended by great risks of shipwreck. Bernard of Angers, in his *Miracles of St. Faith*, tells a curious story of a certain Raymond, who was wrecked at sea on such a journey, and barely escaped with his life. On the conversion of King Stephen of Hungary, the land route by the Danube was opened (R.G. iii. 1), and Adhemar gives us numerous cases of pilgrimages at the beginning of the eleventh century (iii. 46–8). The journeys were difficult and arduous, and they came to have great merit attached to them, and entered largely into the penitential system. Thus, as we have seen, Hugh, the father of Bernard, was a pilgrim for the sake of his soul, and many, including Count Fulk of Anjou, followed his example.

Apart from these considerations, this contact of the West with the East gave movement to life, provided avenues for trade, added immensely to the culture, experience, and utilities of all classes, and helped to maintain the wider outlook of the

Church. The political and economic results were probably greater than the moral and religious ones.

The reverse side of the worship of saints was the FEAR OF DEMONS, which was equally a survival of pagan superstition and early polytheism. Evil deities became local demons. R. Glaber says that they dwell in trees and springs (iv. 3). They take visible form, appearing sometimes like a host of black figures. They appear to monks who have failed to attend matins. They are represented by false teachers and magicians, and appear in visions and dreams. In Flodoard's visions of Frothilde we see life as a great struggle between the saints and the demons for the possession of the souls of people. The office of the exorcist in the Church was in itself a reminder of the power of the demon. The Church was much nearer Manichaeism than it really knew, for the struggle between saint and demon came perilously near that ancient dualism. These demons could be vanquished by the use of the name ' Jesus,' by the sign of the Cross, and by the use of holy water ; but the great spiritual facts symbolized by these forms were often reduced to mere magical formulae acting independently of a change of heart. The saints like Benedict, Ursmar, &c., were mighty to cast out demons, according to contemporary writers like Aimon and Folcuin.

This belief had a pagan origin and flourished in those un-scientific days. The narrow asceticism and close introspection of the monastic life fostered it, and cases of physical infirmity or a storm at sea were equally attributed to the work of demons. This belief inspired terror, yet behind it there lay a moral fact and a religious experience. Men saw the strength of evil, and yet the superior strength of Jesus ; His name, and His Cross did save men from evil in a way which they could scarcely interpret. This belief in demonology, however crudely stated, represented a living issue, for men found life was more than logic. It was rather a struggle, sometimes an agony, in which they could only triumph by securing the help of those forces which come from the One who is stronger than the strong.

The real weakness lay in the conception of God, which had been considerably influenced by Greek metaphysics and also by the Roman ideas of punitive justice, and by the feudal idea of an arbitrary will. The New Testament conception of Fatherhood and the overruling sovereignty of love had been correspondingly weakened. Mankind was not so much a family of the Great Father as the subjects of a mighty chief, who, nevertheless, was so remote that the local magnate, in the form of a local saint or a local demon, took his place for all practical purposes. Religion reflected the political conditions of the time, and a loveless world projected its lovelessness back on Deity, and transferred its feuds to the world of spirits. This sense of the infinite remoteness and mystery of God led to the necessity of priestly mediation, and the habit of thinking of God in terms of power or substance rather than of character led to belief in the magical properties of forms and ceremonies. Fear of such a Being, whose judgement was eternal doom in hell, made religion a burden of penance and confession, instead of a gracious communion with God in Christ.

VII. In a concluding section to this chapter we may summarize the evidence produced in the previous sections, and briefly try to estimate its significance.

There is a marked and, in some senses, an essential difference between the Church of the New Testament and apostolic period, and the Church of the tenth century. The relation between the Church and the feudal world will be discussed in the last chapter, and it will be there seen that the inner life of the Church bore the impress of that feudal world ; but there were other influences affecting the Church. The Christian Church functioned in a certain environment, which modified its pure essence and often weakened its spiritual force.

1. An earlier paganism survived in the belief in the magical properties of names, signs, symbols, in the worship of relics and the honouring of local saints, whilst Eastern dualistic theory not only introduced the Catharist heresy, but marked the Church with a fierce asceticism that waged relentless war against the flesh. Traces of this influence can be discerned in certain aspects of the monastic movement and in the growing emphasis placed on celibacy.

2. Rome contributed to the Church its provincial and diocesan system. Canon Law was largely Roman jurisprudence applied to Church life. The legal mind of Rome helped to develop the penitential system, whilst the Latin genius encouraged uniformity in Church administration, and helped to build up, as an institution, the visible organized Catholic Church.

3. Greece gave its metaphysics to the Church and provided the terminology for its creed.   Thus the Church often thought of God in terms of substance rather than of personality, of grace as a semi-physical force rather than a spiritual attitude, and of the Eternal Life as the immortality of physical existence rather than a quality of fellowship.   As we have pointed out, the Christian sacraments, in their tenth-century form, betrayed the influence of this habit of thought.

4. Jewish ideas of the priesthood, as found in the Old Testament, helped greatly the advance of sacerdotalism in the Church, and the Christian minister was too often identified with the Jewish priest in the capacity of mediator between God and man.

These alien yet inevitable influences were in some senses damaging to the pure ideal of the Founder, and yet in other ways helped to relate the Christian ideal to the actual life of the world ; for the Church, in order to function at all, had to relate itself to the institutions and the ideas of the age.   Though greatly modified, the Christian spirit was not lost.   In the later chapters we shall see that Christianity revealed itself as a principle of reform, as a redeeming and saving influence in society, and we shall see the Christian spirit exemplified in a typical saint.

The explanation of the continued vitality of the Christian religion lay in the fact that it was the religion of Christ.   He was sometimes half hidden behind form and dogma, but He was never entirely lost.   He was always the ultimate authority for life and doctrine, and the revelation of God in a human life. Christianity was also the religion of the Cross, that is, the religion of sacrifice and service with a mighty appeal of love at the heart of it.   Sin was real, so were law and judgement, but men felt the immeasurable influence of a love which in some mysterious way had died for them, to satisfy and atone, to save them from hell and bring them to heaven, and that love was ultimately regarded as an expression of the grace of God.

It would be quite true to say that all the best minds of the Middle Ages were associated with the religion of the Cross, and that the noblest character and endeavour found its incentive and inspiration in the appeal of Jesus Christ and Him crucified.

In spite of grave abuses and alien, unworthy elements in its doctrines, rites, and customs, the Church, by the crucifix, the sign of the Cross, the solemn celebrations of the Mass, the sacrificial lives of noble men and women, and the study of the gospel records, forced its way to the foot of the Cross of Jesus, and always discovered a perennial source of power and virtue in that sacred place. Roman law, Greek metaphysic, Jewish sacerdotalism, and popular superstition could obscure, but could not altogether hide, the face of Jesus ; and, wherever He appeared, He sanctified life and enriched it by calling forth the noblest loyalties of which men are capable.

VII

THE REFORM MOVEMENT

Note

G. = Gerbert's Letters.
O. = Jonas Vita Odonis.
R. = Richer.
Ru. = Ruotger's Vita Brunonis.
U. = Ulric's Consuet. Clun.

THE study of Church history reveals the extraordinary power of revival latent in the Christian Church. This can be explained by the inability of the Church to forget its ideals, and by the fact that fresh contact with the ideals as contained in the life and teaching of Jesus continually produces new movements of reform.

The ninth and tenth centuries have been described as the darkest period of the Dark Ages, and yet it was in these centuries that we come across the revivals associated with Benedict of Aniane and the great Abbots of Cluny, which were endeavours to recover the old Benedictine discipline and culture.

I. First of all, reference must be made to the revival in Lorraine. Chrodegang of Metz in the eighth century had sought to impose the discipline of a common life on the Cathedral Canons, and the Metz district was a reforming centre during the tenth century. Close to Metz was the monastery of Gorz. The older monastery had been founded by Chrodegang, but had degenerated and been destroyed. The new monastery, built in A.D. 933, gained a great reputation as a ' Beehive of Monks.' A great revival of religion had broken out in Lorraine. This movement, unlike the Cluny reform, sprang from the people, and was forced upon the higher clergy by the lower clergy and laity. Men of humble birth, like Humbert of Verdun and the celebrated John of Metz, whose life (Migne 137)

gives us such important details about this revival, sought
refuge in solitary places, and, through fierce asceticism, prayers,
fastings, and vigils, sought a higher life for the soul.   Of this
company Einold, Archdeacon of Toul, was the only man of
culture and position.   It was a popular and democratic attempt
to raise the tone of the Church.   These lonely seekers after the
higher life began to gather in groups.   At last, when they were
about to retire to Italy, Bishop Adalberon of Metz was induced
to grant to them the monastery of Gorz in his diocese.   He
showed at first little sympathy with them, but he was warned
in a vision to grant them further aid, and afterwards became
their generous patron.

Einold of Toul was their first abbot.   John became prior,
and ultimately abbot.   A fierce frenzy of asceticism, illustrated
by the story of John's early monastic life, moderated with the
years, and a system of ordered discipline, similar to that of
Cluny, began to prevail.   Bishop Richer of Liège showed
them great favour, and the monks reformed a number of
monasteries in his diocese.   Adalberon of Metz asked them
to undertake the reform of the monastery of St. Arnulf, near
Metz, and the pious came from all sides to Gorz, as the centre
of monastic zeal.   Like other monasteries, it possessed a
school, and offered education to the sons of the people.   In this
school well-known bishops like Adalberon of Rheims, Rothad
of Cambrai, and Adalberon of Verdun were trained.   It was
a monk of Gorz named Wigbert who founded the monastery
at Gembloux, and, from the latter monastery, Erluin went
forth in an endeavour to reform Lobbes, which had become
greatly secularized.   The story of this monastery (Migne 137)
gives some idea of the great need of reform, for Erluin, in
endeavouring to reform the wild and dissipated lives of these
monks, was actually beaten, maimed, and blinded.

II. Gorz was not the only reforming centre in Lorraine.
Bruno, Archbishop of Cologne, was a great statesman, and
was also a great saint, and exerted immense influence upon the
religious life of the times.   He loved learning.   As a boy he
studied at a school at Utrecht, and later he studied under an
Irish bishop called Israel (Ru. v. 7).   He taught what he himself
had previously learnt.   There was no branch of Greek and
Latin studies that escaped him.   He revived the seven arts,
long forgotten (Ru. 5), and examined, with learned men,

history, rhetoric, poetry, and philosophy. The presence of
Greeks at the Imperial Court helped him to revive Greek
studies. He gave his leisure to study, and carried books about
with him in all his journeys ; and, even when called from the
school to the palace, by no means neglected books. It is
expressly stated that, not content with superficial knowledge,
he sought to solve problems by wrestling with the difficulties
of interpretation. But he was not merely an educationalist.
He reformed monastic foundations either by force or by persuasion, brought the monks back into regular life, and, among
these monasteries reformed by him, stood out prominently
Lorch (Ru. 10). He strove for uniformity in the monasteries
of his diocese, so that in diverse congregations there might be
one heart and soul. He forbade luxury in dress, and everything which seemed indecent or effeminate. He commanded
all to live according to ancient regulations. He provided
liberally for those who lived according to rule (Ru. 33), and
encouraged and helped those seeking the solitary life by providing them with cells and material support. He gathered
relics from every side (Ru. 31), and built and repaired churches
and monasteries suitable for their honour. Some houses he
destroyed that he might rebuild in nobler form, and others
he repaired and increased their size. He was a true pastor
and a great preacher (Ru. 33). He loved peace, and, if he had
to attack robbers, it was only that peace might come, whilst
in all things he sought the well-being of the people, being
severe to the evil, but mild and tender to the good (Ru. 34).
His admiring biographer, Ruotger, notes his humility, his love
of secret prayer, his tears of penitence, his frugality, his sense
of the solemnity of life and the nearness of death, his longing
to be with Christ, his secret doubts, fears, and sorrows, and
his dislike of all luxury in dress or food, more remarkable
because of his royal birth. Making all allowances for the
idealization of hero-worship, we may seek the outline form of
a great soul, sincerely and fundamentally Christian.

Egbert of Trèves, Thierry of Metz, and Wigfrid of Verdun
were all trained in his school, and, like him, though deeply
involved in the politics of the age, were reformers, builders,
lovers of the beautiful, gatherers of relics, and anxious for the
tightening of discipline in the monasteries and churches.
Odelric of Rheims, formerly a Canon of Metz, was a nominee of

Bruno, and proved to be a brilliant scholar as well as a strenuous defender of Church rights (R. iii. 18).

Bruno had also shown considerable sympathy with the celebrated Rathier (890-974). This scholar was born at Liège, and, in the course of a very learned career, was, in turn, monk at Lobbes, Bishop of Verona, then Bishop of Liège, then Bishop of Verona for a second period, after which he returned to his native land to live as a monk for the remaining years of his life. Bruno supported him whilst at Liège, and secured his reinstatement at Verona. Rathier was a voluminous writer (Migne 136), a powerful advocate of celibate clergy, a defender of the rights of the episcopacy, a strong opponent of simony, and a believer in the theory of the sacraments associated with Radbert. His life was very restless and disturbed, for he quarrelled with his clergy at Verona on the division of Church funds, with the princes of North Italy, with his clergy at Liège, and with the Abbot of Lobbes. It is clear that, with all his wisdom, eloquence, and reforming passion, he lacked both tact and sympathy. Nevertheless, he suffered in the defence of Church law, and strove for a higher ideal for the clergy. His life, largely passed in Italy and Belgium, does not directly concern us, but he has a place among the reformers of the tenth century, and interprets to us in many ways the mind of the century. By his residence in Lorraine and Provence, and his correspondence with Flodoard of Rheims and relations with Lothaire, he had some influence on the Church in France. At a later stage Liège became, under Notker, a reforming centre. This prelate figures in Gerbert's correspondence. He was a shrewd man of the world, diplomat, and politician, but he achieved distinction by the construction, enrichment, and renovation of monasteries and churches in his diocese, and for the emphasis he placed on the education and training of the clergy.

III. We must, however, pass to another name, that of Adalberon, student of the school of Gorz, Canon of Metz, and then Archbishop of Rheims. He belonged to the great Lorraine family of Ardenne. His brother Godfrey was Count of Verdun and Hainault. As Archbishop of Rheims, his reputation became an international one. He was a great figure in the politics of the time, but here we are concerned with him as churchman. Richer has given to us an account of his reforms, and further information is given in the history of the monastery of Mouzon (Migne 137). Adalberon was an active, indefatigable reformer, and his aim was to check the feudalizing of the Church by reviving the canonical life of rule and discipline, and by reforming monasteries. All this was, however, to be carried out under episcopal supervision, and, if necessary, he was prepared to draw very near to Rome. His ideals were consistently imperialistic, and even international. Though Chancellor of France, he was a lover of the Empire, and, though sharing in the possessions of, and enjoying the status of, a great feudal magnate, he never forgot that he was a bishop of the Church with an international centre at Rome.

He began his reforms in his Cathedral of Rheims. He constructed a cloister for the canons, and enforced the common life. He imposed silence in the dormitory, the refectory, and the church, and secured the proper maintenance of the ' Hours ' of service. From Compline to Laudes there was to be complete silence, and, before the first hour of the day, only those who had special duties could pass out of the cloisters. The ' Institutes of St. Augustine ' and the decrees of the Fathers were to be read daily for the edification of the clergy. He proceeded to rebuild the church, though it is uncertain what he actually did. Richer's words are : ' Fornices qui ab aecclesiae introitu per quartum pene totius basilicae partem, inde et ampliore receptaculo et digniore scemate tota aecclesia decorata est.' In Flodoard's Additions we are told that Adalberon destroyed ' arcuatum opus quod erat secus valvas aecclesiae Sanctae Mariae Remensis.' Laur, in his edition of Flodoard (p. 161), suggests that there was an atrium, a square place with porticoes which would be equal to one-fourth of the length of the whole church, including the atrium, and that the altar stood not upon, but near, the arched portico, and that this was the arched work destroyed. Adalberon, therefore, probably extended the nave of the church, and made a more imposing front. He made a portable altar, with figures of the four evangelists at the angles, their outstretched wings extending over the sides, meeting in the middle, and also a candelabra of seven lamps illustrating the seven gifts of the Spirit, which he decorated elegantly. He suspended crowns, made towers with bells, and decorated the great altar with crosses of gold and surrounded it with gleaming *cancelli*.

The windows were ornamented with figures in stained glass,
and he provided a reliquary for the relics of saints.   He also
constructed, outside the city walls, the Church of St. Denis
in such a way that the priests of St. Denis, celebrating Mass
towards the east, would see through the door the priest in
the cathedral, and follow his movements, as the doors in the
two churches were immediately opposite.   The cathedral must
then have been quite close to the city walls.

Adalberon was not content with the embellishment of the
cathedral, but he carefully watched all the monasteries and
churches of his diocese.   There was a church at Mouzon served
by canons who were living quite secular lives with their wives
and children, and with property of their own.   Adalberon
was anxious to reform the church.   Now it so happened that
the Archbishop, with his brother Godfrey, had recently besieged
and taken Warg, near Mezières, the residence of a certain
Eudes, who had previously devastated the possessions of the
church of Rheims.   Warg was set on fire, but it was noticed
that a church where the bones of a certain Arnulf were preserved
escaped the fire.   This Arnulf was a poor Lorraine pilgrim
who had been wounded in the forest by brigands, and brought
to Gruyère to die.   Miracles were said to have occurred at
this place, and the fame of the saint spread abroad.   Aimon,
a chevalier of Gruyère, surrendered the body to the above-
mentioned Eudes, who preserved it at Warg.   Adalberon
took the body to his church at Mouzon, July 24, 971, and he
felt that Arnulf the pilgrim was calling upon him to reform
Mouzon.

To the south-west of Mezières there was a small monastic
community consisting of Lietard and eight monks, dependent
upon St. Rémy.   It had been founded by a certain Count
Stephen and his wife Freduile, who, having no children, left
their all to these monks on the advice of Abbot Gerard of
St. Rémy.   The monastery, however, was only poor in resources.
Adalberon was determined to bring these eight monks from
St. Thin to Mouzon, substituting for them monks of St. Rémy.
He therefore visited St. Thin, and directed the abbot and his
monks to follow him to Mouzon.   He himself arrived first,
and, calling the canons together, offered them the choice of
either accepting monastic discipline, including celibacy and
the common life, or expulsion from the church.   The majority

preferred to depart, and Lietard and his monks, appearing at this precise moment, quietly took possession of the church. Having reformed Mouzon, Adalberon proceeded to endow it generously with land belonging to his family, and his brother Count Godfrey became its advocate.

Adalberon was also interested in the monastery of St. Rémy. Having succeeded in obtaining the consent of the abbot for his Mouzon schemes, he proceeded to take steps to strengthen St. Rémy itself. He secured a royal immunity from Lothaire, but he wished also to secure Papal immunity to protect the monastery from the King himself, and he also wished to secure a similar privilege for the monastery of St. Timothy, which he had given to St. Rémy for hospitality purposes, for the use of the poor. He therefore decided to visit Rome to secure a Papal bull, granting the desired privileges and confirming his reforms. According to Richer (iii. 25), he arrived in Rome in time to celebrate Christmas there in the presence of twelve bishops. His reputation secured for him a cordial reception from the Pope, and the Pope granted him what he asked, as Adalberon apparently returned with some provisional statement signed by the Pope and the bishops. Later on, according to the history of the monastery of Mouzon, which says nothing of a personal visit to Rome, Adalberon sent messengers asking for the official bull, that he might present it to a gathering of bishops in May. This bull was definitely signed and sent April 23, 972.

The synod assembled at Notre Dame in Tardenne, and was attended by bishops with twelve archdeacons and presbyters, and Adalberon, presiding, indicated his purpose and explained his recent activities. The signature of the Pope was passed round for observation, and the bishops, convinced of the genuineness of the signature, signed in turn the immunities, which were then sent to the monasteries in question and deposited in the several archives. The synod also approved of certain similar reforms carried through by Rorico at St. Vincent of Laon eleven years before. In this case MacAllan, an Irishman, with twelve monks, had taken the place of the secular canons. This Irishman died in 978.

The Archbishop took the opportunity to refer to the laxity among the monks of the diocese, and another synod was called, presided over by Abbot Rudolf of St. Rémy, which, though bishops were present, consisted mainly of abbots, among whom were Abbots of St. Medard, Corbie, Vincent, and St. Basil. The cases referred to were puerile in the extreme, dealing largely with the use of the term ' Father ' instead of ' Brother,' the passing in and out of certain brethren without the blessing of others, and for the rest, the colour of garments and the use of a particular kind of shoe and stocking were condemned. The synod dispersed, having issued a solemn condemnation of such supposed evils. The immunity received from Pope John XIII for St. Rémy was as follows : ' On account of your intervention, we confirm to your archmonastery, situated in France not far from Rheims, over which you preside, and by privilege of our authority, all possessions both movable and immovable, which are able to be declared, lands, vineyards, servants, female slaves, farm servants, male and female, buildings, dwellings, treasures, ornaments, and whatever money you desire; declaring under the curse of divine judgement, and the prohibition of strong anathema, that no one, either king or archbishop or bishop or any person great or small, shall ever presume to injure or alienate or carry away any of its possessions or interests. If anyone, contrary to our desire, should presume by evil deeds to do anything knowingly against the writing of this our apostolic privilege, let him know that he is excommunicated by the judgement of God and St. Peter, first of apostles, and by our humility, and anathematized with the devil and all the impious for whom eternal torments have been prepared.' The King is warned off, and the Pope is left supreme.

Adalberon proceeded to deal with the monastery of St. Thierry of Rheims. Lothaire had accorded an immunity in 962, but, in spite of this, it was seized by Count Roger of Rouen. Adalberon retook the monastery, drove out the canons, introduced monks with Airard as abbot, and then secured from Lothaire in 974 confirmation of his reforms and the renewal of the immunities. In 976 Adalberon made the discovery of the body of St. Thierry, and begged the King to assist in the elevation of the relics. After some delay, Lothaire and Queen Emma arrived with an army, and, in the presence of the troops, nobles, bishops, and abbots, he himself transferred the relics of St. Thierry into the abbey. We shall find that Adalberon endeavoured to interfere in the internal

M

affairs of Fleury, but he refused, having probably learnt wisdom, to intervene in the internal affairs of St. Denis. Adalberon was concerned for the morals of the clergy. It is significant that, apart from his inquiry into the life of the monasteries, he brought the cases of two bishops of the Province (Theobald of Amiens and Asceline of Laon) before synods for disciplinary purposes. He was also eager for the intellectual progress of the Church, and it was he who placed Gerbert at the head of the school at Rheims.

Gerbert, born of an Aquitaine family of plebeian extraction, became a pupil in the monastery of St. Gerard of Aurillac, governed by Abbot Gerard. Here he had been taught grammar and Latin literature by a monk called Raymond, and probably took monastic vows. In 967 Borell of Barcelona visited Aurillac as a pilgrim, and, taking Gerbert away with him, committed him to Hatto, the Bishop of Vich, from whom he learnt mathematics, the knowledge of which had probably been brought to Spain by the Arabs. Borell took Bishop Hatto and Gerbert to Rome in 970, seeking an archbishopric for Hatto. The Pope introduced Gerbert to the Emperor Otho I, who was then in Italy, and who, being impressed with Gerbert's knowledge, retained him in Italy. Borell returned to Spain, whilst Hatto died at Rome. Gerbert told the Emperor that he wished to learn logic or philosophy, and after he had been a year in Italy, Gerannus, an archdeacon of Rheims, with the reputation of a philosopher, visited Italy as Lothaire's ambassador to Otho. Gerbert sought instruction from him, with the result that Gerbert came to Rheims in 972 and was made *scholasticus* by Adalberon, which position he retained till 983, when he was appointed Abbot of Bobbio by Otho III. This position he had for a year, when, disgusted with the violence of the monks, he returned to Rheims, to take an important place in the conspiracy which changed the dynasty of France. His letters are still a priceless source of information for the period in question, but his educational and political work will be dealt with elsewhere.

Thus we see the measure of the stature of Adalberon. A puritan in his desire for moral discipline, yet thoroughly mediaeval and catholic in his love of the beautiful and his appreciation of art, he was no mystic, and his letters bear little witness to any great religious experience. His zeal for reform went hand in hand with considerable craft and intrigue. He was rather a statesman than saint, and in all his reforms he was careful to hold fast the vast estates which were the real peril to the religious life of the Church.   His spirit was often harsh, his methods open to criticism, but with all his faults he was on the side of discipline and reform.   Before his mind there flashed out the ideal of a Church holy, Imperial, catholic, and by his zeal for knowledge he prepared for better days.

IV. Another centre of reform was Fleury.   This royal abbey had been reformed by Odo of Cluny, but the connexion between the abbeys had not been maintained, and, after the death of Oidbold, who had aroused the indignation of Gerbert, the celebrated Abbo was elected.   Abbo was one of the great scholars of the age, and a great reformer.

He is known to have paid two visits to Rome, one during the pontificate of John XV about the end of 995.   His intention, as described to his friend Leo of St. Boniface, was to exchange relics of St. Benedict for relics of St. Boniface, and receive the Papal confirmation for the privileges and possessions of his monastery.   He had no illusions about the character of the Pope, and mourned the condition of the Roman Church ' widowed of a worthy pastor.'   His second visit to Rome was apparently in 997, when he received a bull from Pope Gregory V, conceding fresh privileges to Fleury, such as freedom from the excommunication which was to fall on the rest of the country, and protection from the Bishop of Orleans.   He returned from the last journey with the pallium for Arnulf, now to be re-established in Rheims (Epistles 1, 15).

He also advocated the claims of the monks of St. Martin of Tours in their controversy with the Archbishop of Tours. These monks claimed that all episcopal rites in the monastery should be celebrated by their own monastic bishop instead of by the diocesan bishop, and took the matter to Rome.   At the synod of St. Denis he defended the rights of monks in the matter of tithes, and was therefore held responsible for the riot which led to the break-up of that conference, and the hurried flight of the bishops.   From this charge, however, he defended himself in an ' Apologia ' addressed to the King (Migne 139). Simony especially aroused his wrath, and his favourite argument was that Christ called the Church His Church and not Peter's, and that therefore the successors of Peter had not

possessions which they could either buy or sell.   His sympathies were manifestly monastic and Papal.   He resented the
claims of the provincial episcopate to control the monasteries,
and criticized the arrogance and avarice of many bishops.   On
the other hand, he maintained the rights of the abbot as
against lawless elements in the monastery itself.   He sought to
restore the Benedictine rule, and strove for a higher moral
standard for all clergy.   He regarded the monk as in a higher
grade than the ordinary cleric.

Called to reform the monastery of St. Rule in Gascony, he
met his death in a brawl caused by a quarrel between his
French monks and the Gascons who resented their intervention.   In spite of his opposition to Gallican sentiments and
his passionate loyalty to the Papacy, he held a high religious
view of royalty, whose divine right and religious prerogative
he strongly upheld.   There can be no doubt that his influence
upon King Robert led to the promotion of monks to a high
position in the Church, which fact provoked the ironies of
Asceline of Laon.   It may be noted that, whilst Fleury maintained its independence of Cluny, there was much friendly
association between Abbo and Odilo of Cluny.

Other centres of reform should be noted.   After the translation of the relics of St. Riquier to Centule, Enquerrand, a monk
of Corbie, with the support of Hugh Capet, replaced seculars by
monks, whilst similar reforms were undertaken by Restold at
St. Valerie.   Hugh Capet also drove canons from the Church of
St. Bartholomew in Paris, replaced them by monks, and deposited
there the relics of St. Magloire, originally brought from Dol.
Similar reforms had been carried through with royal sanction
at Mont St. Michel in 967, St. Eloi of Noyon in 978, St. Aubin
of Angers in 966, St. Bavon at Ghent.   The reforms at Noyon
were also confirmed by Pope John XV in 988.   Thus a perusal
of royal diplomata and Papal bulls, together with a study of
the annals and miracle literature, prove to us how widespread
was the desire for reform and a purer Church life.   This desire
shows itself in all grades of society, and can be traced among
the higher and lower clergy, among the nobility and peasantry.
Bishops, princes, abbots, and even the kings of the age betray
its influence.

V. The history of the Church in France would be incomplete
without reference to the monastery of Cluny and its mighty

influence on the life of Western Christendom. For information we rely on the collection of the charters of Cluny, the customs compiled by Ulric (Migne 149), the Lives of the Abbots Odo, Maiolus, Odilo, &c.

The little town of Cluny is situated on the river Grosne in a valley among high limestone hills. It is twelve miles northwest of Maçon, a town on the Saone. An important road, the Via Agrippa, between Boulogne and Lyons, used to pass this way. In the tenth century Cluny, situated in the Duchy of Burgundy, was a hunting-lodge belonging to Duke William of Aquitaine. It originally belonged to the Bishop of Maçon, who gave it to the Count of Maçon in exchange for three villas. From the Count it passed to Ada, sister of Duke William, and she willed it to her brother in exchange for an alod in the year 893. Cluny consisted then of a villa with churches, chapels, manors, vineyards, meadows, pastures, trees, cultivated and uncultivated lands, and watercourses.

In 910 Duke William granted a charter for the foundation of the celebrated monastery. Berno, a wealthy Burgundian who had sacrificed all secular interests and embraced the religious life, had built a monastery at Gigny, endowed it with his own possessions, and taken vows there. Later, at the request of the monks, he became abbot, and, his reputation for sanctity increasing, he was also asked to undertake the reform of a monastery at Beaume. Here he became known to Duke William, who consulted him with regard to the proposed foundation of Cluny. William's charter (Migne 133) reveals his intentions. He gave the villa with all its belongings to the Apostles Peter and Paul. On this site the monks were to build the monastery and offer prayers unceasingly. The Benedictine rule was to be followed, and Berno was to be its first abbot, but after him the abbot was to be freely elected by the monks without interference from the Duke or any other prince. The monastery was to pay to the Church at Rome a tribute of ten solidi every five years, and in return enjoy special Papal protection. Hospitality was to be given daily to the poor and needy, and pilgrims. The original endowment was not heavy, for R. Glaber (iii. 5) tells us that it consisted only of fifteen *coloniae*, and at first there were only twelve monks there. Building operations proceeded slowly, and the monastery was not completed at Berno's death in 926, for the dedication took place in the time of his successor (O. ii. 3).

Berno's will (Migne 133) shows that he administered six monasteries, Gigny, Beaume, Aithicus, St. Lautenus of Deols, Massay, and Cluny, and in his will he left the villa of Alfracta, part of a meadow belonging to a certain Simon, and four *Cardariae* to Cluny, which formed part of the Gigny estate, in return for which Cluny was to pay twelve denarii to Gigny. Uniformity in the manner of life was commended to all these monasteries. The enjoyment of property in common, and periods of silence, together with a common ritual, were emphasized. Guy was appointed by Berno as abbot of the first three monasteries, and Odo became Abbot of Cluny, Deols, and Massay. The efforts of Guy to retain Alfracta were frustrated by the intervention of Pope John X, and the will of Berno was held to be valid.

Odo, who now took charge of Cluny, had been Canon of St. Martin of Tours, but had been repelled by the secular life of the canons. He had spent much time in lonely contemplation in a cell apart, and he was attracted towards the monastic life. Through a friend, Adhegrinus, who had called at Beaume whilst on pilgrimage to Rome, he had heard of the life and work of Berno (O. i. 22). Cluny attracted him, and he entered the monastery at the age of thirty. Fifteen years later, Berno, feeling his strength failing, summoned the neighbouring bishops, and in their presence laid down the burden of his high office. The monks chose Odo as his successor, undoubtedly on Berno's recommendation (O. i. 38).

Odo was a man of commanding genius and sanctity. Our period does not embrace his career, but under him the influence of Cluny extended far and wide. He himself was a scholar who had studied in the school of Paris (O. ii. 9). He had the advantage of a long training in organization under the leadership of Berno. He completed the building of the monastery (O. ii. 3) and maintained the reform régime. He was, moreover, called upon to undertake the reform of other monasteries like Fleury (O. iii. 8), and certain churches in Italy came under his control, for he enjoyed the patronage of Alberic the Patrician.

Cluny grew in riches, and in the number and power of its monks. It was situated in a favourable position, being in the Duchy of Burgundy and remote from the political influence of the King of Laon and the Emperor. It lay near trade routes, but in a valley into which the invading Normans never seem to have penetrated. The authority of the Duke of Burgundy was never strong, and thus in its sheltered valley it had unique opportunity of carrying out, without undue political influence, free election and other customs of true Benedictinism. But the strong personality of these early abbots had more to do with the rapid development of Cluny than any mere chance of geographical situation. The real kings of men in those days were Berno, Odo, Maiolus, and Odilo, the Abbots of Cluny. Rarely can the historian discover so illustrious a succession of great and gifted men.

Odo showed no exaggerated asceticism. He had a keen sense of humour (O. ii. 19, ii. 7), and his biographer tells us that sometimes the monks 'laughed till they cried' at his words. Other characteristics were his spiritual joy, his unquenchable charity, his powers of statesmanship, his moderation, and his knowledge of human hearts. He was an organizer, a preacher, a writer, a born leader of men, but he was above everything else a saint who loved God and his fellow men, and particularly cared for the needy. He died in 942.

His successor, Aymard, appointed as his coadjutor in 938, spent his brief reign in carefully supervising the secular affairs of the monastery. The majority of charters connected with his rule deal with exchanges of land, and there is evidence that he was, so to speak, rounding off the Cluny estates. R. Glaber (iii. 5) describes him as a simple man, who, though not so famous as other abbots, carefully upheld regular discipline. Odilo describes him as 'one of happy memory and blessed simplicity, zealous in increasing the property of the monastery.' In his later years he grew blind, and, unable to do justice to the office, he called his monks together, and asked them to choose a Father who would lead them in the way of God. As they hesitated, he suggested Maiolus, and the monks elected him as coadjutor. Power increasingly fell to him till, on the death of Aymard, he became sole abbot. Numerous grants of land mark this era. Conrad, King of Burgundy, Louis IV, and Lothaire of France and various counts and bishops gave lands, and in 949 Pope Agapetus confirmed the autonomy of

Cluny with its liberties and possessions. Hence tithes taken by bishops were restored, and the monastery was granted free choice of the abbot and protection from secular and ecclesiastical princes. No bishop could enter the monastery, much less give orders there, without the abbot's permission. Lothaire confirmed in 955 all Cluny's privileges as conceded by former kings (Dip. 15).

It will be well at this point to consider the nature of the reforms carried out at Cluny. Various efforts had been made to establish the pure Benedictine ideal of France, the greatest effort being the one associated with Benedict of Aniane, called Eutychus in the Life of Odo (O. i. 32), but these efforts had not been successful. The desolating effects of prolonged warfare, the growth of feudal anarchy, and the frequent invasions had weakened religious life, and the time in which Cluny was founded was a period of profound spiritual depression. Monasteries were secularized and corrupt, laymen ruled as abbots, and monks dressed as laymen, whilst the hours of service were changed in order to avoid rising in the night (O. iii. 1).

Cluny was primarily a reaction against the feudal control of monasteries. The scandal of feudal lords ruling as lay abbots over worldly monks resounded through the land. France was prepared for a change. The conscience of the age was at last roused, and reacted to the challenge. Cluny stood for free election of the abbot. ' Back to Benedict ' was the cry. This meant a rejection of secular control. It was, in fact, the ideal which later on under Gregory VII was to challenge the whole fabric of royal veto. ' Let the Church choose its own leaders, let the saints be the constituency, let their votes suffice.' The ideal was noble, but it was bound to languish in conditions of heavy endowments and secular entanglement, created by pious donors who had helped to make Cluny a wealthy and privileged institution. Nevertheless, the nobility of the ideal which stood out before the minds of these great abbots must be duly recognized. Government of the people, by the people, for the people, was in a sense true in those early days of Cluny, and the monks had got hold of a democratic principle of some value. The monk of low birth enjoyed, equally with the monk who came from some titled family, his place of dignity in the fellowship of the monastery.

Cluny, however, did strengthen the Papal power, for, seeking Papal help against feudal tyranny, she involved herself in a relation of mutual interest, and Cluny stood out as a stalwart defender of the Papacy.

Three great principles appear at Cluny, obedience, chastity, and common ownership of property. The abbot, once elected, had absolute sway, being in fact responsible to God alone, but he was recommended to consult the council of monks. Monks were expected to render humble obedience. Odo, thinking he had offended in some way, threw himself prostrate before Berno, begging favour (O. i. 33, 34), and this seems to have been a usual custom. The married life was regarded as quite inferior to the celibate life (O. i, 36), and the ideal of celibacy for the clergy received vast impetus from the renewed emphasis on chastity in Cluny's discipline. Every one who went into the monastery gave of his own freewill his possessions to the monastery, so that the monks reserved nothing for their own (O. iii. 9). Private ownership was regarded at the root of all evil, producing jealousies and envies (O. iii. 3). The monks could only use the word ' mine ' in reference to father and mother, otherwise they were compelled to say ' ours.' The community counted for everything, because ' they had all things in common.'

Cluny aroused a new interest in worship. The canonical Hours were to be celebrated regularly, and abstention, except in special cases of sickness, was a punishable offence (U. ii. 6, ii. 6) ; and the monk's attitude during worship was strictly defined, even to the position of his hands, the inclination of his head and the detail of his dress (U. ii. 7). A great increase in the number of psalms and prayers was a feature of the revival under Benedict of Aniane, and, at Cluny, this meant a reduction of the time available for manual labour. Every day there were sung 138 psalms, and there were two Masses every day, one of which was for the dead, and also two litanies (U. i. 6, O. i. 32). The number 138 was later reduced to 124, because otherwise there would be more psalms than prayers. Seventy-five psalms were chanted at Easter and Christmas (O. i. 35). There were special readings in the church and refectory, including, besides the books of the Bible and the Apocrypha, Leo on the ' Incarnation,' with the writings of Augustine and Chrysostom (U. i. 1). Ulric, in his

first books, notes in detail special seasons with their special
services, and thus, year in and year out, the carefully regulated
system of worship, with its psalms and prayers, was maintained intact.   The canonical Hours included Matins, Lauds
or Prime, Tierce, Sex, Nones, Vespers, Compline, and the
times varied with the seasons of the year.   Lauds began at
daybreak, Matins would come about 2 a.m., and the day of
worship and service lasted from 2 a.m. to sunset, with an hour
or two for sleep after the midday meal during the summer
months.   The services in the church consisted of psalms,
Bible-reading with Catholic exposition according to the days,
canticles, litanies, responses, and the Te Deum.

There were prolonged periods of silence, in which the monks
used signs (U. ii. 4, O. i. 32) ; e.g. in asking for bread they made
a circle with both thumbs and fingers because a loaf of bread is
round (U. ii. 4).   In the church, dormitory, kitchen, and
refectory, silence was enjoined (U. ii. 3).   There were stated
and limited opportunities for speech in the cloisters (U. ii. 20)
and chapter-house, and even then speech must be in a low
voice, and only about quite necessary things.   But, in the last
week of Advent and at Easter, silence was profound (O. i. 32).
The abbot had power to call for special silence on saints' days.
Thus the monks gave themselves up to the quiet life of meditation.   Being still, they sought God in a silence strongly
contrasted with the noise of a world at war.

The government and discipline of the monastery was very
carefully regulated, and during the eleventh century a
vast connexional system developed, each monastery forming
an extension of the Cluny principle and governed by a prior.
All the priors met at times in conference, under the presidency
of the one abbot.   In those days the influence and status of the
abbot were immense, and, as he moved about, he was followed
by a large retinue of servants.   Asceline ridicules the imposing
army of monks which followed Odilo in his journeys.   In these
earlier days, however, there was much more simplicity and
freedom.

The abbot was the head of the government.   He was second
only to God, his word and will were law, and he was responsible for the maintenance of discipline.   There was a severe
system of punishment for offences, including stripes, fastings,
and exclusion from church privileges.   Graver offences

demanded public penance, when the person in question, standing before the community, received the imposed penalty.

The prior was the viceroy of the abbot, acting for him in his absence (U. iii. 4). He was elected in the chapter by the abbot in council with his seniors, and his place was at the right hand of the abbot, whilst he had special authority over the deaneries. We also read of a cloistral prior, who was vicar of the great prior, and who went round the cloisters and reported to the chapter anything that he saw amiss. He also visited the kitchen and dormitory, and saw that all was well in the church. In the winter he made another visit between Nocturnes and Matins. Under him were *circatores*, whose duty was to note and report any neglect of monastic rules (U. iii. 7).

There were special rules for boys belonging to the school of the monastery and their masters. The boys were well provided with food and clothes, and had to attend the regular church services. For offences they were punished with stripes, and for such offences were expected to make confession to the abbot or prior. The masters had them in view continually. No boy could pass out of the dormitory at night without the presence of a master and another boy, or without a light (O. i. 33). Ulric says : ' Seeing with what zeal they are guarded night and day, I have said in my heart that it would be difficult for any son of a king in a palace to be nourished with greater care than the humblest boy in Cluny ' (U. iii. 18). In spite of this eulogy and the special care shown towards sick boys, the boys were obviously subject to a most rigorous discipline, even espionage, which left little room for freedom, initiative, and real happiness. The hard theological dogma of original sin left its mark on education till quite recent times. These boys had been devoted to the monastery by pious friends and parents according to an old custom, e.g. William of Dijon, Abbo, and Odo.

The estates of Cluny were divided into deaneries, over which monks called ' Deans ' had control. These deans had servants who worked for them in the fields, for they took responsibility for the cultivation of the fields and vineyards, and also the care of sheep and cattle. The dean made his report to the prior, who visited the estate at harvest and vintage.

The Chamberlain (Camerarius) was the chief buyer for the monastery, and gave all gifts received from estates to those directly concerned, hangings and vessels to the sacrist, money to the cellarer for food and to the guesthouse. He had to provide clothes and bedding for the monks out of his resources, and there were careful arrangements made for the washing and mending of the clothes.

The Apocrisarius was the official who guarded the treasury of the church, and in his hands was placed anything offered by the people to the altar (U. iii. 1). He had the keys of the church, was responsible for its lighting at service time, and for the necessary church furniture. In order that his resources should not fail he possessed certain villas, with tithes of vines and fields. He sounded the gong for the Hours, lighted the candles in the church, gave candles also to the infirmary, guest-chambers, and refectory.

The Cellarer had charge of the food arrangements, and, under him (U. ii. 18), there were keepers of the granary, who gave him information as to available grain, the gardener, (U. iii. 20) and the bakers. Benedict had allowed considerable discretion in eating and drinking, increased the allowance for special work, and allowed a special diet for the sick. A meat diet had been rejected by Odo (O. 33), but meat had in certain cases been allowed by Benedict and was apparently given to the sick in Ulric's time (U. iii. 27). The usual allowance of food was one pound of bread a day ; but, if the monk were to eat his pound for dinner, he was allowed another half-pound for supper (U. iii. 21). Benedict had allowed a pint of wine, and each monk received his portion according to rule from another helper of the cellarer called the keeper of the wine. Dinner consisted of three courses. The first consisted of dried beans, the second course was cooked by servants in the kitchen, and on Sundays and Thursdays it consisted of fish, and on other days of eggs or cheese, four or five eggs being allowed to each monk (U. iii. 18). The third course, prepared by the monks themselves, consisted of vegetables from the garden. The cellarer had charge of the sheep-folds, piggeries, and the fisheries (U. iii. 18), and he had lands near Cluny where he grazed horses, and waters in which he set nets for fish. On special feast days, onions, spiced wine, and cakes were substituted for beans. Two meals were provided, at midday and about 5 p.m., but in Lent only the midday meal was allowed.

The infirmary stood close to the Church of St. Mary, and the chief official was called the Infirmarius. He drew his supplies from the cellarer or money from the chamberlain, and had under him a cook and three other servants. The *infirmàrius* kept ginger and cinnamon, candles, fruits and pepper, for emergencies, and in case of sudden illness was able to supply special spiced wine.

The monks, if well enough, were expected to attend service at church. It was customary to sprinkle the beds daily with holy water.

The Almoner, or the Guestmaster, was a very important official. He had charge of hospitality and charity arrangements, which formed a marked feature of Benedict's original scheme. Cluny was not only a place of worship and meditation, but also of hospitality. The almoner had consequently a certain allowance for this purpose. He drew thirty portions of food and wine for thirty days in case of a monk's death, also two extra portions if the news of death had been delayed, and, on the anniversary of the death of a brother, he drew a monk's full allowance. Portions in memory of kings and princes were added at a later period, and half of what was left by the monks in the refectory, beans, fish, eggs, as the case might be, were appropriated for the almoner's use. For every pilgrim, one pound of bread was given the first day, and half a pound the second, and also half a monk's measure of wine daily. To nuns at the gate he gave a pound of bread and wine. Pilgrims and travellers ate together in the guesthouse, but if the pilgrim had a tired or sick wife in the town, she also received help. Pilgrims who were monks were allowed to dine in the refectory, but laymen remained at the guesthouse. Each day the guestmaster received from the keeper of the granary twelve tarts of three pounds' weight for orphans, widows, and the sick. Once a week he went round the town with a servant carrying provisions, and, if it was a case of a sick woman, he sent his servant into the house with the allowance whilst he remained outside (U. iii. 24).

In the guesthouse eighteen pensioners lived, who had special allowances. There were five servants employed. There were special charities also. On the first Sunday in Lent the chamberlain provided salt pork for all the poor who came. Ulric says that in one year 250 hogs were divided among 17,000 poor

(U. iii. 11), and that on the feast of Trinity twelve poor men were fed with bread, meat, and wine (U. i. 26).

The Constable (Constabulus) not only looked after the horses belonging to the monastery, but also the horses of the guests (U. iii. 23), and he provided horseshoes and barley and oats for the horses.

Another official was called the Precentor, or Armarius, and he obtained his name because in his hands were placed the service books, called the *armaria* (U. iii. 10). He had charge of the singing arrangements, which included the responses in the refectory as well as in the church. He also carried sacramental elements to sick or dying monks, and under him was one who taught singing to the boys.

The dying monks were specially provided for. They confessed to the abbot or prior, and then were carried into the chapter, where they confessed. Whilst the prior invoked absolution, they suitably replied with ' Amen.' Then the dying monks were carried back to their beds. The priests anointed them with oil, making the sign of the Cross, and administered the sacraments, using bread dipped in wine, whilst the dying monks kissed the crosses which were placed on their faces during the night. Candles burned through the night, and the Hours were chanted, and at last the monks, lying on ashes, passed away in the presence of their brethren, who had been summoned by the sounding of bells. The funeral arrangements included anointing the body with holy water and incense, and there were special Masses for the dead and special gifts for the poor in the guesthouse.

Other customs to be briefly noted were solemn processions, the daily Masses for living and dead, the frequent or daily confession of sins, the reception of relics with songs of praise, the special processions at stated seasons, the use of holy water. Lay brothers (Conversi) served the monks in the monastery in various capacities, and had their own rules of discipline.

Benedict had emphasized the necessity of manual labour. As the monastery grew, the actual manual work of agriculture on the estate fell more and more to lay servants and serfs, of whom we read so much in charters. But the idea of the worth of labour, which did so much in the early days to improve land and reclaim the fen, was not lost, though the actual manual labour in Ulric's time consisted in little more than shelling beans, plucking weeds and useless herbs out of the garden, and making bread in the bakery (U. i. 30). Nevertheless, the monks retained an interest in agriculture.

Benedict had found a place for culture in his scheme. Reference is made in his rule to special times for reading and the use of books out of a library. We know that Cluny had its library, for Maiolus once held the office of librarian. The abbots were famous for their love of reading and they were cultured men. There was a weekly reader who read to the monks at table (U. i. 30), we read of monks who retired quietly with a book to the cloister (U. ii. 24), and we know that the Fathers were closely studied (U. i. 1). Secular literature was not altogether abandoned, for Maiolus, whilst resisting the ' lies of Virgil,' did not refuse philosophy, but simply exercised discretion in the use of it. There was evidently a school for boys at Cluny, of which Odo was once master (O. i. 23, 30). The tradition of learning was thus maintained, and Cluny, with its ideal of manual and intellectual labour, thus formed a splendid contrast to that world outside devastated by war. Here in this return to quiet, peaceful study, the healthy exercise of the field, the harmony of organized government, the fellowship of a common life, and the beauty and peace of the sanctuary, Cluny was pointing, not backwards, but forwards. It was, in fact, laying the foundations of a better social order, where peace is loved better than war, and where life is a partnership of services and of worship.

It was not an unworthy endeavour to introduce the Kingdom of God into the life of the world. We notice throughout a certain moderation in the whole institution as compared with other forms of ascetic life, and in this it was but following out the teaching of Benedict himself, who, whilst emphasizing certain principles of obedience and the common life, allowed some discretion in detailed application. The whole system was constitutional, and, powerful though the abbot might be, he was as much bound by the rules as the humblest monk. Stern though the discipline was, it was the discipline of a home, where the abbot was the father and the monks brethren. The long list of duties, such as loving God with all the heart, respecting all men, clothing the naked, and loving one's enemy, speaking ill of none, hating no one, and returning good for evil, and never despairing of God's mercy, show how

completely Benedict entered into the spirit of the Sermon on
the Mount.   Whilst these maxims show the essential Christian
mind, the regulations, the reasoned uniformity, and the
supremacy of law, reveal the presence of the Latin mind.
Benedict was a product of the latinized Christian mind.

VI. We have thus seen that the reform movements consisted
largely in the substitution of monk for secular and the extension
of Benedictine ideals and practice in the Church.

The weakness of monasticism, at Cluny and elsewhere, is
obvious enough.   Its discipline and piety were too rigid,
external, and uniform, and its obedience too abject.   It was
founded upon an unnatural separation of the sexes.   It was
too introspective and too far removed from the ordinary
relationships of life.   Yet, within limits, monasticism offered
a noble witness to certain truths.

It broke with nationalism, and stood for an international
brotherhood of monks.   It broke with caste, and took peasant
and noble alike into its fellowship.   It broke with unrestricted
individualism which used the word ' my,' and held forth a
type of socialism which spoke of ' ours.'

Now the monks were originally solitaries, turning from the
organized Church to find God in lonely communion, and, even
when the solitary became a coenobite, a type of personal
individualism was preserved. The monk entered the monastery
by his own acceptance of the vows of his order.   He confessed
his own sins, sought a remedy for his own soul's ills, and, in
contemplation and introspection, found God for himself, and
his own way to heaven.   The moral and religious responsibility
of the individual is here recognized.   But the monks were
nevertheless socialists.   They grasped the idea that no man
can, or ought to try, to live alone or for himself.   Each man
was to surrender his own possessions, so that he possessed only
in common with others.   Each monk was to find himself in
accepting the will of the community, and to realize life's
significance by cultivating loyalty to that which was higher
and bigger than himself.   Self-denial, sacrifice, discipline, and
law were to be substituted for self-indulgence, self-assertion,
comfort, and licence.   They recognized the fact that life must
be both individual and social, and that individualism and
socialism can be transcended by a higher synthesis of love and
loyalty.   Above all it placed the Church in the midst, for the

monastery existed for the Church, and the Church stood for the highest loyalties. The Church in the midst was a declaration that all the loyalties that make life sweet and strong must presuppose a higher loyalty to God, that all authority and discipline must presuppose the sanction of a divine law, that the fellowship which is to endure must be related to fellowship with God, and that, for the perfecting of society here, there must be a contact with the realities of the spiritual and unseen.

In this, monasticism, within serious limits of course, pointed the way to the Kingdom of God, as the establishment of the divine order of love and service in the world. At its best, it represented Puritanism in its moral discipline, and Mysticism in its silent meditation and intense religious experience. Oliver Cromwell and George Fox could have found points of contact with these early Cluny saints.

N

VIII

LIFE AND CHARACTER OF MAIOLUS

Note
   E. = Eudes's Life of Burchard.
   O. = Odilo's Life.
   S. = Syrus's Life.

THE greatest and most influential figure in the Europe of the tenth century was not the Emperor Otho, nor the King of France, nor the Pope, but Maiolus, and his greatness was not achieved by diplomacy and military success, but by the compelling power of sheer goodness. France, Burgundy, Italy, and Germany looked to him for inspiration and guidance ; kings and emperors sought his advice and humbled themselves before him ; and the weakest peasant did not appeal to him in vain. He was a great saint, and won his way to the conscience and heart of the feudal world. Fortunately we are not without trustworthy information about his life. Two biographies, written by the monk Syrus and his successor Odilo, give us almost contemporary evidence. The letters of Gerbert also refer to him, whilst the later writings of R. Glaber (Migne 142), the Life of Burchard by Eudes or Odo of St. Maur, and the Chronicles of Dijon (Migne 160), give supplementary evidence of considerable value. Though there is an exaggeration, possibly, in the glowing panegyric of Odilo, there shines through every page of these biographies the pure, clear light of sanctity, and one feels the heart-throb of a great passion of love. The abbots of Rheims called him ' star most brilliant ' (G. 95), and his biographers discovered in him the four cardinal virtues and the fulfilment of the Sermon on the Mount. He lived in a stirring time, and saw a change of dynasty in France and the reign of three emperors in Germany.

   The date of his birth is unknown, but he came of an old

Provençal family of noble blood, and his native city was Avignon. His father's name was Fulcher and his mother's Raimondis. His father was wealthy, for we learn that he bestowed large estates on his wife at marriage, including villas and churches at Aix, Sisteron, Apt, Riez—in all, one hundred manors and thirty serfs. There were two sons, Maiolus and Cynricus. Maiolus may have been the younger, but his future greatness was foretold, and his parents destined him for a literary career and the Church. His name means *Magnus Oculus*, and the significance of the name was not lost on Syrus. He preserved unsullied chastity during the perilous times of adolescence, and showed early indications of piety, but sad experiences tested his faith.

He lost his parents while still young, and the ancestral possessions were devastated by barbarian invaders. Compelled to leave Provence, he came to Mâcon, where apparently one of the chief men of the city was related to him and was prepared to befriend him. He remained at Mâcon for some time, and gave himself up to literary pursuits, to the study of the Latin classics. His reputation became so well established that the bishop wished him to join the College of Canons, but he was desirous of further study, and proceeded to Lyons, described as ' The Mother of all Gaul, nourisher of philosophy, excelling all towns far and near in opportunities for the study of the liberal arts and religious culture.' The scholar to whom he committed himself was one Anthony, a learned and prudent teacher, and from him he received a training in philosophy, whilst he kept himself from vice and lived as if already a monk. He returned to Mâcon, and his piety became known to the Church authorities. Having been ordained a priest, he was, at the express wish of the bishop and citizens, made archdeacon, which position carried responsibilities in matters of discipline and brought him into close relation with the bishop.

He sought to make himself useful, and gathered round him clergy from different parts and taught them free of charge. His love for the poor was particularly noticeable, and, in time of famine caused by the devastating wars which were so prevalent, many came to him for help. His sympathies were strong, but he had not always the resources out of which he could meet the demand. One day, as he prayed to God, he saw seven solidi lying on the ground before him, which fact was

to him a direct answer to prayer, and to those who heard the
story a miracle. He gave the money for the relief of distress.
In every respect he sought to be an example and a true apostle,
whilst his love of the monastic life had led him to seek retirement in a certain solitary oratory of St. Michael, where he
often prayed and found the consolations of silence.

Meanwhile, the archbishopric of Besançon fell vacant, and
Maiolus was invited by the clergy and people and the local
patron to fill this important see, but he declined. The simple
monastic life was a greater attraction to him than all the
secular pomp and splendour of such a see. The life of a monk
surpassed in religious value the life of a secular churchman.
Here we distinguish that trait of humility so noticeable in
these early Abbots of Cluny. As Syrus put it, ' Following the
example of Jesus, he withdrew from the multitude to pray.'
He began to think seriously of entering Cluny. He had often
visited it, and was well known to the monks, who earnestly
invited him to take the necessary vows and share their
life.

Aymard was abbot at this time. Maiolus asked permission
to enter, and this was easily obtained. ' The grace of God
generated in him a contempt of the world. He spurned worldly
nobility, left behind the society of friends and relatives, and
chose to serve Christ as King, submitting himself wholly to the
heavenly Teacher ' (O.). His humility and obedience were
most marked. He learned the rule of Benedict, and devoted
himself wholly to its practice, and, from being a Doctor of
Grammar, he became the disciple of simple men (S.). Aymard
was attracted to him, and appointed him *apocrisarius* and
librarian. Maiolus was ever studious, and loved books, but
we are given to understand that he turned away from ' the
lies of Virgil ' and the vanities of philosophy to seek heavenly
knowledge and the word of God. Syrus tells us, however, that
he did not break completely with secular subjects, but, reading
intelligently, simply retained what he found useful and threw
away what he regarded as superfluous, making the Scriptures
in every respect the supreme authority. In other words, he
did not reject his former literary and philosophical studies,
but read them in the light of the Bible and the Church, and
interpreted accordingly.

He had been nine years a monk when Aymard, growing

blind and ill and very weary, called the brethren together and bade them choose a successor. He suggested to them Maiolus, who, however, hesitated, preferring the privilege of obedience to the responsibility of authority. The abbot insisted, and the monks were unanimous in their decision. Three days passed, and the monks earnestly prayed that he might be induced to accept. At last he had a vision of St. Benedict, who said to him : ' You are secure by divine help, which will not fail you, so do not hesitate to undertake the duty.' Therefore, throwing his care on the Lord and surrendering his will to God, he prostrated himself before the brethren, beseeching them not to regard his obstinacy, but remember his inability and his fear of so great a care. ' If you had only known me you would never have compelled me to this office, but I cannot refuse. I am changed by your unchanging judgement ' (S.). So he was elected at last, and led by the aged abbot to the abbot's throne, whilst all rejoiced.

This occurred in 954, and he seems to have acted as coadjutor with ever-increasing power until Aymard's death about 965. The life he now began to live was a very busy one, and, though harassed by many cares, his influence became very great. He visited Italy, and at Pavia he met the Emperor Otho I and the Empress Adelaide, and he was asked to undertake the reformation of numerous monasteries in Italy, such as St. Saviour's of Pavia, and St. Apollonaris, near Ravenna. Conrad, the king of Burgundy, was devoted to him, and Maiolus received from him St. Amandus, St. Paul-Trois-Châteaux. Lothaire confirmed this gift in 960 (Dip. 2), and in 964 Maiolus received Peterlingen in the Juras, founded by Queen Bertha of Burgundy and completed by her daughter, the Empress Adelaide.

The Othos were his constant friends, and he acted frequently as an intermediary between them and those seeking their patronage. One day, returning to Cluny, he said : ' Last night as I slept I saw a mighty lion in a cage, and it burst through the cage. Of a surety Otho I will die.' Soon after there arrived the news of the old Emperor's death.

Otho II continued to favour him, and he is said to have offered him the Papacy—probably in 974, after the death of Boniface II. This story is only told by Syrus, but its truth need not be doubted, because such action on the part of Otho II was such as might have been expected.   But Maiolus refused, giving as his reasons: (1) He had not the qualities for such an honour ; (2) He was unwilling to forsake Cluny ; (3) He and the Romans could not find moral unity.   These reasons show us that Maiolus knew only too well the corruption of the Papacy, and evidently he regarded such elevation, not only as the choice of a lower religious ideal, but as a veritable peril for his soul.   To leave Cluny for Rome would seem to him like going back into the world.   At the same time, by one of those contradictions so strangely prominent in the Middle Ages, Maiolus continued to view with great respect the ancient see of St. Peter, and sought from the Pope various immunities, which were readily granted.   Cluny reverenced the Papacy just because Rome was the premier see of Christendom, being the Imperial city and the throne of St. Peter, but Cluny had no misgivings in regard to the actual character of individual Popes, and the perils of their situation.   Maiolus paid more than one visit to Rome, but his character was a standing rebuke to the character of the Popes.   No wonder he felt himself out of sympathy with Rome in regard to morals. Incidentally this story shows us the measure of Imperial interference in the Papal election.

About this time there was trouble between Otho II and his mother Adelaide, possibly caused by the Empress Theophania, who was always jealous of her mother-in-law's influence. Adelaide, unjustly charged with conspiracy against the authority of her son, fled to the court of her brother, Conrad of Burgundy.   Some have thought that this family quarrel gave Lothaire and Emma a pretext for their attack on Otho and Theophania, but there is no actual proof of this.   Many who had received generous treatment from Adelaide refused now to speak for her, and there seemed no way of bridging the gulf between mother and son, until at last Maiolus intervened. He possessed the confidence of both parties in the dispute, and, believing the Emperor was in the wrong, he was not afraid to risk his displeasure by boldly denouncing his unfilial conduct.   He met the Emperor at Pavia, warned him of divine displeasure, and conjured him by the example of Jesus to show respect to his mother.   His appeals were not delivered in vain, for Otho, learning that there was no truth in the charges made, threw himself at his mother's feet, asked forgiveness, and the reconciliation was complete.

Maiolus strongly dissuaded Otho II from his Italian wars. At Verona, taking Otho's hands into his own and looking him straight in the face, he said: 'Open thine ears to the counsels of Brother Maiolus, and return whence thou camest, for know surely, if thou goest to Rome, thou wilt never see another Christmas, but in Rome find thy grave.' His admirers noted that his prediction concerning the death of Otho II was as true as his prediction concerning Otho I. Otho II was defeated in battle by the Greeks and Saracens in Calabria, 982. He died of disappointment and grief at Rome, December 7, 983, at the early age of twenty-eight. His plans had miscarried and his heart was broken. His wife, the Greek Theophania, had not concealed her joy at the victory of the Greeks, and this fact had added to his troubles.

As we have seen, Maiolus had no illusions about the character of the Pope, but, as Cluny was under Papal protection, and respect for the Papal see was always considered as something apart from respect for the individual Pope, he had to make official visits to Rome. It was whilst returning from one of these journeys that his companion Hildric fell ill. Maiolus, full of anxiety, prayed for his friend's recovery. The illness was serious enough, but one in white reminded him of James's advice to anoint the sick with oil (Jas. vi. 4). As soon as Matins were over, he poured oil on the sick man, and he was healed. The incident redounded to the honour of Maiolus, whatever the ultimate explanation may be. This visit to Rome seems to have preceded his entrance upon his duties as abbot. In his first visit in the capacity of abbot, 967, he repaired and reformed the Church of St. Paul, from which the supposed ashes of Paul and Peter were sent to Cluny for safety.

On another occasion, returning from Italy, he was attacked in the mountains by the Saracens. These people had ravaged the coasts of southern France and Italy from their base in Africa. In 810 they ravaged Nice, in 838 they arrived at Marseilles, and in 846 they appeared in the Cannes neighbourhood, occupied the mountainous district to the north, and established themselves at Fraxinet, from which place they raided the towns of Provence and interfered with travellers from France to Italy. The date of this attack on Maiolus is

uncertain, but it occurred in the earlier days of his reign at
Cluny. He was accompanied by monks and clergy, and, as
he was crossing the Alps, the Saracens attacked him from
the heights. The monks fled and were pursued. Maiolus
remained with his companions, and was taken prisoner as he
sat, wounded in the hand, upon a stone. He was put in chains
and imprisoned in a cave. The Saracens demanded a ransom.
He said he had nothing to give, but he had friends at Cluny,
who would pay a ransom price for him. He was allowed to
send messengers to Cluny, and, according to R. Glaber (i. 4.),
the import of the message was : ' The sons of Belial have
encompassed me, the snares of death have taken hold upon
me. If it please you, send a redemption price for me, and
those with me.' Meanwhile he had managed to save the book
of St. Jerome on the Assumption (S.) under his clothes. He,
remembering that there were twenty-four days before the
festival, asked the Mother of the Lord to obtain from her Son
his release by that day, and then he slept for grief. When he
awoke, he found to his astonishment that the fetters were
loose, and he took this as a sign of coming liberty. He is
said to have taught the Saracens the superiority of Christianity
to Mohammedanism by pointing out from the Bible that the
real succession was in Isaac, not Ishmael. Miracles were
wrought. A man treading on the Bible was immediately
struck by the divine displeasure, and the Saracens were duly
impressed. The saint endured with patience the hardships
of captivity, counting it a privilege to be a confessor of Christ.
In due time the ransom price, raised by the distressed monks at
Cluny, secured his release and the release of his followers, and
he returned in safety to the monastery. The Saracens were
completely defeated by William, Count of Provence, in a great
battle at Fraxinet, and the hundred years' occupation of the
Alps by the Saracens was brought to an end. The Chronicles
write with relish of the thousands who, trapped in the mountain,
sought death by throwing themselves from the heights. The
victory was popularly believed to be due to the merits of
Maiolus, and a judgement on the Saracens for having detained
so great a saint.

This Count William greatly loved Maiolus, and it is said that,
when he knew death was drawing near, he summoned the saint
to Avignon, where he lived. To avoid popular demonstration,

the interview was held on an island in the Rhone, but many attempting to cross in boats were shipwrecked. However, through the merits of Maiolus, according to the story, all reached the shore in safety, being gently carried there by the waves (S.), and certain loaves were taken out of the water unharmed. These stories show the immense impression Maiolus made upon the people of his time.

In the late years of his life there is the case of Fleury referred to in Gerbert's letters (80, 86, 87, 88, 95, 142, 143). This royal abbey craved to possess the bones of Benedict. It had been reformed by Odo, but, once reformed, resumed its independent course. A certain Oidbold had been nominated to the abbey by Lothaire, and, in spite of a tribute from Aimon, he seems to have been a man of doubtful character. Gerbert calls him ' a man of perfidy and infamy.' Whatever his character was in reality, Gerbert and Adalberon of Rheims called upon Maiolus to ' heal the contagion of an alien flock.' ' If you are silent, who will speak ? ' Maiolus replied with the restrained refusal to interfere in the affairs of another monastery, and, whilst he condemned the conduct of the man in question, he did not apparently withdraw from all fellowship with him. Adalberon wrote (G. 87) and strongly condemned Maiolus, arguing that the Church was one throughout the world, and that the affairs of Fleury really concerned both Rheims and Cluny. He tried to involve the abbot in inconsistency. ' You condemn him, then why communicate ? You speak magnificently against the usurper, but what is the good of talking without doing ? ' and he finished this heated letter by urging Maiolus to break off all relations. Such action would bring the weight of his great influence against the usurper, and Adalberon would be only too glad to follow such a leader as Maiolus in such a cause. Maiolus did not change his ground. He condemned the unworthy abbot, whose infamy he had known previous to his election, and he promised to warn the people against him and to stand aloof himself ; but he refused to intervene actively in the affairs of a monastery outside the jurisdiction of Cluny. A letter of the abbots of Rheims to the brothers at Fleury expressed sympathy with them, and made reference to the judgements pronounced on their abbot by Maiolus, whom they termed ' the most brilliant star.' This letter quotes from Maiolus's letter to Adalberon, and proceeds : ' Withdraw yourselves, O sheep of Christ, from him who is no shepherd, but a wolf ravening the sheep. He has not blushed to thrust himself forward. Let him boast that, by the favour of kings, princes, and dukes, he is set over monks, but, condemned by two such Fathers as Maiolus and Edward (of Tours), he is cut off from our fellowship.' Nothing further seems to have occurred, and Oidbold enjoyed his position till his death two years later, in 988, when Gerbert (143) wrote with joy of his death, ' which is for the safety of many.'

The whole incident has an interest of its own. It shows the possibility of corruption through the abuse of royal nomination. It shows the independent relation in which Cluny stands to Fleury. Above all, there is a revelation of the respect in which Maiolus was held by such men as Adalberon and Gerbert. If only he could be induced to condemn, all would be well. Then the moderation of the abbot, his gentleness and prudence, stand out in marked contrast to the passion and bluster of Gerbert and Adalberon. Maiolus knew his own powers, and was not prepared to go beyond the limits set by these powers. Fleury was a royal appointment, and it seems clear that the King and many of the monks had approved of the election. Maiolus did not feel the occasion warranted a challenge to the ancient rights of the King to choose the abbot in conjunction with the monks. The election of Abbo with the King's consent brought the controversy to an end.

The incident shows the wise discretion of Maiolus. The time for an attack on royal nomination was not yet, and Cluny held a high view of the royal prerogative, as also did Fleury. It may be said that this policy indicated lack of courage, but it must be remembered that the kings and many of the principal lords were willing to further reform. This being the case, Maiolus may well have thought that the well-being of the Church would be best served by co-operating with such rulers. A premature assertion of the rights of the Church as against the King's nomination might have proved disastrous to both Church and State. Apart from all this, Maiolus's natural humility prevented him from assuming authority over a brother abbot, and we must remember that the references of Abbo and Aimon to Oidbold suggest that Gerbert's statements only represent one aspect of the case.

Maiolus was called in for advice in another direction. Bruno, the saintly Bishop of Langres, favoured the monks, and was enthusiastic for reform. The deplorable condition of the church of St. Benignus of Dijon shocked the Bishop. His policy was to introduce discipline and piety where there was laxity and corruption, and this meant the removal of the worldly Abbot Manasses and the introduction of monks who would be prepared to live holy lives. At first he secured the services of Azo of Deventer, but after two years this monk returned to his own people, and Manasses was once more in possession. Bruno appealed to Maiolus.

Now, Maiolus had but recently called at the monastery of St. Michael at Locedia, in North Italy. Here he had met a young man, William, who, born of a noble Lombard family, had been committed to the care of the Church at an early age by his pious parents. He grew up in the monastery and gained reputation as a scholar. He studied at Ticinum and Vercelli, and became a teacher in the monastic school. When asked to become deacon by the Bishop of Vercelli, he refused to render homage to the Bishop, protesting against the feudal obligation which it seemed to suggest. He mourned the decay of religious life at Locedia, and sought opportunity for severer discipline in the monastery of St. Michael the Archangel, high up in the Alps. He returned to Locedia, and there continued his duty as a teacher of music and grammar.

It was at this stage that Maiolus arrived *en route* for Rome. His wise insight soon perceived the earnestness of the young man, and they had heart-to-heart conversations. Maiolus gave him time for thought, and promised to call again on his return from Rome, but William considered the question of becoming a monk, and, though he had to face the claims of kith and kin, his hereditary lands and the attraction of his native soil, he determined to commit himself solely to God. When Maiolus returned, he found William fully prepared for life at Cluny ; and, receiving him into spiritual sonship, led him to Cluny, where a suitable welcome was given to him by the monks, prepared for his coming. He lived there for a year, and was then judged worthy of the priesthood, but he pleaded his limitations, and the matter was allowed to rest for a time. The abbot and the new recruit were drawn to each other by common sympathies, and, when certain brethren from St. Saturninus, beyond the Rhone, asked for a leader in

the way of salvation, William was chosen. He taught them
a uniform way of singing and praying in the Cluny manner,
and urged the grace of charity.

Then the request of Bruno reached the ears of Maiolus.
Who better able to deal with the situation at Dijon than
William ? So, with twelve monks he was sent to Dijon to
further the reforms dear to the heart of the Bishop. Bruno
ordained him priest, and secured for him election as Abbot
of St. Benignus in 990, which post he held till his death in
1031. This appointment was only the beginning of a great
work, for he travelled throughout France and northern
Italy, reforming decayed and decaying monasteries like
Vezelay, Besua, Fécamp, St. Germains of Paris, St. Favon
of Milum, St. Aprus of Toul. He also founded a monastery
on his ancestral land at Fructuare, in Lombardy. In each
of these monasteries he introduced the strict discipline of
St. Benedict as interpreted by Cluny. At Fécamp he opened
a school for the study of the divine offices, and himself taught
there without charge. He also established an important
school at Dijon, where he rebuilt magnificently the Church of
St. Benignus in the form of a T, into which he transferred the
bones of the saint, discovered through a dream. He rebuked
the Pope, and called on him to restore discipline, saying :
' If the sources are tepid, will the flow of the stream increase
in warmth ? ' He defended the claims of the Church of the
West against the East. He was not afraid to rebuke the
passion and rage of the French King Robert, and to call to
mind his unfilial conduct towards his father. Throughout,
his relations with Bruno were always happy and friendly, and
Bruno generously supported him, committing monasteries
of his diocese to his care, and earning for himself the title
of ' Father of Monks.' Adalberon of Metz and Bertold of
Toul were among the prelates of Lorraine who sought the help
of his reforming zeal. It is said that William brought new life
to over forty monasteries, and ruled 1,200 brethren. He was
a scholar who loved the music of the Church. His dress was
simple and his food frugal. He condemned unsparingly
new extravagance in dress brought from Aquitaine by Queen
Constance, and rebuked the pride of the clergy. He felt
instinctively his own sins, and mourned over them, but he
believed no crimes could outbalance the gifts of mercy secured

by the Cross of Christ, if there was faith enough to receive them.   He died while visiting Fécamp in 1031, having gained an international reputation.

The tendency of his piety was towards a too rigid asceticism, and he was once warned in a dream by St. Gregory against undue severity to his monks ; but he was a great preacher, seeking to draw men by persuasion from the evils of the world, whilst he himself panted for the heavenly kingdom and sought to bring all men with him to that desired goal.   He was called ' Father William ' by the many spiritual sons whom he loved.   We have dwelt upon this life to show the type of men whom Maiolus introduced into the work of reforming monasteries.

Another incident in the life and work of Maiolus is related in the Life of Count Burchard.   The monastery of St. Maur du Fosse was a royal abbey controlled by Hugh Capet.   Maginard, the nominal abbot, was of noble birth, but he lived a secular life, devoted to the chase, and, when he went forth to hunt, he used to clothe himself in rich garments, divesting himself of the monastic dress.   The example set by the leader proved attractive to the followers, and a general lack of discipline prevailed.   A hermit called Adacus, moved by this scandal, approached Burchard, one of the associates of the King, who was Count of Corbie, Milum, Vendôme, and royal Count of Paris.   This Count had recently married Elizabeth, widow of Eudes of Champagne, and both husband and wife sought to end the scandal of impiety in the monastery. Burchard promised the hermit sympathetic consideration, and then approached the King for the patronage of the abbey. The King hesitated, for it had long been a royal abbey, and he feared lest the successors of Burchard might deprive the monks of their rights, and thus bring a sin on the soul of the King.   The Count stated that he only wanted control for a time in order to restore discipline, and Hugh Capet, sincerely anxious for reform, yielded to his friend's persuasion.

The Count at once thought of Maiolus as the best exponent of reforming principles, and took a journey to Cluny, where he was received with becoming courtesy.   He threw himself on the ground before the saint, who naturally asked the reason for so long a journey.   Burchard, having explained the situation at St. Maur, said : ' I ask that it be restored by your help, so that the institutes of Benedict may be preserved. I want no help but yours.' Maiolus replied : ' Since there are several monasteries in your country, why not go to them ? For the journey to those regions, unknown to us and remote from us, is weary and long, and involves leaving our people, to seek yours.' The Count continued, however, until at last he conquered the abbot by his importunity. Arrangements were made by the Count for Maiolus to meet the Abbot of St. Maur and his monks by the River Marne. These were quite ignorant of the Count's intentions. When they reached the appointed place, they were told plainly by the Count that only those who obeyed Maiolus could return with him to the monastery, and that others were to be deprived of everything except the clothes they wore. Many refused to follow Maiolus and were expelled. Maginard, being of noble birth and a kinsman of Ansoald, a rich citizen of Paris, retired to St. Maur of Glenfuil, where he became abbot.

Maiolus at once began to impose discipline, but, realizing the poverty of the wasted monastery, asked the King for the increased endowment, and the King gave, at the request of the Count, a ville and churches between the Seine and the Marne (E. 4). Maiolus meditated a return to Cluny, and committed the care of the monastery to Teuton (E. 5), one of the Cluny monks. Robert, on his accession, gave the monastery definitely to Teuton, whilst Cluny sorrowed because the return of a brother was thus denied to them, and perhaps because Cluny's direct control was weakened by the King's influence. Teuton rebuilt the Church on a larger and grander scale, and gifts were bestowed by the Count and others. Teuton developed strong ascetic tendencies, and, intent on fasts and lonely vigils, he retired to a small possession near Rheims belonging to Du Fosse. He sent the insignia of office to one Walter (E. 8), whom he had trained, and asked the monks to elect him. He himself lived as a solitary, and, when at a later stage he desired to see the monks at Nogent-sur-Marne, they refused to see him, because he had suddenly left them, and because they now had another abbot. Teuton then returned to Cluny, where he survived his two immediate successors at St. Maur.

The King again intervened, and gave the monastery to Theobald, a step-son of Burchard. Royal influence had evidently triumphed over the pure Benedictine idea of a free election.   Perhaps in this case there is something more than appears on the surface.   Do we gather that both Maiolus and Teuton had striven for more freedom, and that their return to Cluny was due to the determination of the King and Count to have some say in the control of the monastery ?   If so, Maiolus and Cluny were not quite so unconcerned about royal interference as would sometimes appear.   There was certainly, however, no open breach, and the relations between him and Hugh Capet were friendly to the last.

Maiolus was also called in to reform the great monastery of Tours, and there is said to have been much feeling in Cluny when the monastery preferred to have its own abbot rather than a Cluny prior, but, as this story is not contemporaneous, it may be an ante-dating of later customs.   It also appears that Maiolus was approached by Duke Richard of Normandy in regard to the reforming of Fécamp, but, Maiolus being unwilling to attempt the reform without the fulfilment of conditions unacceptable to the Duke, this matter was left, as we have seen, to his illustrious disciple, William of Dijon. He restored St. Germain of Auxerre at the request of Duke Henry of Burgundy (G.P.A. 47), and left there Hildric.

Maiolus had grown old and infirm, and longed for the retirement in which he could enjoy his books.   Odilo, a descendant of an old family of Auvergne, had drifted to Cluny, and had won the love and confidence of Maiolus, who, feeling the infirmities of age, recommended him to the monks as his successor in the same way in which he had been recommended half a century before.   Two years before his death he retired to smaller monasteries, where he devoted himself to stimulating the faith of the brethren, whilst he himself gave himself up to God, and waited for the time when he could ' depart and be with Christ.'

Hugh Capet, who had learned something of his work at St. Maur, was desirous that a similar reformation should be accomplished at the Abbey of St. Denis, of which he was lay abbot.   The riotous Council of St. Denis shows there was abundant need of reform.   Maiolus was old and infirm, and in great need of rest, but he could not refuse this appeal, for he believed in honouring the King as well as obeying God. He started on his last journey, but he fell ill whilst passing through Avignon, and, though he struggled on to Savigny, he could get no farther, and he breathed his last in the Abbey of Savigny, surrounded by his monks.   To his sorrowing friends he said : ' You will have Jesus as your pastor and protector ' ; and he continued to repeat verses of Scripture and familiar psalms till the end came.   To one asking if he were in any pain he answered : ' There is no trouble, for all is quiet.'   He absolved and confirmed his monks, made the sign of the Cross with his right hand, and, with his eyes towards heaven and with joy on his face, he passed peacefully away in the eighty-fourth year of his age, in 994.   The King, hearing of his illness, hastened to his side, but arrived only in time for the funeral celebrations.   Cluny desired the body of one so holy, but Savigny claimed him, and there he remained, with the result that the little monastery became a famous shrine, where miracles were said to take place.

Throughout his life the influence, wealth, and power of Cluny had steadily grown.   He had enjoyed the favour of neighbouring kings and powerful dukes, and this meant endowments for his abbey.   Numerous bequests made by the Archbishop of Lyons, the Bishops of Maçon and Autun, and numerous clerics and laics, are recorded in 1,372 charters, which were issued during his rule.   The Popes were always friendly.   There is the letter of John XIII (967), commending Cluny to the protection of neighbouring bishops, including the Archbishops of Lyons, Vienne, Arles, Besançon.   Then Benedict VII issued a chart granting Lerins to the monastery in 978.   On the other hand, it cannot be denied that Maiolus did grant lands to laymen as *precaria*, which proved to be a dangerous precedent, though it did possibly secure at first the interest and protection of powerful barons.   But these privileged laymen often used the lands for their own selfish ends.   We also read of sales and exchanges of land, which show that there was a very secular side to the administration of those vast estates.   Even in the great days there were secular interests at work endangering the spiritual life of the monastery.

The character of Maiolus was a very noble one, even if we allow for the inevitable idealization of admiring biographers. There is a certain moderation about Maiolus which is in striking contrast to some forms of contemporary asceticism.   It is quite a mistake to suppose that Cluny stood for an excessive asceticism. Syrus tells us that there was nothing extreme about Maiolus. At the tables of the rich he drank what was placed before him. He adopted the middle course in dress, being neither too spruce nor too abject. He was moderate in fasting, and used discretion in food. He drank a little wine, and avoided public demonstration of ascetic discipline, lest he should get praise for it. In all these matters he ate and dressed so that the necessities of the body might be met. We find no self-torture, no pride in filth or rags, but the moderation suggestive of a trained and well-balanced mind. He was very generous, but in almsgiving there was no indiscriminate giving, for he gave according to the needs of the people.

His attitude to education provides another illustration of his moderation. He had been famous as a philosopher, and had taught in the schools, and, though later he abandoned the 'lies of Virgil,' he did not throw aside all literary pursuits. He was an inveterate reader, and, like John Wesley, whom in some respects he resembled, used to read as he travelled on horseback. We read of his sitting late at night reading Dionysius the Areopagite by the light of a candle till sleep overcame him. He was a great student of the Bible, the Fathers, and the Rule of Benedict, but he also used secular literature with discrimination. It is significant that he held the office of librarian before he became abbot. His moderation appeared again in his attitude to the secular authorities. He defended the autonomy of his monastery, and could rebuke kings and emperors, and defend against them the weak and helpless; but he honoured the King and showed reverence to the powers that ruled, and he certainly never took up the uncompromising attitude of Gregory VII and Thomas à Becket. He did not so much challenge the royal nomination as he sought to influence the kings towards reform. Yet, in emphasizing this moderation in matters of food, clothing, alms, politics, we must not therefore conclude that this was a cold nature, swayed by pure reason. On the contrary, it was an intense nature, with immense reserves of emotion and passion On the essentials of all true religion he was very earnest. He loved God with passion and renunciation. There were many things in which he could use discretion, but there were factors beyond the realm of compromise, and the secret of his power

O

is discovered in the depth of his religious feeling and the reality of his love to God.

There were tears in his life. He wept as he read of the saints and meditated at the holy places. He wept for his own sins, and often professed himself the greatest sinner. Like another Isaiah, he saw himself in the light of the holiness of God. He suffered intensely for the wrongs of the poor, for, ' afflicted by the calamities of the poor, he groaned at the iniquities of evil men.' There was much to excite his pity in those wild days. We hear of his pouring out his soul in prayer for the people in time of famine, and the money which he obtained he gave freely to feed the starving. Syrus tells us that, in journeying, he loved to find secret places remote from men and near to God, and there he used to weep till the ground near him was wet with his tears.

But, though he possessed the grace of tears, there was a rich joy in his life, for he rejoiced with all who rejoiced, and his arrival in a certain town was once the cause of riotous joy. There was laughter in the monastery, and Odilo refers to his happy face, and describes him as dignified in bearing, cheerful in manner, with face serene like an angel. He possessed a voice of rich tone and the gift of eloquent speech. Every movement was graceful, for to Odilo he seemed to be of all mortals the most beautiful.

After all, it was the gentleness and kindness of his character which most arrested the attention of the age, for he was so unlike the proud baron who ruled by force. ' Beloved by God and man, he studied to please men that he might not be displeasing to God, and to please God that he might be useful to men,' so clearly did he perceive the connexion between the love of God and the service of men. Almsgiving and prayers were not just endeavours to secure the salvation of his own soul, but the overflow of a great heart which sympathized with the people because they were God's people and his brethren.

Odilo says the Sermon on the Mount was lived by him, and unquestionably, as his love flowed out on the world, something like the fulfilment of our Lord's precepts came to view. On a journey he took off his cloak and wrapped it round the shoulders of a poor man who was without one.

Odilo extols his prudence, temperance, fortitude, justice,

his patience in adversity, his humility in prosperity, and his devoted love of the saints. He delights to see in him the true leader, fighting the good fight, holding fast the faith, and running faithfully the race of life.

To Syrus he possessed all the virtues. The root of all is the love which radiated from his nature, the streaming light of pity, gentleness, and grace, enlightening the darkness of the Dark Ages. He never allowed his busy life and the multitudinous cares of his extensive pastorate or his relations with kings and princes to rob him of his quiet times with God. ' I have loved Thy house,' said the dying saint. ' Who will help us ? ' was the agonized cry of his monks. ' Christ is your protector,' was his triumphant reply, and in that sentence lies the significance of his faith. He restored peace to the Church, reconciled kings and princes, maintained the observance of rules, delivered men from the power of the devil, and raised those dead in sin to life.

They said he performed miracles, healed the sick, and foretold events. They said that, while in Pavia with Gerard, the Bishop of Toul, water was changed into wine for his sake. Much of this is due to the fervent imagination of credulous admirers. At the same time, we can well believe that in his many wanderings he had picked up much medical knowledge ; that he had singular knowledge of human nature in its motives and purposes, together with psychic gifts ; that he had influence with the rich and strong, who could help him materially out of their resources ; that he was a careful observer of the world's life, could read the possibilities of a situation, and see the inevitable trend of events ; above all, that he had great power with God in prayer, and in faith had access to all the resources of the spiritual world. Such a man would inevitably gain reputation as a worker of miracles. His biographer well says that as the mind is greater than the body, so it is a greater thing to raise one spiritually dead than one physically dead.

The charm and grandeur of his life consisted in the supremacy of love. He left behind him the society of the world, friends and relatives, to serve King Christ, and submitted himself wholly to the Heavenly Teacher. And so he renewed the religious life of three countries, and threw across the dark background of the feudal age the light of a saintly life. No wonder that men honoured and loved him. They thought the water in which he washed had healing powers. They brought their sick to him for healing. They believed in him, and he led them to believe in God. We may smile at the beliefs of that age, we may say it was a credulous age, but it was one which could appreciate the purity and tenderness of one of Christ's saints. There is sufficient evidence, in spite of all idealization, that Maiolus, who so impressed his age, is worthy of the appreciation of a later age. He was a man who loved God, and found that loving service for his fellow men was the truest expression of his love to God, and he sought to enshrine his ideal in the ordered fellowship of the common life.

IX

THE CHURCH AND THE FEUDAL STATE

Note

A.	=	Abbo.
Ad.	=	Adhemar.
B.	=	Burchard.
Dip.	=	Actes of Lothaire.
Fl.	=	Flodoard.
G.	=	Gerbert.
G.P.C.	=	Gesta Ep. Com.
R.	=	Richer.
Rath.	=	Rathier.
St. R.	=	Ch. of St. Riquier.

See also works of Carlyle, Beer, Lot, Luchaire, and Pfister.

OUR purpose is now to see the relation of the Church to this feudalized State and learn to what extent it had yielded to feudalism. Across this France the Church organization was thrown like a survival of the ancient Roman Empire. The result of such a blend was a series of interesting paradoxes. Feudalism and imperialism lay across each other, but fusion was impossible, and thus there was a vast contradiction at the heart of mediaeval French society. Two mutually antagonistic ideals of private and public law were struggling together, and neither emerged uninfluenced by the other. The various counties of the feudal system cut right across the Church system, and in very few cases were these political and ecclesiastical divisions coterminous.

A brief sketch of ecclesiastical France is necessary. The dioceses and provinces of the Church corresponded with the territories and provinces of the ancient Empire. The pagans overthrew the Empire, but Clovis, as we have seen, accepted baptism and made terms with the Church, which was allowed certain privileges and permitted to retain and even increase its power. A dual system prevailed from the beginning, but the Church maintained Roman forms, used its languages, its dress and its law, and thus preserved a principle of continuity in French history. The relation between the Empire and the Church can easily be seen thus :

LYONS I. was identical with the Church province of Lyons, and included bishoprics of Lyons, Autun, Mâcon, Langres, Châlons.

LYONS II. with Rouen, Avranches, Bayeux, Coutance, Évreux, Liseux, Siez.

LYONS III. with Tours, Angers, Le Mans, Nantes, Rennes, and other Breton sees.

LYONS IV. with Sens, Auxerre, Chartres, Meaux, Nevers, Orleans, Paris, Troyes.

BELGICA I. with Trèves, Liège, Verdun, Toul, Metz.

BELGICA II. with Rheims, Noyon, Châlons, Beauvais, Arras, Soissons, Cambrai, Senlis, Amiens, Laon, Tournai.

BELGICA III. : Besançon, Lausanne, &c.

AQUITAINE I. : Bordeaux, Angoulême, Poitiers, Saintes, Périgueux, and Agen.

AQUITAINE II. : Bourges, Limoges, Clermont, Le Puy, Albi, Cahors, Mende, Rodez.

NARBONNE I. : Narbonne, Toulouse, Béziers, Nîmes, Lodz, Agde, Uzes, Maguelone, Barcelona, Gerona, Roda, Urgel, Elne, Carcassone.

NARBONNE II. : Aix, Riez, Fréjus, Antibes, Apt.

VIENNE : Vienne, Grenoble, Valence, Geneva, Die, Viviers, but in this case after prolonged discussion this province was separated from ARLES, which with Viason, Orange, Avignon, Cavaillae, Carpentaria, Marseilles, and Toulon, formed a separate province.

AQUITAINE III., or Novem Popularia, with Auch, Dex, Lectoure, Aire, Couvenae, Bizorre, Oleum, Bezus, Lescor.

ALPES MARITIMAE with Embrium, Vence, Castillac, Cimiez, Nice, Senez, Digne.

ALPES GRATIAE with Tarantaise, Sion, Aosta.

GERMANIA I. : Mainz, &c.

GERMANIA II. : Cologne, &c.

Of course the last two provinces lay inside modern Germany.

The Alpine provinces do not concern us, for they were well within the kingdoms of Italy and Burgundy. In regard to the provinces more particularly related to modern France, it will at once be noted that these provinces were identical with Church boundaries, and that the cathedral cities were the principal cities in the provinces. The archbishops of the tenth century had charge of the capital cities of the ancient provinces, and the bishops ruled important cities in those provinces. The dioceses were the survivals of the ancient city territories. Some of the sees came into existence at a later period to meet advancing Christian needs, and thus Laon, Nevers, Carcassone, Elne and Maguelone were created in Merovingian times. Enough has been said to show that the Church was the heir of the Empire, and it now remains for us to see the extraordinary way in which this diocesan organization lay across the new feudal France.

The archbishoprics of Vienne, Arles, Besançon, Aix, with their dioceses, lay well within the new kingdom of Burgundy, and outside the France of the tenth century ; in fact Besançon was the capital of the Burgundian kings. The province of Lyons was in a very peculiar position, for, in the time of the last Carolings and early Capetians, Lyons itself was in the kingdom of Burgundy, whilst the remaining bishoprics of the province were in the duchy of Burgundy and therefore within the borders of the French kingdom. There had apparently been a time when Louis IV and Lothaire claimed Lyons, but these claims had been sacrificed as a marriage dowry. We find Conrad of Burgundy nominating his own son Burchard as Archbishop of Lyons, and this Burchard is called in to consecrate Bruno, Bishop of Langres, a nominee of Lothaire Thus the principal bishopric is in one kingdom and the remaining bishoprics are in another kingdom. We can thus see that this very anomalous and difficult position rendered synodal administration dependent largely on the goodwill of the two kings concerned. Fortunately Lothaire and Conrad were in agreement, but Hugh and Conrad were not so friendly, and there are hints of trouble in Gerbert's Letters (G. 144, 146).

The province of Rouen corresponded with the duchy of Normandy, being the one case in which the Church administration coincided with feudal boundaries. This exceptional case strengthened enormously the position of the Duke, and gave him complete control through the metropolitan of Rouen, who was his nominee, over all the bishops and churches of his duchy.

As regards Tours (Lyons III.), the Brittany bishoprics were held to be part of this province by the Pope of Rome and the Archbishop of Tours ; but, in spite of Papal warning and much correspondence, the Celtic bishoprics vindicated their practical independence under the Bishop of Dol. Tours itself was an important city of the county of Tours and under the suzerainty of Hugh, Duke of France. Richer shows us Hugh introducing Lothaire to Tours as one of his own cities. On the accession of the Capetians it became a royal appointment, and Archbishop Archembald, in solemnizing the marriage ceremony of Robert and Bertha, showed his dependence on royal power. Le Mans also became a royal appointment with the change of dynasty, but at a later stage Henry I sold his rights of nomination to the Counts of Anjou. Angers, Nantes, and Rennes seem to have been controlled by local counts.

In the province of Sens (Lyons IV.) the power of the Carolingian dynasty remained great to the last, and was handed on by them to the Capetians. Thus Lothaire nominated at Sens, Chartres, Auxerre, and apparently also at Meaux and Troyes. The sees of Paris and Orleans were in the nomination of the Duke of France till he became King, when they became royal appointments. Nevers seems to have remained in the nomination of the local count. The bishoprics of the province of Trèves (Belgica I.) lay within the kingdom or duchy of Lorraine, and at the end of the tenth century were controlled by German kings and princes.

In the province of Rheims (Belgica II.), Cambrai was the one bishopric which lay outside the kingdom of France and in the nomination of the Emperor, though Mouzon and part of the diocese of Rheims lay across the frontier also. Rheims, Laon, Beauvais, Châlons, Noyon, Amiens, Soissons, were all royal appointments in the time of the Carolings, and Senlis, originally ducal, also became royal on the accession of Hugh Capet. The right of nomination to these sees, powerful and wealthy, was a great source of strength to the crown. Tournai was at this time united to Noyon, and was thus under royal control. Arras was united to Cambrai, but Lothaire took possession of the city of Arras and the see, and exercised regalian rights.

Terouanne, the principal Flemish bishopric, also seems to have been under royal control, and the failure of the Count of Flanders to maintain his hold over these Flemish churches would considerably weaken his political position, and place him at a disadvantage in comparison with his rival the Duke of Normandy, for the control of the bishopric meant control of wealth and lands with their military contingents.

When we turn to Aquitaine we find great complexity in the government of the Church and less royal influence. In the province of Bordeaux (Aquitaine I.), the archbishopric of Bordeaux and the bishopric of Agen were actually in the duchy of Gascony, whilst all the other sees of the province were in the duchy of Aquitaine. The nomination of the archbishop seems to have been claimed by both dukes, for they unite in nominating Godfrey, 1028 (Adhemar), but the influence of the Duke of Gascony, living there, must have been very great. He certainly had rights at Agen, where we find his brother Gombaud bishop at the end of the tenth century. The Duke of Aquitaine preserved rights of nomination in his own city of Poitiers and at Saintes, and probably at Angoulême and Périgueux also, though twelfth-century writers have connected these bishoprics with Hugh Capet. It is clear that the harmonious working of the Church in the province would be imperilled by this dual control of the principal see, and by the local influence of numerous local counts, not always friendly to each other, in other bishoprics.

The King had a certain control in the province of Bourges (Aquitaine II.), for Lothaire nominated Guy to Le Puy, and Bourges was most certainly in the nomination of the Capetian kings (Adhemar) ; but Cahors, Albi, and Rodez were under the control of the Marquis of Toulouse ; Mende became associated with the Count of Givaudan ; Limoges was under the Duke of Aquitaine, though the kings had previously exercised control and still claimed it (Ad. iii. 25, 37), and Clermont was under the Count of Auvergne, though the Carolings had intimate relations with Bishop Stephen, and may have shared control with the count.

The province of Narbonne (Narbonne I.) escaped royal nomination entirely, and the fifteen bishoprics were controlled by various local counts and viscounts, who in some cases shared this control with the duke or marquis. Toulouse was under the marquis, who also possessed bishoprics, as we have seen, in the province of Bourges, whilst Narbonne itself was shared by the Marquis of Gothia and the local viscount. Barcelona and the bishoprics beyond the Pyrenees were in this province, and these likewise were under local control, the Count of Barcelona, for example, nominating to Barcelona, Gerona, and Vien (see Benedict VII, diploma xi. and xii., and John XIII, diploma xix.). In this section of the province, however, the Caroling and Capetian kings had considerable influence, for they gave numerous immunities to monasteries and churches.

The province of Auch (Aquitaine III.) corresponded with the duchy of Gascony, and the various bishoprics were controlled by the duke or local counts, the king's power being practically nil.

Thus we realize how the Roman episcopal system cut across feudal France. The Duke of Aquitaine controlled bishoprics in the provinces of Bordeaux and Bourges, the Count of Toulouse in Bourges and Narbonne, whilst the archbishoprics of Bordeaux and Lyons lay respectively in the duchy of Gascony and the kingdom of Burgundy. The Duke of Normandy was the only ruler whose duchy was identical with the ecclesiastical province. We realize the extraordinary complexity of the situation, and the difficulty of Church administration, when we remember that there was constant friction between the various dukes and counts and barons.

The situation was further complicated by the presence of great monastic foundations, which sought protection against the bishops of the province, and resisted the episcopal right of visitation. Many of these abbeys were under lay control, and some, like St. Germains, were governed by powerful counts in the capacity of lay abbots. Some abbeys were in the gift of the Crown, and thus the Caroling kings nominated to St. Martial in Limoges and to Fleury near Orleans. Great monasteries like Vezelay and Cluny were looking away to Rome for protection. But the various dioceses contained abbeys which were in constant conflict with the bishops, and which claimed autonomy. These abbeys possessed lands, a large number of vassals and tenants, and prodigious wealth, and therefore the local lord was tempted to usurp the position of the abbot, or exercise close control over him.

Among these 600 monastic foundations, special mention might be made of the abbeys of St. Bavon at Ghent, St. Bertin, St. Peter at Ghent, St. Amand, which belonged to the Count of Flanders; St. Wandrille, the Holy Trinity at Fécamp, Jumièges, St. Ouen, Mont St. Michel, belonging to the Duke of Normandy; and St. Denis, St. Martin of Tours, St. Germain, St. Maur du Fosse, St. Riquier, Corbie, belonging to the Duke of France. The possession of the monasteries added enormously to the resources of these dukes. It must be remembered that the Caroling kings, besides possessing the right of nomination to St. Martial of Limoges and St. Benedict of Fleury, controlled monasteries in numerous dioceses like Rheims, Sens, Auxerre, Laon, &c. The royal diplomas witness to the king's authority in these affairs. There was urgent need of reform, but the Cluny movement, with its reformed abbeys all under one abbot, all under obedience to Rome, situated in various countries and duchies, came not only to threaten the bishop's authority, but also to check the authority of the king and counts by drawing the Church away from feudal ideas to those of Imperial order and unity.

It is certain that the Church became dangerously influenced by the feudal spirit of the times. Thietmar shows us that in Germany the Emperor presented the newly appointed bishop with crozier and staff as insignia of office, and that the homage which the newly-elected prelate offered differed little from the homage rendered by a secular lord. The see possessed, besides the tithes and offerings and first-fruits, the ' regalia,' an endowment of land which made the bishop a landed magnate. He did homage for these lands, but no clear distinction was drawn between his material and spiritual duties. The struggles about investiture lay yet in the future, but the general confusion of ideals made it inevitable. The bishop ranked as a duke, the presbyter as a count. Their landed possessions in a society based on the land gave them power, influence, wealth, prestige. They had their retainers, their castles, forts, palaces, their tenants and vassals, and we constantly find bishops at the head of their armies fighting neighbouring lords in a manner not distinguishable from ordinary feudal war. The pastor is often lost in the feudal magnate, and the prophet in the politician. The wealth and political influences attached to a see made it expedient for the count or king to keep control by nominating prelates likely to support his interest. Flodoard (Fl. 962), describing the election of Archbishop Odelric of Rheims, uses the phrase ' Lothaire favouring,' and in the account of the election of Bishop Asceline (Fl. 977) we find the sentence, ' By gift of King Lothaire.' Again Gerbert (G. 155), in reference to the election of Archbishop Arnulf, speaks of ' orthodox kings consenting.'

In the time of Hugh Capet, who united the power of the duchy of France with that of the kings of Laon, it has been estimated by Professor Lot that, of the seventy-seven bishoprics in the ten provinces, twenty-five were in the nomination of the king, and that the rest were largely controlled by the local magnates. He has also shown us that the great majority of the 660 monasteries were under secular control. To this nomination of bishops was attached the right to hold a see during a vacancy and enjoy its revenues, and also a claim for military service in time of war, and financial aids. Thus the Archbishop of Rheims sends a military contingent to the siege of Verdun (G. 53) and also to the sieges of Laon (G. 122, 125).

The inevitable result of this secular control was the election of a certain type of prelate, chosen for dynastic or family reasons. The king or duke placed his own friends in these wealthy sees. Lothaire nominated nephews to Noyon and Langres. A Count of Troyes secured the see of Sens for his own son, whilst another count obtained the see of Paris for his son. The bishops were for the most part of noble, if not of royal blood, and many of them, e.g. Asceline of Laon, Hugh of Auxerre, Archembald of Sens, and Sifroi and Avesgaudus of Le Mans, were thoroughly detestable prelates. They intrigued, robbed their churches, assigned lands to their friends, misappropriated church funds, went forth like warriors to battle, raided neighbouring baronies, quarrelled over disputed boundaries, surrendered themselves frequently to the pleasures of the chase and indulgences of the table, and, in some cases, acknowledged openly their concubines. But they watched the interests of their families, and that sufficed.

The fact that so much wealth in land and so much power and status were associated with the bishopric, together with the dependence of the bishopric upon the secular power, produced the evil called ' simony,' which roused the fierce indignation

of the reformers.   It was called simony because it was the sin
of Simon Magus, who offered money for spiritual gifts.   It was
to those reformers a glaring anomaly that the bishop's office,
which they associated with the grace of God, should be a
matter of buying and selling.   That which the bishop received
freely from God, namely the grace of God, should be given
freely.   Buying or selling grace was a contradiction in terms.
Yet, after the death of a bishop, a see was often granted by the
king or count to the highest bidder.   Natranmus bought the
bishopric of Nevers for a sum of money.   The Count of
Toulouse offered the bishopric of Cahors to a monk, Bernard,
at a price.   Azeline offered money for the see of Cambrai
(G.P.C. i. 22), whilst Gerbert implied that Arnulf offered gifts
to secure Rheims.   The custom was widespread, and the
inevitable result of the feudal hand upon the Church, and it
led to the great controversy between Pope Gregory VII and
the Emperor.   But it is a curious fact that no writer of the
period seems to have realized that simony was the inevitable
result of the immense possessions of the Church (A., Canon 13)
(B. i. 22–23).

There are noble characters among the bishops, like Bruno
of Langres, and we may suppose that the vicious clergy were
in the minority, but the general effect of secular nomination
was depressing to the spiritual interests.   Christian character
was a secondary feature in many of these elections, and political
and dynastic interests often influenced the appointment.
That so many men of really noble character secured election
seems to indicate the piety of many of these kings and lords.

The secular influence is also seen in the composition of the
synods called to deal with Church affairs.   Hugh Capet and
his ' palatins ' appeared at the Council of St. Basil, Rheims.
King Robert presided over the Council of Chelles.   Laymen,
including Count Godfrey with his sons, were present at the
Synod of Mouzon (R. iv. 99).   We know that women as well
as men were present at Charroux.   This principle of lay representation in the government of the Church is a sound one, for
the Christian laity has its rights ; but in actual practice, under
the condition of those times, lay representation probably
meant little more than the presence of the king or local baron,
and stood for a measure of feudal control and influence.   The
presence of Christian laymen moved by the Christian spirit

is a tremendous asset to the Church, but the presence of lustful kings or greedy barons, only nominally Christian, and using their position in the council for their own ends, could only demoralize the Church.

Bishops were also present at the king's court and undertook many secular duties. Some were actually military leaders; others, by reason of superior learning, were employed as diplomatic agents. Two bishops mediated between Hugh the Great and Louis IV. Arnulf of Orleans accompanied Hugh Capet to Italy when he sought peace with Otho II (R. iii. 84), and the correspondence of Gerbert shows us bishops working alongside counts in a conspiracy which will ultimately change the dynasty in France. The bishops of Langres and Laon were appointed by Lothaire, 967 (Dip. 29), and Hugh Capet respectively, counts of their cities. They took control of the economic as well as spiritual life of the city, of markets, mints, ramparts, taxation (Dip. 29). Asceline of Laon quarrelled with his people on a question of economies. Bruno, Archbishop of Cologne, was both Regent of France and Viceroy of Lorraine, and was constantly engaged in secular diplomacy, military affairs, and problems of administration. Rorico of Laon and Gibuin of Châlons accompanied the King in his military expeditions, whilst Archbishops of Rheims were often warring with neighbouring counts. Thus we arrive at the conclusion that the Church was in close relation with the State, and in considerable danger of losing its essential ideals.

The local lord exerted an influence over the monasteries as well as over the parish churches. In reference to the monasteries he sometimes held the position of advocate. Thus Godfrey was the advocate, or protector, of Mouzon. The Chronicle of St. Riquier informs us that Hugh Capet took Abbeville and Foresta Cella from the monastery and placed them under the jurisdiction of his son-in-law, also called Hugh, who was termed 'advocate' because he had been appointed defender of the Church. This custom avoided direct lay government, which many monasteries like St. Riquier had experienced (St. R. Ch. iii. 9–11). The advocate represented the temporal power. He could call out the soldiery, administer the returns, and exercise a more or less definite control over the monastery. As a matter of fact, the advocate was, as often as not, a robber in disguise. Aimon (Miracles of B.)

mentions a certain advocate called Gauzlinus, who, whilst professing to defend the abbey from external foes, did himself lay waste more violently than any other. He refused to hear the pleading of the monks, and was struck at last with divine judgement while sitting at the seat of ' justice ' among the peasantry of his estate. Abbo (Canon 2, and Aimon's Vita St. A. 17) denounced certain advocates who reduced the Church to poverty, robbed it of its possessions, appropriated its returns, and, laying waste that which they were supposed to defend, ill-used the *coloniae*. He regarded it as an abuse of the right of *usufructuarius*.

The feudal hand was heavy on the rural churches. The local barons sometimes provided churches on their own estates, and, having nominated the priest, claimed a share in the returns and general oversight. Here we see the beginning of lay patronage and all its attendant evils. Canons were issued dealing with the situation, and efforts were made to limit the patron's power (A., Canons 11, 30, 32, 37). The nomination had to be made .only with the bishop's approval, whilst the churches, in their worship, ministries, and endowments, were to be under episcopal authority (A., Canons 25, 35) (B. iii. 8). It was further held that no local cleric should receive or retain money without the knowledge of the bishop. Yet, however anxious a church was to maintain its ecclesiastical rights, the position of the local magnate would be very strong, and dangerous in many cases to the spiritual life of the church.

It must not be forgotten that both the king and the count claimed to exercise ' regalian rights,' i.e. they claimed to hold a see during a vacancy and use its possessions during the recess. Thus Lothaire seems to have exercised regalian rights at Arras. Some monasteries were actually governed by secular princes under the title of lay abbots. Hugh Capet was himself at one time lay abbot of St. Martin of Tours, St. Denis, and St. Germain. This meant that the feudal lord did not trouble to nominate religious abbots, but held the abbey for himself and his heirs. The reform movement was directed against this scandal, which of course did not obtain in regard to bishoprics, a lay bishop being a contradiction in terms to that age.

The situation was further complicated by widespread alienation of Church lands to secular control through the customs of *praecariae*, *commutationes*, and *libellarii* (A., Canon ;

Rathier, Qual. Con. xiii.). The first word means that one
form of alienation was by way of a petition. There were
various causes for this alienation. The bishop perhaps needed
some strong protector, sometimes he was anxious to make
provision for kinsmen, or to secure better cultivation of the
land. An Abbot of St. Riquier, Engelgard, whilst seeking
to recover land already alienated, found himself compelled to
endow laymen with monastic lands for these last two reasons
(St. R. iii. 7). Now Canon Law forbade the alienation of
Church lands, and in form this was avoided by the system of
usufructuarius, by which the layman was only given the use
of the land for a limited period on certain conditions. A certain
sum of money, for example, is paid down to meet certain
Church needs, and then a certain amount is paid annually as
long as the estate is held. Sometimes there is a provision that
this arrangement can only cover one life, sometimes it can
cover two or more. The Church often lost heavily on the
transaction, because those in possession often refused to yield
it, and handed it over to their heirs as if it were their own land.
The annual payment was sometimes only a nominal sum,
yielding no proper return on the land given. Sometimes a
church would be compelled to exchange a large estate for a
smaller one. Rathier would therefore seem to be right when
he declared that Church land was alienated by fraud as well
as by necessity. These holders of Church lands were not
easily displaced, and could use their post of vantage to overawe
the Church, their nominal landlord.

Thus the secularizing of the Church is seen in the following
ways :

1. The Church held immense landed possessions through
the gifts of pious benefactors, and for these lands the bishop
rendered homage in the feudal manner to the lord, and in
his turn let out land to seculars called advocates, or received
services of various kinds as a landlord from his tenants.

2. The clergy enjoyed the privileges of a feudal status.

3. They were employed in quite secular negotiations.

4. The Church was also under feudal influence by reason of
royal or baronial nomination and the regalian rights which
accompanied it.

5. The Church leaders themselves belonged very largely to
the nobility, and were often elected for dynastic rather than

ethical reasons. They often shared the pride and pomp of the feudal lord, and fitted only too well into the feudal system. Pride of birth, contempt for the common man, a passion for intrigue, reliance on might rather than right, appear in the writings of such a prelate as Bishop Asceline. In fact we see the dangers of a too close connexion between State and Church.

This is, however, one side of the picture, for there is another, often overlooked. The Church was in peril and gravely compromised, but it never became wholly feudalized, and, by retaining a certain emphasis which was fundamentally non-feudal, proved to be a powerful factor in breaking down the system or preventing its further development. The non-feudal aspect of the Church can now be discussed in detail.

I. The Church was not without a certain theory of life which influenced its practice, softened its manners, and widened its sympathy. That theory was a non-feudal conception derived from the early Fathers, through Isidore of Seville, who were influenced by Roman law, by Greek thought, and by such writers as Cicero, Seneca, and more particularly by the Scriptures. This view of life expressed itself in that complex body of opinion called Canon Law, which was codified and harmonized in one orderly system in the thirteenth century.

The mediaeval theory accepted by the Church distinguished between the Divine Law or the Law of Nature, defined as the principle of justice or the Golden Rule, and Human Law founded on custom, including the Law of Nations (Jus Gentium) and Civil Law (Jus Civile). By the Law of Nature it was believed that man was originally free and equal, with a common right to all things. This represented the Golden Age before the Fall, but represented not only the primitive in time, but the ideal and eternal in values, and the principle of justice inherent in life, which is the standard by which Human Law must be judged. Now the Fall of Man introduced wildness and anarchy, because it brought in the acquisitive spirit, the love of power and gain, and this made control necessary. Thus the State came into existence, with its coercive jurisdiction and use of force, not as the highest good, which was the free spirit of love, but as a relative good, relative to the actual condition of a fallen world. Private property, slavery, and other institutions were, according to this theory, created by the State, and therefore indirectly results of the

P

Fall of Man. It will be noticed how closely political theory is related to the Church theology.

There was a little uncertainty as to the exact value of the State. Regarded as a result of the Fall, and compared with the highest good, the reign of love, Augustine and Pope Gregory VII used language derogatory to the State. This, however, was not the general view, for as a relative good the State came to be regarded as the divinely-appointed way to control evil, and lead the world back again to the 'highest good.' Thus, as Carlyle puts it, the State is a 'necessary accommodation to a corrupt State of Human Nature,' and this is justified by the ultimate purpose of setting forward the principles of natural right (vol. ii. 113, 119), and he adds, 'The punishment is also a remedy by which evil dispositions are restrained.' Thus the Fathers and the mediaeval thinkers were able to accept the State, slavery, private property, and even war, and justify them to their own consciences as having divine authority; but, as M. Beer has well said, 'Why is it that only the slaves have to bear the consequences of sinfulness? Are not the slave-owners sinful?' (p. 51). This view of the State was clearly taught by both Rathier and Gerbert (Letter of Sylvester Ep. 12) in the tenth century, and found expression in Canon Law (B. xv. 43).

The Church, however, never forgot that love was a higher principle than force, and that all men were originally the children of one Father, free and equal. Monasticism was essentially an endeavour to return to the socialism of Natural Law, and M. Beer has indicated that many so-called heretical sects bore the impress of this primitive idealism. In actual practice this view, which impressed itself on Canon Law, led to an earnest emphasis being placed on the duty of alms-giving. No man ought to possess beyond his needs, and should be willing to share his superfluity with others. Thus practical benevolence, alms-giving, helping the poor, monasticism, and the genuine Church interest in the people may be regarded as an endeavour to apply Divine Law or the Law of Nature to the life of the world. Moreover, Augustine's great work, *The City of God*, left its mark also. It was a favourite work of Charlemagne. It was found in the libraries of the monasteries. Asceline quoted it. There the Church saw the two cities, the City of God, the order of love and service, on the one hand,

and the City of the World, of force and greed, on the other hand, and recognized that the Church was the institution in which men should find the City of God and the reign of love.

It was also believed that the Law of Nature, the Divine Law, was expressed in the Scriptures, partially in the Old Testament, fully in the New ; and the Bible, with its picture of Jesus, lay open before the teachers and scholars of the tenth century. That picture of Jesus is always inspiring and producing character. Overlaid in dogma and obscured by feudal thought, that picture was never altogether lost. The student of the literature of this period cannot but notice how often the Bible is quoted. Gerbert, Abbo, and Rathier quote freely. The Sermon on the Mount is often referred to, especially the Beatitudes, and Parables, such as Dives and Lazarus and the Unjust Steward. The bishop's duties are again and again quoted from the pastoral Epistles, whilst an endeavour is frequently made to justify the sacramental position of the Church by quotation from the New Testament. The Scriptures are used theologically, sometimes in a forced and artificial manner, but the words and works of Jesus are there, and the possession of the Bible raised the Church above the narrow feudal world to a higher world of love and grace.

The Church retained the right of excommunication, and exercised it, through confession and penance, as a moral factor in society (B. i. 94). The difference between the Church and the State was recognized in theory, and each had its special province ; but the Church, whilst not claiming political supremacy, made certain religious and ethical claims which gave her a very important place in the political world. The State represented the temporal and material side of life, the body, so to speak ; the Church represented the eternal and spiritual side of life, in fact, the soul. It was easy to declare that, as the soul was higher than the body, so the Church was higher than the State. The Church condemned usury and various forms of oppression, limited wars, and administered the whole system of inheritance dealing with testaments, wills, and oaths. The Church spoke on these matters not on political and economic, but on moral, grounds, and sought to control by means of spiritual penalties. In a sense, no part of life was really left out, because the Church stood for the law of God, and this law was supreme everywhere. The Machiavellian State, and an industry divorced from morality had not yet come into being. Once a bishop did protect in a quite modern way, but the Church felt that it ought to have a corporate mind on these problems of life's relationships; and, in so thinking, it emphasized its belief that business and politics shade off into morals and religion. In fact, as all life consisted of personal relationships, and as all personal relationships involved character, economics and politics must ultimately be found to be branches of morals.

The claim is a big one, and when material force is substituted for spiritual penalties, and where the will of one man, often very fallible, is substituted for the will of the many, united to each other and to God in a rich spiritual experience, the claim may be a dangerous one and liable to terrible abuse. At the same time, that claim is not without truth and wisdom. At any rate it is a nobler attitude to life than that of abandoning whole realms of life to economic necessity and political expediency. The Church dared to excommunicate those who broke peace and injured their neighbours, and it could on occasion place a duke or a king or even an emperor under discipline. Thus in the ninth century the Church deposed the Emperor Louis I for his sins, and in the tenth century placed King Robert under penance. We are learning to-day, after bitter experience, that all life must be moralized, that the law of Christ has something to say on the relations between employed and employer, and between various classes in the country and the nations of the world. To-day many feel that the terrible conditions of the industrial revolution ought not to have been allowed to exist without a Church protest, and that the Church, having pronounced on intemperance and gambling, ought to have a mind on war and the proper ordering of society. This is the Copec movement, and we may learn something from the social and political theory of the mediaeval Church.

II. It must not be forgotten that the hereditary principle, which was the nerve of feudalism, never really gripped the Church. In Brittany and the Celtic Churches we read of the sons succeeding their fathers as bishops, but the conscience of the age generally rejected the marriage of clergy, and thus prevented sees passing from bishops to legitimate offspring.

Thus, at the death of the bishop, the see fell back to the king or count, until another bishop was substituted by the consent of the king or count. The constant change of bishops, the introduction of new men from new families, prevented that growth of powerful family traditions, so prevalent among the lay barons. The episcopal estate was not something which the bishop could leave to whomsoever he willed, and this ever-recurring break in the family interests put the Church outside a system which was on an hereditary basis. The call to celibacy of the reformers of the tenth century, revolting as it seems to us when enforced, was not without some reasoned basis in the best minds of the age. If it opened the door to insincerity and even immorality, it most certainly prevented the Church from becoming a mere feature of the feudal system, and left open the door to reform.

III. Then the Church was certainly damaged by its close connexion with the State, but at the same time the relationship with royalty had other consequences. The King had power in the Church, but, when he gave immunities and confirmed privileges, he was more to the Church than chief feudal lord. He was, in fact, a sacred person, and royalty a sacred and divinely-ordered institution relative to the fallen world. Phrases in the royal charters are significant. Thus we find 'Lothaire, King by the grace of God.' We also have Latin terms as follows: '*Deo volente*,' '*Permissu Dei*,' '*Dei clementia*,' '*Divino ordinante*,' '*Favente providentia*.' Lothaire said that God had committed to him the protection of the Church and the kingdom (Dip. 25, 28), and refers to his '*regia auctoritas*' and '*regius fiscus*.' The Archbishop placed the crown on the head of the King on the Lord's Day, and the coronation was a religious festival. Luchaire has clearly shown that the King was more than the chief feudal lord. He was, in fact, the King reigning by divine right. It is doubtful, however, whether Luchaire is justified in describing this divine right as the power of absolute sovereignty, limited only by the King's conscience. He admits that the King's authority is limited in practice, and it would seem that it was severely limited in theory. Divine right was not an irresponsible tyranny outside the law, but an authority based on justice, and justice was not only the conscience of the King, but rather the moral instincts and the essential life of the community (Abbo,

Canon 9), expressed in immemorial custom, which was the foundation of all national laws. To rule by divine right meant to rule according to justice, which was identified with the divine will.

It is true that Abbo, e.g., regarded disobedience to the King's authority as both perjury and sacrilege, for it was a sin against the Lord's anointed, and authority came from God ; but Abbo tells us emphatically what he meant by the authority of the King. The King ruled that he might make just judgement for all, and that he might judge the people, not with his own, but with the judgement of God (Apol.). Authority is therefore identified with justice. He (Canon 3) has left us a description of kingship as he understood it. The ' justice of the king ' is ' to judge the accused without respect of persons, to defend strangers, minors, and widows, to hinder robbers, to put to death adulterers, not to exalt the wicked, to exile the impious, put to death parricides and perjurers, to defend the churches, to nourish the poor with alms, to entrust the government to good men, to take counsel with wise, sober, and experienced men, to defend the country against all enemies, to live for all things in God, and to preserve in God the Catholic Faith,' &c. No words could more expressly declare the moral character of the King's authority. That authority is only justified when used to establish the law of justice. Gerbert quotes I Pet. ii. 14 to show that government exists for the securing of justice (G. 217). Certain diplomas of Hugh Capet, quoted by Luchaire (p. 43), show the necessary connexion between justice and the King's authority. Rathier (iii. 1, Prae.) says that the King must be prudent, just, brave, and sober, and goes so far as to say that a man who lacks these qualities, though he held the monarchy of the world, could not rightly be called a king, for the man who governs wrongfully loses authority. Here it is stated in unmistakable language that divine right means divine duty. Canon Law declared not only that the King was under Law, but that he was also under the discipline of religion. He had no right to do what was prohibited to his subjects. Moreover, the higher the position, the greater was the sin and the severer would be the judgement (B. xv. 41 and 42). The way is open for the distinction between the tyrant and the king, with right of rebellion against the former which is found in Isidore, Hincmar,

Hraban, John of Salisbury, &c. (Carlyle, i. 221), and also hinted at in Burchard's Collection of Canons (B. xvi. 23, xix. 5).

It was recognized by Abbo (Canon 7) that the divine right is exercised through the choice of the people, for he says that the King is appointed by election and not simply by hereditary right, like the feudal lord, that the agreement of the whole kingdom is needed for the election of a king, and that the King, unequal by himself to the task of ruling, must seek the *counsel* and *aid* of the bishops and princes. Hugh Capet admitted that to govern without such counsel would be an abuse of the royal power (G. 107). The views of Adalberon of Rheims have already been quoted in the account of Hugh Capet's election. He emphatically asserted that kings must reign by election.

This royal authority, springing from God and acknowledged by bishops and people, with duties as well as rights, dependent for its continued existence on the pursuit of righteousness, was something more than a feudal relationship. The Church and the mass of the free-men and traders came to see that their own interests were bound up with the interests of such a monarchy. The Church needed the protection of the King from feudal licence, and the King needed the support of the Church in order to render his title sacred. A common interest in culture, peace, and law bound Church and Throne together, until at last there appeared the triumphant monarchy of Louis IX, called by the Church St. Louis. By relating secular authority to divine law and the principle of justice the Church helped to undermine feudalism, based, for practical purposes, on force and licence.

IV. The Church was an international factor. It transcended local, feudal, and even national limits. It was one Church, universal, apostolic, and, as such, represented a standing protest against feudalism. The Church was a survival of the Roman system. Its diocesan and provincial organization cut right across feudal boundaries, and witnessed to the tradition of the ancient Empire. Its episcopal cities were, in most cases, ancient Roman cities. Its language, culture, art, government, and discipline betrayed the Latin genius. It was the Roman Church in the Teutonic world. As the various cities and provinces had once looked to the Imperial city, so the churches in various cities and districts looked with reverence toward the church of that city, which was also traditionally the church of St. Peter.

As we have seen, the acceptance of the Forged Decretals witnessed to this innate reverence. Now this reverence for Rome was not a reverence for a particular Pope, nor only for one particular church as distinct from others, but it implied a recognition of the unity and solidarity of life, both secular and religious. God ruled in this world, on the spiritual side through the Church, with the Pope as chief bishop, and, on the secular side, through the State, with the Emperor as chief ruler. The glamour of the Roman name was the glamour of the eternal and universal, for which Rome stood, at any rate in imagination and tradition. The Church, thus centred in Rome, was believed to be a world system, in theory co-extensive with life. The Church might, in fact, be partly feudalized, and might even become national; but in theory it was neither; for when the Papal authority was most bitterly attacked, it was not to substitute baron or king, but to place over against the Pope the Universal Church, which had spoken at the great councils, and through various decrees and canons. This reference to the canons will remind us that there was a system of Canon Law in process of compilation—the codifying, so to speak, of the customs of the Church in relation to the divine law contained in the Scriptures and moral instincts of man (B. iii. 124-126). The study of Canon Law reveals the international mind. Gerbert and Abbo could quote African, Spanish, Italian, as well as Gallican councils, and regarded the decisions of such councils as precedents for the guidance of the Church in France. The great canonists were really international lawyers. Isidore, Reginon, Burchard, Abbo, wrote and compiled for the whole Church.

Then there is an active association between the Churches in different countries, which also indicates an international spirit. There is real movement and interchange. The Papal legate, the bishop, the abbot, the monk, the student, the pilgrim, pass from place to place, consulting freely, co-operating in synods, seeking relics, or collecting books. The Papal legates preside over councils attended by French and German bishops. The Archbishop of Rheims attends Italian synods in Pavia and Rome. Rathier is at one time Bishop of Verona, at another Bishop of Liège. Gerbert passes from Rheims to Ravenna and then to Rome. The significant fact is that the bishop's status and authority are the same in every country.

The monastic movement strengthened this fellowship. The Abbot of Cluny and William of Dijon enjoy international reputations. They pass with incredible speed and energy from one country to another. Cluny has daughter or sister houses throughout the west of Europe. Abbo visits English monasteries, and Anglican bishops, like Dunstan and Oswald, visit Flanders and Fleury. Benedictine monasteries present the same essential features wherever they appear.

Pilgrims are passing frequently to Rome and other sacred places. They visit Jerusalem and the holy places, and it is thought that through this interchange of Western and Eastern ideas the Catharist heresy came into France.

This interchange of thought and life, this exchanging of bishoprics and building of new monasteries, all witness to an underlying unity. Bishop and monk belong not to a feudal or a national institution. They appeal to Rome or a Universal Council. They journey to Jerusalem for the inspiration of sacred sights, and show thereby that they belong to a world order.

Christian theology and Church ritual and orders presuppose this international ideal. The whole of mankind had fallen in Adam, and could only find salvation in Christ. Salvation as well as sin were international factors. The sacraments, the appointed means of grace, for their validity were not dependent on local conditions. The sacraments were binding on all, were privileges open to all, and, through them, the same grace could be conveyed to all. The duties of the priesthood, the authority of the bishop, the validity of the sacraments, were not dependent on the whim of some local baron. They belonged to the essential significance of the Church, and were universal in their range of operations. The Church possessed the Bible, belonging to no class or section, and it presented Jesus as an ideal in whom Gentiles and Jews were transcended. Therefore we may assert that the Church, in its theology, its law, its discipline, its ethical ideals, its Scriptural appeal, and its presentation through the Mass of the universal atonement for universal sin, preserved and proclaimed international factors.

It is easy enough to show the immense difference between the theory and practice of the mediaeval Church. There were corruption, superstition, and imperfect ideas of God and salvation, and many pagan survivals. There was often more emphasis placed on creed and institutions than upon experience and character. The Fatherhood of God and the gracious figure of Jesus were often obscured. A reformation both in morals and theology was needed. Puritan and evangelical protests were along the line of progress in the Church, but the mere substitution of national Churches for the internationalism of the mediaeval Church represented no spiritual gain, for to the extent that a Church is just Gallican or Anglican, to that extent it is no Church. The Church of the tenth century, with all its faults, had a universal setting, and tried to express an international ideal. Asceline called the Church the ' Kingdom of God.' In a sense he was right, for the Church did try in some imperfect way to transcend conditions of class, climate, and colour. We need to preserve all the gains the Reformation secured for us, but we must not lose the international conception of Christianity. The Church in this country, as in others, has too often identified itself with the political interests of the State, and accepted the pernicious doctrine that the war is just because it is the country's cause. In these days of fierce national quarrels, which have taken the place of the older feudal quarrels, the Church must cultivate the international mind and imagination, and help to create international fellowship, which is the Christian life.

V. The Church resisted feudalism when it emphasized the value of education. Feudalism despised the culture of the schools. In the Church alone the educational tradition of the Graeco-Roman world survived. All scholars were churchmen, and the schools of the day were either monastic schools, like Fleury and St. Riquier, or cathedral schools, like Rheims, Chartres, Orleans, Paris, and Laon. The head of the episcopal school was called the *scholasticus*, and he was appointed by the bishop. The education provided in both types of schools was limited, but we read of the ' Seven Arts ' taught at Fleury by Abbo and at Cologne by Bruno, and these included grammar, rhetoric, and logic, known as the ' Trivium '; arithmetic, music, geometry, and astronomy, known as the ' Quadrivium.' Bruno and Rathier seem to have been acquainted with the Greek language, and Abbo and Gerbert use certain Greek words, though it is doubtful whether they knew much of the language as a whole. Gerbert could only study the Greek classics in Latin translations. Abbo's use of Greek seems to be derived from Latin writers. Nowhere does he quote directly from Greek authors.

Gerbert was the greatest scholar of the age. Richer (iii. 46) gives us an interesting list of the books which Gerbert used, and, as a student of Gerbert's school, Richer could write with authority on this matter. He mentions the *Isagogue* of Porphyry, translated by Victorinus, which he interpreted according to the principles of Boethius ; also the *Categories* of Aristotle, and the *Topica*, translated from the Greek by Tullius, and also expounded by Boethius. Gerbert taught literature and rhetoric from the poets Virgil, Terence, Statius, Horace, Persius, and Lucan. Richer also informs us that Gerbert was acquainted with arithmetic, concerning which he wrote a book on the multiplication and division tables, and made an *abacus* for reckoning ; that he also studied astronomy (G. 2, 5, 24), and could show the position of constellations on the sphere and trace their movements. Confirmation of these statements are found in Gerbert's letters. He frequently refers to a book on the ' tables ' by one Joseph of Spain (17, 25), and writes to one Lupo of Barcelona about a book on astrology (24). Richer also states that Gerbert knew something of music, and his own letters indicate that he knew something of organ construction (R. iii. 49 ; G. 92, 112).

Gerbert divides philosophy into theoretic philosophy, which includes physics, mathematics, and theology and practical philosophy, which includes ethics, economics, and politics ; but actually the philosophy of the time was little more than a form of logic, which was often of a curiously formal and abstract character. In the debates between Otric and Gerbert, described in such detail by Richer (iii. 5, 6), and considered to be of such importance as to warrant the presence of a busy Emperor, the main question debated was whether physics should be subordinated to mathematics, as species to genus, or whether, in the categories of substance ' mortal ' should come before ' reasonable.' The same line of thought is seen in a book, attributed to Gerbert, on the relationship between a ' reasonable ' nature and the ' use of reason.' There is a danger of losing reality in a jugglery of words, yet there is a definite seeking after truth, and an endeavour to train the mind in these curious debates. Gerbert's logic was certainly greatly influenced by Aristotle. He distinguishes between ' potency ' and ' act.' He is acquainted with the *Categories* of Aristotle, understands the syllogistic form of argument and delights in the relation between *genus* and *species*. He was, however, also under Platonic influence. Richer (iii. 63) tells us he quoted from Plato in the debate with Otric. The only work of Plato's known in the West was his *Timaeus*. De Wulf (155) suggests that Gerbert had become acquainted with Plato through John Erigena, and is inclined to place Gerbert on the side of the Realists in the great debate which characterized mediaeval scholasticism. Certain statements of Gerbert's point in that direction ; as, e.g., his statement that good can be ascribed to the creature only in so far as he participates in the ' Good ' will of God. But Gerbert is mainly concerned with logical formula and definition, and his metaphysic is not clearly expressed or distinguished from his logic.

His geometry had a very practical relation to land-surveying, and his teaching of rhetoric had in view the training of the student for practical and useful service in the courts of the Church and State. He claimed that correct speech had a definite relation to correct life (R. iii. 48 ; G. 118). It is also certain that Gerbert had some knowledge of medicine, and medical works are referred to in his letters, particularly one called ' Ophthalmicus,' written by the philosopher Demosthenes. His students Fulbert and Richer were both interested in medicine. Richer (iii. 50) gives us an interesting personal reference to a visit paid by him to Chartres for the purpose of acquiring a knowledge of pharmacy and surgery, which were taught there by a cleric, Hildebrand, from the books of Hippocrates, Gallienus, and Suranus.

Gerbert had a profound and detailed knowledge of Canon Law and the writings of the Fathers. The story of the controversy with Rome, in the matter of the election to the see of Rheims, gives ample proof that Gerbert had read widely in Church history and Canon Law (G. 217). Gerbert's letters reveal a positive passion for knowledge. He is always engaged in building up his library. He is continually borrowing, exchanging, or buying books dealing with all kinds of subjects, and he became a perfect encyclopaedia of knowledge culled from Latin, Greek, and perhaps Arabian sources (Letters 124, 142, 77, 89, 55, 63, 60). He was credited by an ignorant and superstitious age with the arts of a wizard, and, though he may not have made any great original contribution to thought, we must not underestimate his intellectual powers. He was remarkably free from the superstitions of popular religion. His acquaintance with the Latin classics gave an unmistakable breadth to his mind. He was free from theological prejudices. His love of inquiry, passion for knowledge, his sense of the many-sidedness of truth, his belief in the order of the universe, based on scientific inquiry or experiment, and on some acquaintance with astronomy and history, medicine and mathematics, and finally his trust in that order as wise and strong, link him to the modern world, and suggest a strikingly modern attitude to some of life's problems. The world he entered, as he pondered over his books and looked at the stars from the high tower of the Lateran whilst Rome slept, was God's world, and he would retire into it from the maze of things with the quiet confidence that somehow the ways of truth were the ways of God. He was a philosopher rather than a theologian, and his mind was rationalistic rather than mystical. He did not believe much in demons, and cared little for relics, but he lacked the moral passion and the intense devotion of the Cluny saints, and a strain of intrigue ran through his nature. Perhaps if he had believed a little more in the power of sin, and fought it more earnestly, and thereby combined the saint's intensity of experience with the thinker's love of research, he might have made a greater contribution to the progress of the race. He was no saint, but his earnest search for truth will always give him a great place in the world's history as well as in the life of the mediaeval Church.

Gerbert influenced society through a number of distinguished men who studied under him, among whom were King Robert, son of Hugh Capet, Fulbert, John of Auxerre, and Richer the historian. The last-named wrote a history of his times. It is very valuable for the information it gives about the last Caroling kings and the struggle between Hugh Capet and Charles of Lorraine. Until 965 his narrative is largely based on the Annals of Flodoard, Canon of Rheims ; but, for the events with which he was strictly contemporary, his writing is invaluable. The acceptance of the False Decretals shows clearly the limitations of historical research, yet the writings of Flodoard and Richer show that the compilation of historic annals was not without merit, and that there was some understanding of the movements of nations and the motives of persons. Richer's account of the betrayal of Charles of Lorraine shows considerable power of vivid narrative. Richer imitates the classical style of Sallust, and many of the histories contain much legend ; but there was undoubtedly much painstaking effort to find out the truth of things.

Rheims was not the only centre of culture. Maiolus attended lectures at Lyons under Anthony, and his biographer describes Lyons as the ' Mother of Philosophy.' Abbo, in the pursuit of knowledge, travelled from school to school, and, in the words of his biographer, Aimon, ' gathered honey from many flowers like a fruitful bee.' He visited Paris and Rheims, where he learnt philosophy and a little astronomy, whilst at a school at Orleans he studied music. Under him Fleury became a centre of knowledge. He wrote books on arithmetic, astronomy, grammar, and logic. His special forte was law, and he drew up a very valuable collection of canons. It has been sometimes said that the monastic schools were behind the episcopal schools in their intellectual standard. This assumption, however, is hardly borne out by the facts. The revival of religion at Cluny was certainly accompanied by a distaste for the legends and general teaching of the old pagan classics. A process of selection was encouraged by Maiolus, and special emphasis placed on the Christian Fathers, but Maiolus himself did not refuse all secular knowledge. Rathier, whose writings are full of classical quotations, was trained at the monastic school of Lobbes, whilst Adalberon of Rheims, who was also well acquainted with the classics, was a student of Gorz. Gerbert received his first education at the monastery of Aurillac. Abbo himself is a witness to the educational standard of the monastic schools. Classical quotations can be read in his works.

The library at St. Riquier (iii. 3), in the ninth century, included, among its 250 books, not only the writings of Augustine, Jerome, Chrysostom, Gregory the Great, but also of the historians Josephus, Eusebius, Sozomus, Socrates, Bede, Gregory of Tours, together with certain works of Cicero and Donatus, glosses of Virgil, extracts from Philo, with various chronicles, missals, books of law, both sacred and secular, and numerous homilies and epistles.   The works of Boethius and Cassiodorus were much in evidence in all the libraries.   The whole of the Scriptures and the Rule of Benedict received the greatest emphasis, but there is sufficient evidence to show that the Seven Arts were not neglected, though of course the teaching may not have been of a very searching character.   It is certain that all the historians, philosophers, doctors, grammarians, were always either monks or clerics, and the Church represented, in a feudal world, the non-feudal ideals of culture and learning.

VI. THE CHURCH SOUGHT PEACE :

It is true that the voice and example of the Church was often compromised by material considerations, favour, fear, and interest, but it represented, nevertheless, the only institution which stood for peace.

1. *In its Ideals.*

The Church has to be judged, not by its lowest, but by its highest expression ; not only by what it was, but what rather it knew it ought to be, and by its aspiration towards the ideal. Notice the type of saint honoured.   His characteristics are always humility, unselfishness, and the willingness patiently to bear injuries.   Odilo saw in Maiolus the fulfilment of the Beatitudes of the Sermon on the Mount.   Ruotger is very anxious to prove that his hero, Bruno of Cologne, was a peacemaker ; and this endeavour, whether successful or not, is a significant illustration of the Church mind.   The lives of men like Adalberon of Metz, Bruno of Langres, and William of Dijon, all reveal this interest in peace.   It should be remembered that the worship of saints and their relics meant generally the raising aloft of the ideal of peace, for these saints were rarely men of war, but rather men of peace.   St. Martin of Tours, for example, who was greatly honoured in France, was a man who left the army because he could not harmonize a soldier's life with his conception of Christianity.

The Church distinguished between ' those who pray ' and ' those who fight,' and the Church represented, with its clergy, the former class.   In early days Origen justified the pacifism of the early Church by making a similar distinction, though using it in a wider sense.   The Christians in those days, said he, did not fight for the Empire, but fulfilled their duty by praying for the Empire.   Now the ancient witness to the distinction between fighting and praying, limited now to the ordained clergy and monks, but showing within the narrower limits the sense of the incompatibility of the service of Christ and war, can be dimly discerned.   Fulbert of Chartres uses arguments from the example of Jesus which could apply on a wider scale, and are found on the lips of pacifists at the present day.   Christ, says he, would not fight, though He might have called legions of angels to His side, and He was always willing patiently to forbear and forgive.   Rathier is equally opposed to clerics who engage in warfare.   Canon Law asserted that those dedicated to the service of Christ should stand off the battle-field and follow Christ in the pursuit of peace (B. ii. 211–212).

Those who killed in war were brought under discipline and their motives for fighting carefully analysed.   The Church distinguished between those who killed by the order of the Prince in public war and those who killed in a wrong cause or on their own responsibility, but penance was imposed in both cases, implying that to kill in war was a form of homicide.

2. *In Actual Deed.*

Now we should do well to study the Church efforts to put into practice these ideals of peace, and this period of history affords a few interesting examples of a genuine peace movement.   Dudo informs us that it was the bishops who first took steps to deliver France from the ruthless invaders whom the Duke of Normandy had introduced, and it was a Bishop of Chartres, Wulfald, who opened up negotiations with the Duke. Bruno of Cologne sought peace for Lorraine, and was ever reconciling enmities by successful diplomacy and the influence of his great personality.   Maiolus of Cluny was ever engaged in a ministry of reconciliation ; e.g. he established peace between Otho II and his mother.   His successor, Odilo, earnestly sought peace in Burgundy when Robert invaded the land, and, along with Fulbert of Chartres, took an active part in settling disputes and arranging peace pacts.

Apart from these considerations, attention must now be directed to a very definite movement for peace which developed in the central and southern portions of France.   It has been suggested that the movement originated in the south, because there more refined manners witnessed to surviving memories of the Pax Romana.

In 989 (Mansi xix.) a council was held at Charroux, presided over by the Archbishop of Bordeaux, supported by the Bishops of Poitiers, Limoges, Périgueux, Saintes, and Angoulême, and Christians of both sexes, and judgement was passed on those who robbed churches, peasants, unarmed travellers, or clergy. Such robbers were to be excommunicated till satisfaction was given for the offence. The following year at Narbonne, a council, attended by neighbouring bishops and counts, issued anathemas against any one who invaded Church land or injured the clergy. In the same year, a council (Mansi xix.) held at Ansa issued decrees to protect the possessions of Cluny from the excesses of neighbouring barons. The Archbishops of Lyons and Vienne were present, with numerous bishops and prominent laymen.

Another important council was called by Guy, the Bishop of Le Puy, in 990 (Ch. de St. P. du Puy). He exhorted all to become sons of peace, because ' without peace no one could see the Lord.' Here peace is advocated on distinctly Christian ground. The Archbishops of Bourges and Vienne were present, with numerous bishops from the three provinces of Bourges, Narbonne, and Vienne. There were also present neighbouring princes and nobles, as well as humbler laity. They agreed to meet again in October of that year, having passed various measures for the maintenance of justice and peace. When the day became due, the Bishop called upon all the peasantry and nobility who were present to sign a pact of peace, guaranteeing the maintenance of the provisions recently enacted, with the promise of the forgiveness of sins as the reward. When they showed some hesitation, he introduced his nephews, Pons and Bertrand, with their forces, and secured thereby the signing of the first of the series of pacts establishing the ' Truce of God.' As the acceptance of the pact brought remedy for sins, so the breaking of the pact meant excommunication.

In 997 another pact was introduced into Aquitaine, according to Adhemar. There had been a terrible pestilence, and a solemn three days' fast was held at Limoges at the initiative of the Abbot of St. Martial, Bishop Alduin, and Duke William of Aquitaine. The Archbishop Dagobert of Bourges, Gombaud, Bishop of Agen, along with the Bishops of Saintes, Périgueux, Clermont, Angoulême, and Anicy, were summoned to a council. Relics were introduced, and the body of St. Martial brought from his

Q

tomb. The plague ceased, and the grateful people swore solemn oaths of peace, and those who violated them were to be banished from the Church. This pact was also signed by the duke and neighbouring lords.

In 999 another council was held at Poitiers (Mansi xix.), when Duke William was present, along with Archbishop Seguin of Bordeaux, and the Bishops of Poitiers, Limoges, and Saintes, and twelve abbots and certain laymen. It was agreed that any disputes about theft should be examined by the chief men of the district. If justice was not enforced locally, there was to be an appeal to the nobles and bishops who had attended the council, who would then meet and judge the guilty. Hostages were to be given, and the provisions of previous councils were confirmed.

Thus efforts were made by the Church to bring in peace by excommunicating those who made war, and by establishing local covenants or pacts between all the people of a given area, including all classes and both sexes. The movement continued into the next century, and was supported by King Robert. Various councils were held and various pacts of peace were renewed in one form or another. When the Church found it difficult to suppress war, it sought to limit war to a given period—between Monday and Wednesday—and to modify its ferocity by the custom of chivalry, whereby the young knight, after the nightly vigil in the church, swore only to fight for the oppressed. History, however, shows that neither then, nor at any other time, can war be regulated or controlled, for the wild spirit of war always passes beyond these attempted regulations. War by its very nature is barbarous and lawless. This carries us beyond our period. It is sufficient to note that, by the end of the tenth century, the Church in its organized form, apart from the peace-loving activities of individuals, had been forced by its own interests, by the miseries of the land, and by the challenging ideal of its own teaching, to seek peace, for 'without peace no one could see the Lord.'

In considering this peace movement, due credit must be given to pious kings like Robert I, or men like William IV of Aquitaine, who spent the last four years of his life in a monastery, and William V, whose deeply religious character is sketched by Adhemar iii. 41. But the initiative was undoubtedly with the Church, and can probably be attributed to the great revival of religion which had broken out in different parts of the country, particularly at Cluny, and which meant renewed emphasis upon the value of love, fellowship, and loyalty as the essential features of Christianity.

So the Church resisted the warring spirit of feudalism by upholding the Christian ideal of peace, and endeavoured to apply the ideal by means of leagues and covenants of peace.

VII. THE CHURCH TAUGHT SOCIAL JUSTICE.

It was the one institution which cared for the rights of those sections of the community that lay outside the feudal hierarchy. We have seen that its theory of life was influenced by the theological doctrine of the Fall of Man. It is quite true that Asceline of Laon, representing the secular clergy, and Abbo the monks, regarded the order of society as the best possible order under the circumstances of the Fall. There were three classes—those who pray, those who fight, and those who work. Therefore the Church accepted the threefold order as divinely sanctioned, but sought, nevertheless, to control it in the interests of all parties by securing justice for all. There are various ways in which the Church sought to carry out this programme.

1. In seeking peace by limiting or abolishing private war, the Church was defending social interests. War was, and is, the outcome of hatreds and jealousies, private or public, and always results in various conditions of oppression, along with pestilence and famine, disorder and crime. It is always the common people who suffer most. The burden of war was, in the Middle Ages, borne by the peasant and the trader, living in the unfortified villages and towns. Thus peace meant social welfare for the worker. The limitation of private war by the action of the Church must have been a great boon to the mass of the people, for social welfare, which presupposes law, cannot exist in a condition of war, which really means lawlessness.

2. The Church took over the protection of certain classes of people. Canon Law gave bishops authority to interfere on behalf of those injured by injustice in the courts (Burchard xx. 1). From the earliest days the Church had shown a special interest in widows, orphans, strangers, captives, and the poor. It never forgot the Master's words in Matt. xxv., in

Q*

which He identified Himself with the sick, the imprisoned, and the needy. The story is told about a certain Count of Anjou, Fulk the Good, that he carried a leper to the Church of St. Martin at Tours, and that, on arrival at the church, the leper vanished, and he discovered that he had carried the Christ. Many similar stories are found in the 'miracle' literature of the period. These stories teach that Christ can be honoured in the service of the poor. Maiolus believed that the love of God is the service of man. Alms-giving may have often sprung from selfish motives, for many gave alms for the remedy of their souls. Alms-giving was certainly a form of discipline which was supposed to give merit and cover sin ; but it was not always so, for it was often the expression of the kindly and sympathetic feelings of Christian men and women, who were conscious of the needs of their neighbours, and wanted to help them for their own sake, and for the sake of the Christ whom they all served. Further, it was believed that alms-giving was a duty, and the appointed means for reducing the great inequalities of the social system, and the duty of generous hospitality was commended to the laity.

Rathier may be regarded as a representative writer. He quotes Jerome to the effect that ' the rich man is either unjust (*iniquus*) or the heir of the unjust. For it is unjust that what God bestowed on all collectively (*generaliter*) certain should gather singly (*singulariter*) ' ; and in another passage, claiming the Epistles of James and John as authorities, he points out that alms-giving may be called justice and not pity, because the money given belongs to the One who teaches us to give alms (Prae. iv. 23–5).

Alms-giving may be criticized as economically unsound, but it must not be thought that it was necessarily indiscriminate in its operation, for its distribution was controlled by the ecclesiastical authorities, who may be supposed to have had some system of administration. By Church custom a fourth portion of the Church finances was set apart for the poor, and was to be administered by the bishop (B. iii. 138). Then it must not be forgotten that the monasteries were great centres of social service. They provided pensions and hospitality for certain poor people, hospitals for the sick, homes of refuge for the abandoned, and schools for the children, to whom they gave free education as well as food and clothes. These functions of the monasteries were fulfilled by specially-chosen monks, who worked according to rule and plan. These monasteries must have been a source of great benefit to the poor and sick of the district. The fact is that the only infirmaries, pension offices, and homes for the aged were Church institutions.

The Church also protected the man charged with crime from hasty and violent treatment, by providing at least a temporary refuge for him in ' sanctuary,' even if a slave (Burchard iii. 190–194; Abbo Intro. to Canons). The only condition was that the refugee must surrender arms and trust to the Church. This must have meant a real protection for the poor and helpless in violent times.

3. It legislated for the merchants, labourers, and peasants. It excommunicated not only the robber of the church, but the men who robbed the merchant and wronged the peasant. The regulations of the Council of Le Puy, 990, are interesting in this respect. No one was to steal from a worker his horses, oxen, asses, nor what these animals carried, nor his fowls, goats, pigs, or eggs, and no one was to take a villein in order to force him to buy himself out of servitude. No one was to carry home for his own use what belonged to another. The corvée was strictly limited. No man was to be called upon to build a castle unless special reasons were given, whilst merchants, travelling unarmed along the road, were specially protected from attack. Provisions of this kind show that the trader and the peasant had rights which the Church sought to defend by ecclesiastical sanction. The practice of usury was condemned by the Church.

By usury was meant not only the exorbitant interest associated with the word in these days, but every arrangement whereby money was lent for purposes of gain. Usury or interest was associated with covetousness and love of money, and was forbidden to clergy and laity alike. The Church appears definitely on the side of the worker. Wealth should have some correspondence with service, and service is valued in terms of labour, which produced that wealth. In estimating this aspect of Canon Law, it is fair to point out that there is a difference between the simple rural life of the Middle Ages and the complex industrialism of massed capital and labour so prominent to-day, and to show that what may be both necessary and serviceable now might have been exploitation of labour then. Nevertheless, it seems to many that the

Industrial Revolution of the eighteenth century would have been associated with less misery and pain had the Church of a later age been more concerned about the rights of the workers, and about giving Labour its just returns.

The Church attitude to usury indicated the Church attitude to economic problems, and must be related to its demands for just weight (B. xix. 48) and fair prices in the market (B. ii. 168). The profiteer came under the discipline of the Church, which did not uphold the principle of buying in the cheapest market in order just to sell in the dearest. The Law of Christ ought to apply in the market as everywhere else (B. ii. 119–127, and i. 94).

The Church also endeavoured to maintain Sunday as a day of rest from servile labour, and encouraged the use of saints' days for relaxation and worship (Rath., Syn. 2 Ep. 12). These provisions, though rising from a religious interest, must have made life easier for the worker. The Church encouraged labour on other days by recognizing its dignity and its value as a form of service for the community. We find that Erlwin opened a market for trade in Cambrai, whilst the monastery of St. Philibert of Tournus secured a market for the neighbouring town.

The Church also directly encouraged the development of the land. We hear of bishops carrying out extensive clearing operations and bringing waste land under cultivation, whilst an Abbot of St. Riquier (St. R. m. 27) gave land to certain people who were willing to make it habitable and fruitful. The work of the monks in this respect must never be forgotten. Under the inspiration of Benedict they drained the marshes, cleared forests, made roads, constructed bridges, ploughed land and developed agriculture, extended sheep farming, and produced the wool trade. Large clearings of forest led to a trade in timber, and increased the opportunity for trade and travel. Therefore by example and precept the Church encouraged the worker, who ranked far below the fighter in the feudal grades of value. There seems little doubt that the trade corporations, which were making some progress unseen in these days, and which would develop into strong guilds, were helped by the patronage of the Church, which provided for them some patron saint and a religious sanction for their work.

Apart from actual legislation and the encouragement of labour, the teaching of the Church in these matters is interesting, showing that the Church had a mind on economic problems. Rathier may be taken as an example, for he was not only an Italian bishop, but had close relationships with Lorraine and Gaul. In his work *Praeloquiorum*, Rathier was not afraid to remind those in authority that government was only a form of service. He told the nobles, proud of their blood, that all men were equal under God in sin and redemption, and came of a common ancestor. He reminded the rich of the doom of Dives, of the perils of wealth, of the need for rendering service, and of discharging adequately what was really only a stewardship entrusted to them by God. At the same time he urged honesty on the merchant, honest toil on the worker, and uprightness on the public officials and lawyers. He reminded the serf of his true liberty in God. Such words—and they are representative—show that the Church was not afraid to speak its mind on the relation of the classes, and had a definite attitude to the problems of the hour.

Reference should be made here to the Church's attitude to slavery—or serfdom, to use a better word. We have seen that all men were considered equal by the law of Nature, but, by a curious use of the doctrine of the Fall, the Church had justified slavery as a divinely-appointed judgement and remedy for a fallen world. The Church had never explained why the slave alone should pay the penalty. The Church was, in fact, an owner of slaves. It must be remembered, however, that a mediaeval slave was in a very different position from the slave in the old Roman days or on the American plantations. There was very little buying or selling, in the open market, of the person of the slave, as distinct from the land on which he worked. The slave was, in fact, a serf bound to the soil, and thus ownership of land meant ownership of serfs ; but his actual condition was probably not very different from that of the free peasant, working for some landowner and paying heavy dues. It is true that the Church refused to ordain the serf (B. ii. 21), and discouraged the emancipation of its own serfs. They were regarded as the property of the Church or monastery, and thus the freeing of the serf might be regarded as the alienation of Church property, which was strictly forbidden. In this respect serfdom might also be considered a privilege, as an attachment to the Church, however servile, brought material protection and salvation to the soul.

The Church had taken a prominent part in the destruction of the ancient system and the slave trade, and whilst, therefore, upholding the institution of serfdom, and benefiting by it, sought to ameliorate the condition of the serf. It recognized his moral personality in the sense that, whilst denying him civil rights, it brought him under the criminal law. He was responsible for his own crimes, and, on the other hand, the master who killed the slave was guilty of homicide, and if he ill-treated one, or dragged him out of sanctuary, he was liable to excommunication (B. iii. 194). The Church's offer of sanctuary to the injured slave was a valuable privilege, whilst his right to marriage and family life was recognized. Rathier (Prae. i. 29) drew an interesting distinction between the body of the man, which was in slavery to another, and the soul, which might possess both freedom and authority. A survival of the old belief in natural law and equality can be traced in references in Canon Law to the Brotherhood of Man under the One Father (B. xv. 32), and in Rathier's estimate of the Christian life as a brotherhood in Christ, for, writing concerning those who serve, he declared, ' We are all brothers in Christ.' Whatever may be, therefore, the external condition of society, in the inner life of the man and his relationship to God these class distinctions disappear. It is clear that brotherhood in Christ and inner freedom would ultimately demand brotherhood in the world and outward freedom. It should also be noted that the emancipation of slaves was regarded by Canon Law as a meritorious act, bringing a remedy for the ills of the soul of the master (B. ii. 29–30).

Before passing from this section we might call attention to the exalted position of womanhood in the teaching of the Church. The position of women in the tenth century was a very prominent one. Great queens and princesses are constantly referred to in the correspondence of Gerbert, such as the Empresses Adelaide and Theophania, the Queens Emma and Adelaide, the Duchess Beatrice, the Countess Matilda, and the Lady Imiga. These ladies share in the correspondence, meet in councils, take an active part in negotiations, and help to make both war and peace. Richer tells us that Lothaire left his queen in charge of the captured city of Verdun, and that she took an active part in her husband's diplomacy ; whilst the queens of Hugh Capet and Robert had great political influence at the Kings' Courts. It is not only a question of royal ladies, for it is distinctly stated that women as well as men were present at the Councils of Charroux and Narbonne, and these are undoubtedly women of humbler estate. Many of the women shared in the vices of the feudal era, in the intrigue and cruelty of the times ; but the respect for women in these days represented a serious modification of the feudal conception of the supremacy of physical strength.

The Church had something to do with the improved status of women. It held up a high standard of womanhood when it exalted the Virgin Mary ; and, whatever may be our opinion of Mariolatry, there can be little doubt that the reverence for the Virgin Mary had a softening and refining influence on the feudal world, and that, in her, her sex was honoured. Moreover, many other popular saints were women, like St. Faith, whose miracles were recorded by Bernard of Anjou in the eleventh century, and St. Frothilde, whose visions Flodoard recorded. The 'miracle' literature of the time gives us instances of the saints' interest in women and their welfare. Benedict avenges, for example, the wrongs of a poor widow, and women of both high and low birth are healed by his merits. Various biographers sing the praises of pious women who were benefactors of the Church, and many churches and monasteries were memorials of the generosity and piety of women, some of royal birth, others of much humbler parentage. The Church gave special attention to widows, and in various religious houses found place for those who were devoted to the Church, the *Ancillae* of the Lord.

Finally, whilst the Church honoured and exalted the celibate life, it also sanctified and made permanent the marriage bond, and gave a sacramental and spiritual meaning to the relationship of the sexes. Thus the Church honoured womanhood.

VIII. From all that has been said before, we may now conclude that the Church, in spite of its feudal connexion, contained all that was found of democracy in those days. The Church now limited the priesthood to the priestly orders in the Church, but it never quite lost the democracy of apostolic times, which rose out of the conception of the priesthood of all believers and the equal standing of all men before

God in sin and salvation, and, as children of the one Father, within its own priestly ranks the Church gave the man of humble birth a chance which no other institution gave. The feudal world consisted of a series of self-contained classes, and it was wellnigh impossible for the peasant to rise into the higher orders. Birth and ancestry counted for everything in that world. Within the Church these barriers did not obtain to the same extent. Asceline used a great phrase when he said, proud aristocrat as he was, that in the priesthood the child of the worker and the child of the king could find an equal place. The monasteries welcomed into their cells men of all ranks. Sons of the nobility or sons of the poor were educated there. Gerbert was a striking example of this democratic spirit. He was born of moderate parentage. His parents' names are unknown, nevertheless he rose to be Pope of Rome, the equal of emperors and kings. He rose through merit and knowledge, and the Church organization gave him the chance of obtaining knowledge and of using it. It is believed that Fulbert of Chartres, the great Councillor Bishop of King Robert, sprang from the lower orders. King Robert promoted to the bishopric many men of humble birth, such as John of Auxerre, for which he was loudly criticized by the more aristocratic section of the Church, represented by Asceline. That proud prelate taunted the King with the selection of men from the plough and other humble occupations. At a later stage the carpenter of Tuscany becomes the greatest of all the Popes, Gregory VII, and an emperor of high birth awaits his pleasure in the snow at Canossa. There are other ways in which the Church showed its democratic sentiment. Sometimes the honoured saint was only a poor, insignificant pilgrim like Arnulf, whose relics were brought to Mouzon, or a poor woman like Frothilde ; and, if the saint himself was of higher standing, he made no distinction in his favours, for Benedict at Fleury cared for the poor as well as the rich. All classes enjoyed his protection and shared his healing power.

The Church not only gave the peasant a chance of promotion in its own order, but it sought to give him a place of responsibility in the secular world. We have already noticed that Bishop Guy of Le Puy brought peasants and chevaliers together for the maintenance of peace in the locality. This was an event of considerable importance, of which we should be very glad to have further details. The significance of the bishop's action lies in the fact that the peasants of a district are called in to share with the nobility the responsibility for peace and justice. They are apparently to associate on equal terms in a league of co-operation, bound by a covenant of mutual oaths to make war on war. Pfister, in his *Robert le Pieux*, goes so far as to say (p. 167) that this was ' a great event in our history, the entry of the lower orders into political life ' ; and he further points out that the peasant would have, in certain circumstances, ' the right and duty of making war on the lords.' This incident shows, at any rate, that the Church was anxious to give the lower orders a responsible place in society.

The Church maintained in theory the principle of election which it had inherited from the early Church, and in this way parted company with the feudal system, which was based upon hereditary right, privilege of birth, and the pride of power. In theory the bishop had still to be elected by all the inhabitants of the city. In the Benedictine monasteries the rule was that the abbot should be chosen by all the monks of the monastery. The king himself, as distinct from a feudal lord, must be elected by the bishops and the princes, with the consent of all the people. The practice in these matters was very different from the theory, but the survival of the theory of popular election, in which all classes took part, meant much for the future. The Church, in fact, received from the earlier days the democratic principle which it handed over to the modern world, when it could be more easily and successfully applied.

CONCLUSION

IN estimating the position of the Church in the tenth century, it would not be an exaggeration to say that it saved society from utter collapse, and helped to lay the foundations of a strong and enlightened political order. The Church sinned greatly against its ideals, but we must judge every institution by its best expression. The Church produced Maiolus, Bruno, Gerbert, and in the Dark Ages was seen the light of moral and spiritual reform, the proof of the reality of an inner light that was always there. This religious revival was associated with a revival of letters, a desire for peace, and an effort to maintain justice in society. The Church defended the interests of the worker, the trader, the peasant, the poor, the sick and the needy, and the helpless. It provided the only charitable institution which existed. It held up before the age a high ideal of love and service. It reached beyond the national limits to international ideals. The Empire which Gerbert and Adalberon loved was not merely a German monarchy, but a world order, embracing all the nations; in fact, an international ideal of the Kingdom of God. In spite of all its failure, it represented law, loyalty, the unseen spiritual forces of righteousness, and a fellowship grounded in divine reality. It called to mind the words of Jesus, set forth His cross by the presentation of His sacrificial love in sacrament, and, by uniting justice and mercy, saved the soul of Europe.

APPENDIX I

LIST OF AUTHORITIES CONSULTED

ORIGINALS

RICHER : *Historiarum Libri iv. (in usum scholarum Pertz)*
GERBERT : *Letters (ed. Havet, Coll. de Textes)*
    Acta Consilii Remensis ad Sanctum Basolum, and other
    writings in Migne 139
FLODOARD : *Annales (Coll. de Textes Laur.)*
ABBO : in Migne 139
AIMON : *Miracula Sancti Benedicti,* Migne 139
    Vita S. Abbonis, Migne 139
BURCHARDI DECRETORUM LIBRII VIGINTI : Migne 140
RATHIER : Migne 136
THIETMAR : *Chronicon (in usum scholarum Pertz)*
RUOTGER : *Vita Brunonis (in usum scholarum Pertz)*
HARIULF : *Chronicon Centulense (Coll. de Textes)*
ODO DE ST. MAUR : *Vita Burchardi (Coll. de Textes)*
R. GLABER : *Historiarum V., Libri v. (Coll. de Textes)*
Gesta Pontificum Cameracensium, Migne 149
Gesta Pontificum Autissiodorensium, Migne 138
Gesta Abbatum Lobiensium, Migne 137
Gesta Episcoporum Leodiensium, Migne 139
Gesta Episcoporum Virdunensium, Migne 132
Chronicon Mosomensis Monasterii, Migne 137
DUDO : *De Moribus et Actis Primorum Normannie Ducum,*
    Migne 141
ADHEMAR : *Chronicon, &c.,* Migne 141
ASCELINE : *Carmen,* Migne 141
Sigebert de Gembloux, Migne 160
Hugues de Fleury, Migne 163
Hugues de Flavigny, Migne 154
Odoran Chronique, &c., Migne 142
Vita Joh Gorz, Migne 137
Jonas Vita Odonis, Migne 133
Syrus Vita Maioli, Migne 137
Odilo Vita Maioli, Migne 142
Ulric Consuet. Clun., Migne 149
Chronicles collected in *Historiens de France,* ix., x.
Decrees and Epistles of the contemporary Popes (Migne)
MANSI : *Consilia* (Vol. xix.)

Actes de Lothaire et Louis V., Halphen and Lot
MABILLON : *Annales Benedictini*

MODERN WORKS

LOT : *Les Derniers Carolingien*
    Études sur le Règne de Hugues Capet
PFISTER : *Études sur le Règne de Robert le Pieux*
LUCHAIRE : *Histoire des Institutions Monarchiques de la France*
LAVISSE : *Histoire de France* (Vol. ii. and 1 and 2)
LAIR : *Études Critiques sur Divers Textes des Dixième et Onzième Siècles*
CAMBRIDGE : *Mediaeval History* (Vol. iii.)
LAGARDE : *Latin Church in the Middle Ages*
FOAKES JACKSON: *Introduction to History of Christianity* (590–1314)
CARLYLE : *Mediaeval Political Theory* (4 vols.)
CARLYLE AND BARTLETT : *Christianity and History*
DE WULF : *History of Mediaeval Philosophy*
POOL, R. L. : *Illustrations of Mediaeval Thought*
BEER : *Social Struggles in Middle Ages*
GRAHAM, R. : *Life at Cluny*
SMITH, L. : *Early History of Cluny*
GASQUET : *Rule of Benedict*
WATKINS : *History of Penance*
WORKMAN : *Evolution of Monastic Ideal*
HANNAH, IAN : *Christian Monasticism*
FREEMAN : *History of Norman Conquest*
PALGRAVE : *History of England and Normandy*
COULTON : *Mediaeval Garner.*
    ,,   *Mediaeval Studies.*
BRYCE : *Holy Roman Empire.*
DURUY : *History of France.*
TOUT : *Empire and Papacy.*

APPENDIX II

HISTORIANS OF THE PERIOD

FOR the period in question the writings of Flodoard and Richer are invaluable. Flodoard is the painstaking annalist, and, until his death in 965, is the main authority for the history of France. Richer wrote his history at the end of the century, and is the principal authority for the period A.D. 965–1000. He, however, imitated the classical style, and therefore we cannot be quite sure whether the speeches he quotes are the exact words used. He is not always accurate in detail or the order of events, but is generally trustworthy for the principal events with which he is contemporary. He is remarkably free from personal political bias, and evidently desires to do justice to the parties concerned. The one exception to prove this rule is his habit of calling the Normans ' Pirates.'

Gerbert's Letters and edition of the Acts of Synod of St. Basil, &c., represent our authority for the events connected with the change of dynasty and the trial of Arnulf. His works may be used to correct or supplement Richer, as he was often in the inner circle of events ; but we must not forget that he was a party to the dispute, and therefore not always above the suspicion of bias. Havet and Lot have rendered great service in editing these Letters.

Adhemar and R. Glaber (1048) must be read with caution for the events of the tenth century, as their active lives were connected with the mid-eleventh century. Various chronicles and *Gesta* of bishops and abbots contain much valuable information. Hariulf, for example, though he wrote the Chronicle of St. Riquier at the end of the eleventh century, obviously had access to the archives of the monastery, and he included many early documents into his work. Nevertheless, there are many grave errors in some of these chronicles, and they must always be controlled by earlier writers like Richer or Gerbert.

Aimon's works throw a valuable light on the manners and general social life of the period. For the religious life of the time the writings of Abbo (*d.* 1004) are important, as he was a careful student of Church law and customs. Burchard's Collection of Canons made at the end of the tenth century or beginning of the eleventh century have special value for this period. The lives of the early abbots of Cluny, written by contemporary writers, give much information about the monastic life of the time, whilst Asceline's *Carmen* is interesting because it reveals the point of view of a contemporary prelate who was critical of the monks. Thietmar (*d.* 1018) gives us information concerning contemporary events, secular and ecclesiastical, in Germany. The writings of

Fulbert, though strictly relating to the eleventh century, are not without value for this period, as being the work of a representative French prelate who was a student of Gerbert at Rheims. Rathier (*d.* 975), though spending part of his life in Italy, had close relations with the Churches of Belgium and France, and his works are a mine of information on the doctrine, government, and customs of the Church of the tenth century.

Ruotger's Life of Bruno and Constantine's Life of Adalberon of Metz show us the type of saintliness that appealed to that age, whilst Folcuin's history of Lobbes monastery, written at the end of the tenth century, gives us the light and shade of a typical monastery.

The student of this period cannot fail to pay a tribute of gratitude to the exhaustive works of Lot, Luchaire, and Pfister in elucidating the events of the period, whilst R. W. and A. J. Carlyle's volumes have explained the mediaeval theory which is expressed in Canon Law with singular clearness.

Lot, however, in his anxiety to do justice to the Carolings, has done less than justice to the real abilities of Hugh Capet and Gerbert. These men were surely possessed of more than average ability and not a little genius. Otherwise it is difficult to account for the impression they made on history. Lot has done full justice to the real greatness of Lothaire, and his detailed studies on the order of events are very valuable.

Pfister's work is unduly critical of the monks and Cluny, whilst Carlyle's view of the Divine Right of Kings is to be preferred to the view of Luchaire. These defects do not greatly mar the fine contribution of these French scholars to our knowledge of this period.

Carlyle's estimate of mediaeval theory can be supported by quotations from tenth-century writers, and a definite relation between the theory and practice of the Church has been suggested in the above pages. There is less trace of a relationship between the theory and practice of feudalism. Carlyle gives reason for believing that loyalty and mutual contract entered into the theory. A perusal of the tenth-century writings has convinced the writer that there are few traces of either in practice.

Reference should be made to two important works bearing upon this period, which, however, came to the notice of the writer too late for use in the production of this Treatise. Dom Butler's *Benedictine Monachism* describes in detail, with much inside knowledge, the ideal and purpose of the Benedictine movement, but does not seem to invalidate the substance of Chapter VII. Dr. Coulton, in his *Five Centuries of Religion*, using his immense and detailed knowledge of the 'Middle Ages,' shows the great disparity between the Ideal and the Real. This cleavage unfortunately applies to all ages and institutions, and has not been ignored in this work. Nevertheless, the author still thinks that the Church must not only be judged by what it has accomplished, but by what it strove to be in its best moments and by what it knew it ought to be all the time.

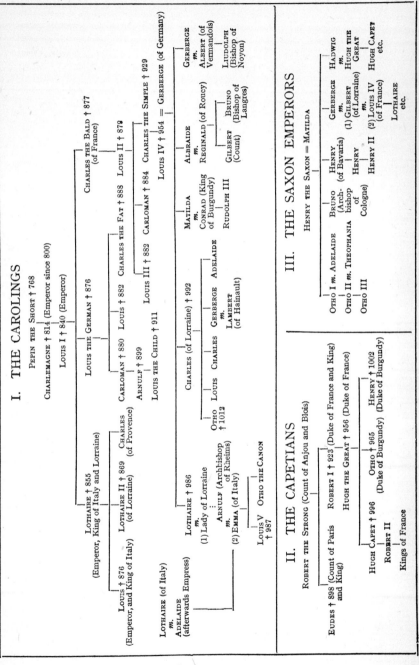

GENEALOGICAL TABLES

I. THE CAROLINGS

II. THE CAPETIANS

III. THE SAXON EMPERORS

INDEX